PRIESTS
FOR THE
21ST
CENTURY

The Boston College Church in the 21st Century Series

Patricia De Leeuw and James F. Keenan, S.J.,
General Editors

Titles in this series include:

Handing On the Faith: The Church's Mission and Challenge

Sexuality and the U.S. Catholic Church: Crisis and Renewal

Inculturation and the Church in North America

Take Heart: Catholic Writers on Hope in Our Time

The Church in the 21st Century Center at Boston College seeks to be a catalyst and resource for the renewal of the Catholic Church in the United States by engaging critical issues facing the Catholic community. Drawing from both the Boston College community and others, its activities currently are focused on four challenges: handing on and sharing the Catholic faith, especially with younger Catholics; fostering relationships built on mutual trust and support among lay men and women, vowed religious, deacons, priests, and bishops; developing an approach to sexuality mindful of human experience and reflective of Catholic tradition; and advancing contemporary reflection on the Catholic intellectual tradition.

PRIESTS
FOR THE
21ST
CENTURY

DONALD J. DIETRICH, EDITOR

A Herder & Herder Book
The Crossroad Publishing Company
New York

The Crossroad Publishing Company
16 Penn Plaza – 481 Eighth Avenue, Suite 1550
New York, NY 10001

Printed in the United States of America

The text of this book is set in 10.5/14 Sabon.

Library of Congress Cataloging-in-Publication Data

Priests for the 21st century / editor, Donald Dietrich.
    p. cm. – (The Boston College church of the 21st century series)
   "A Herder & Herder Book."
   Includes bibliographical references and index.
   ISBN-13: 978-0-8245-2437-1 (alk. paper)
   ISBN-10: 0-8245-2437-3 (alk. paper)
   1. Priests. 2. Priesthood. 3. Pastoral theology. I. Dietrich, Donald J., 1941-
II. Title.
BX1913.P76 2006
262′.142 – dc22

                           2006027442

1 2 3 4 5 6 7 8 9 10   12 11 10 09 08 07 06

To Catholic Priests

Contents

Part Three
IN UNION WITH BISHOP AND LAITY

Part Four
CHALLENGES FOR THE FUTURE

Preface

Donald Dietrich

T HE CHURCH IN THE 21ST CENTURY initiative at Boston College,
begun in September 2002, was designed as a two-year project to
respond to the sexual abuse crisis rocking the Church in the United
States and, as subsequently became apparent, in much of the rest
of the Catholic world. William Leahy, S.J., the president of Boston
College, wanted to make the university's environment available as a
forum for symposia, lectures, and conferences, as well as published
papers, all of which would assist the Church in moving forward
through this troubling time. The Church in the 21st Century Center
ultimately emerged as a permanent commitment on the part of Boston
College to act as a resource for renewal.

The Center was charged with organizing activities to respond to
three challenges: how the Catholic faith can be shared; how relationships based on mutual trust and respect can be fostered among the
laity, vowed religious, priests, and bishops; and how perspectives on
sexuality resonating with human experience and Catholic teaching
can be developed. The conference "The Roman Catholic Priesthood
in the 21st Century" (June 15–17, 2005) at Boston College grew out
of this initiative and was supported through the generosity of the
Knights of Malta, Eastern Division, Boston College, and the regis-
tration fees of nearly one hundred participants. Donald Dietrich and
Michael Himes, professors of theology at Boston College, assisted by
Dawn Overstreet, assistant director of the Church in the 21st Century
Center, organized the conference.

The papers presented and included in this volume are the attempts
of the participating scholars to offer their research on the priesthood

and its historical development in the Roman Catholic tradition and are designed to serve as the basis for an ongoing conversation that could lead to envisioning the meaning of priesthood in the twenty-first century. Professors Himes and Dietrich asked several participants to respond with some formal remarks, and these smaller essays, or "reflections," are also included in this volume. Fr. James Burns, who led a "break-out" session at the conference, has offered a formal essay for the volume.

As the essays show, the conference participants focused on the current state of the question forty years after Vatican II, on the history of sacramental ministry, on the development of the meaning of "pastor," on the challenges and opportunities connected to creating provocative homilies, on the rights of priests, on the relationships of priests to the bishops and to lay ministers, on the so-called "priest shortage," and on the complex issue of "priestly burnout." The conference ended with a summary presentation of the priestly charism today and of how it can be nurtured into the future.

The presentations sparked very animated discussions and are designed in their published form to plant the seeds for future symposia on the meaning of ministry, especially on the more specific issues that concern priests and laity. The scholars did well to present the complex and sometimes problematic research on the issues currently convulsing priests in their ministry. What made the conference really successful, however, was the enthusiastic participation of the priests and laypersons who attended it. On behalf of Boston College, Michael Himes and Donald Dietrich want to thank both the scholars and the other participants who helped in the project of constructing a vision for the priesthood in the twenty-first century. We dedicate this volume to the Catholic priests who struggle to understand their own roles in the post–Vatican II Church.

Part One

GRASPING
THE HERITAGE

Chapter 1

Priesthood

Forty Years after Vatican II

SUSAN WOOD, S.C.L.

❦

F ORTY YEARS AFTER VATICAN II finds us with a plethora of books on the priesthood, with a widespread acknowledgment that priestly identity today is in crisis, with an indisputable shortage of priests as parishes cluster, with priests who serve multiple parishes, and with lay ecclesial ministers who appear to be minding the store, so to speak, in the absence of a resident pastor. Meanwhile, we have also experienced a burgeoning growth of lay ministry exercised often by women and men who are professionally trained, but at other times by those who have had no formal theological or pastoral training. The emergence of this lay ministry has led to some rich collaboration and diversification within ministry, but at times it has also resulted in what may be called "defensive driving" on the part of the ordained. This essay lays out the state of the question regarding a theology of ministry with special emphasis on the priesthood. It does so by identifying the major themes, developments, and tensions within this theology.

A theology of ministry does not develop in a vacuum, within an ivory tower of theological speculation or behind closed doors of ec-clesiastical offices. A theology of ministry is always influenced by its cultural and historical context. It is always contextual, which means that a theology of priesthood or of lay ecclesial ministry is never once and for all developed. Such a theology is in dialogue with the theology that preceded it and with the pastoral needs that confront it. It is organic, dynamic, adaptive, characterized by both continuity

3

and change. To discuss the state of the question today, it is necessary to begin with the major contributions of Vatican II, for today's
theologies of priesthood are in dialogue with that event.

Although a major achievement of Vatican II was the development
of a theology of the episcopacy, it did not achieve the same level of
explication for the presbyterate. Only one section of *Lumen Gentium,* no. 28, treats a theology of the priesthood. The Decree on
the Training of Priests (*Optatam Totius*) addresses the fostering of
priestly vocations and the principles and regulations for priestly training. The Decree on the Ministry and Life of Priests (*Presbyterorum
Ordinis*) initiates a theology of the presbyterate, but much more development is needed. The evolution of the title of this last document,
as Daniel Donovan has noted, indicates that the emphasis was on
priestly ministry before priestly life or identity. "Originally called *de
clericis* (on clerics), it became *de sacerdotibus* (on priests), then *de
vita et ministerio sacerdotium* (on the life and ministry of priests),
and finally *de presbyterorum ministerio et vita* (on the ministry and
life of presbyters)."[1]

The bishops at Vatican II broadened the theology of the priesthood from its Tridentine forerunner, which was predominately a
cultic and priestly theology with an emphasis on the priest's role
in the Eucharist. Vatican II expanded this theology through its use
of the threefold office of priest, prophet, and king corresponding to
the sanctifying, teaching, and pastoral leadership duties of a priest.
It particularly identified preaching the gospel as the preeminent responsibility of a bishop, and by extension, a presbyter. The council
identified the presbyterate with reference to the episcopacy by identifying the bishop as a "high priest" possessing the "fullness of
the sacrament of orders" (*Lumen Gentium,* no. 26), by identifying priests as "prudent cooperators with the episcopal order," which
makes their bishop "present in a certain sense in the individual local
congregations of the faithful" (*Lumen Gentium,* no. 28). It also identified priesthood as a communal ministry. Subsequently, theologians
have argued that these three offices do not exhaust a theology of
priesthood and are actually more unified with one another than the
council documents would suggest, but this move by the council broke

down somewhat the distinction between sacramental and ecclesiastical jurisdiction, by situating governance and pastoral leadership within the sacrament of order. Preaching, teaching, and pastoral leadership as well as sacramental ministry derive from the sacrament of order. This is particularly evident in the theology of the episcopacy, where the council identifies the authority of the bishop as "proper, ordinary, and immediate" (*Lumen Gentium*, no. 27) and identifies episcopal consecration as conferring "the fullness of the sacrament of order" (*Lumen Gentium*, no. 21). Ironically, where the theology of the threefold office articulated by Vatican II expanded the priesthood beyond the cultic model of the post-Tridentine years, the practice of priesthood in recent times has again restricted it to a primarily cultic model as priests serve as sacramental ministers of multiple parishes and as lay people assume responsibilities of pastoral leadership.

Both Vatican II and the ordination rites revised after the council stress the ecclesial task of building up the Church, a ministry that unifies the threefold office. *Lumen Gentium*, no. 10, and *Presbyterorum Ordinis*, no. 12, teach that the ministerial priest "forms and rules the priestly people," "shepherds the faithful," and "builds up the body of Christ, the Church." The emphasis is clearly on the priesthood as ministry rather than as primarily a state in life. Furthermore, the focus of this ministry is on preaching the gospel and celebrating the sacraments, especially the Eucharist.

Vatican II emphasized the communal and collegial character of both the presbyteral order and the episcopacy. In the later development of communion ecclesiology after Vatican II, the communal character of ministry parallels the structure of the Church as a communion. Bishops represent their particular Church in the communion of Churches, which is represented in the college of bishops. They are charged in their office with the connection of the Church with its apostolic past, the communion within their own particular Churches, and the communion of that Church with the universal Church through the bishop's hierarchical relationship with the bishop of Rome.

Communion is also a principle for understanding the presbyter in terms of his relationship to other presbyters, his bishop, Christ, and the Church. Priests constitute one priesthood, the presbyterium, with their bishop. Priests and bishops preside over the Eucharist, the sacrament of unity and communion, because in their pastoral leadership they are charged with the communion and unity of the Church,[2] either as a bishop with respect to the particular Church, the diocese, or a priest with respect to the parish.[3] The priest is in the Church, not above the Church or apart from the Church. The Church in communion with Christ, its head, is the *totus Christus*, the whole Christ. The priest as a representative who recapitulates the community functions liturgically as head of the community, speaking *in persona Christi capitis*, in the person of Christ the head of the community, on behalf of his ecclesial body.

The literature on priesthood since Vatican II is of two genres: ecclesiastical documents and the writings of individual theologians. It is difficult to gauge how influential the latter is with respect to the self-identity of priests since this depends on whether they are used in seminaries and if priests read them. Needless to say, they represent the theological spectrum of various positions regarding priestly identity. The starting points for theological analysis may be any one of the following: office or word, as in Rahner; minister or community leadership, as in Schillebeeckx; Church, as in Kilmartin; or Christ, as in Ratzinger and Galot.[4] Frequently there may be a tension between the theology of ecclesiastical documents and the intellectual formulations of theologians. Both of these are in dialogue with the cultural situation, but have different solutions to perceived problems.

For the purposes of an overview of the state of the question on priesthood today, it is best to begin with a survey of the themes of the ecclesiastical documents. Even if it is difficult to judge the influence of particular theologians, it would be safe to say that the ecclesiastical documents provide the basis for the articulation of priestly identity in seminaries.

"The Ministerial Priesthood" from the synod of 1971 was the first major document on the priesthood after the council.[5] The document is situated within the post-conciliar period on the heels of the social unrest of the late 1960s and the corresponding exodus from the active ministry of many ordained priests. New contextual situations cited in the document include the problem of obsolete methods insufficient for the modern mentality, the secularization of the world, whether the emphasis of the council on the proclamation of the gospel raises doubts about the meaning of a sacramental and cultic ministry, the growing diversification of ministry, and whether teaching on the common priesthood of the faithful obscures the position of the priestly ministry.[6] Thus, priestly identity is being challenged by questions of the relevance of the sacramental ministry at the core of priesthood as well as by the ministry of lay people. A deeper underlying question is whether the present-day Church is too removed from its origins to credibly proclaim the gospel.

The document asserts the essential difference of the ordained ministry from the common priesthood, affirms the threefold office exercised by hierarchical communion, notes that priestly ministry reaches its summit in the celebration of the Eucharist, which can be presided over and effected only by a priest acting in the person of Christ, and asserts that the Church cannot have full certainty of her fidelity and of her visible continuity apart from the presence and activity of the ministry.

Unity becomes a central theme of the document: ministry serving the unity of the whole Church, the unity within proclamation of the word and sacramental life, and the unity of priests with the order of bishops. The general direction of the document, however, is to affirm the priestly identity of the presbyter and to emphasize what distinguishes a ministerial priest from the common priesthood. The document addresses the crisis of priestly identity by reaffirming the centrality of sacramental ministry, particularly in the Eucharist. This is also the one area that cannot be duplicated by lay ministry. Where Vatican II emphasized the ministry of priests, this document focuses on the way of life of priests in its warnings concerning secular and political activity, the fairly extensive section on celibacy, its treatment of the community of life among priests, and the modest lifestyle fitting to their state in life.

The Priest and the Third Christian Millennium: Teacher of the Word, Minister of the Sacraments, and Leader of the Community

(1999), a second post-conciliar document issued by the Congregation for the Clergy, provides an apologetic for the priesthood, which
is evident in the section titled "The Necessary and Indispensable Role
of Priests."[7] As the subtitle indicates, it takes its cue from the structure of the threefold office of Vatican II. Increasing secularism and
the dangers of relativism provide the context for this document and
its themes of "new evangelization" or "reevangelization." In order
for priests to assume the pastoral responsibility of new evangelization, it advocates holiness of life and a profound and proper training
in philosophy and theology. It recognizes that this new evangelization must find a form for the exercise of priestly ministry consonant
with contemporary conditions.[8] Although it integrates priestly life
and ministry in its insistence that proclamation of the word is related
to the personal prayer and sacramental life of the priest, it is also
careful to distinguish the priest from the lay faithful. For instance it
states: "Since priests participate in the authority of Christ they differ
notably from the faithful." It expands the idea of a priest acting *in
persona Christi capitis* by extending this interpretation beyond the
liturgical role of the priest in the Eucharist to his role in governance.[9]
The implication is that not only is the priest's liturgical role essentially
different from the role of the lay faithful, so also is his authority essentially different in the pastoral leadership of the Church. Although
episcopal authority has been a frequent theme in documents, priestly
authority has been addressed much less often. The theme also occurs
in this document's admonition that objective spiritual authority must
be complemented with a subjective authority deriving from sincerity
and holiness of life and pastoral charity.[10] Finally, one observes that
the pastoral ministry of priests in this document is directed towards
individuals rather than the Church as a community.

John Paul II's post-synodal apostolic exhortation *I Will Give You
Shepherds, Pastores Dabo Vobis* (1992) has had enormous influence in seminaries and hence in priestly formation.[11] It begins by
situating the priest in his time, naming positive factors such as a
powerful thirst for justice and peace, a new call for ethics as a quest
for meaning accompanying developments within science and technology, an increased love of Scripture, and the witness of martyrdom in

the Churches of Central and Eastern Europe.[12] Negative contextual factors include a lack of knowledge of the faith, a practical and existential atheism, widespread rationalism, the break-up of the family, a perversion of the true meaning of sexuality, a desperate defense of personal subjectivity which results in a distorted individualism, and consequently a misunderstood theological and pastoral pluralism.[13]

John Paul II attributes a crisis of priestly identity, which emerged in the years following the council, to an erroneous understanding or "even a conscious bias against the doctrine of the Conciliar Magisterium."[14] The response to this crisis by the 1990 Synod was to stress the "specific ontological bond that unites the priesthood to Christ the High Priest and Good Shepherd."[15] John Paul II stresses that "reference to Christ is the absolutely necessary key for understanding the reality of priesthood." In fact priests are called "to prolong the presence of Christ." It would probably be fair to conclude that for John Paul II, the priest's relationship to Christ is the defining characteristic of his priesthood.

John Paul II also notes the fundamental relational and communal nature of the priesthood: "Reference to the Church is therefore necessary, even if it is not primary, in defining the identity of the priest." According to John Paul II, the ecclesiology of communion is decisive for understanding the priest's identity and his essential dignity, although he does not develop the nature of this communion.[16]

John Paul II adopts the view that Christ called the Apostles, who in turn appointed other men as bishops, as priests, and as deacons. This view contrasts with the sacramental views of Rahner and Schillebeeckx for whom Christ is the sacrament of the Father, the Church is a sacrament of Christ, and the seven sacraments, including holy orders, are sacraments of the Church.[17] The issue is whether priesthood exists primarily for the Church or whether the emphasis is primarily on a priest's relationship with Christ. Even though John Paul II emphasizes the priest's relationship to Christ, he nevertheless strives to strike a balance, noting that the priesthood is not to be thought of as existing prior to the Church, but neither should it be considered as posterior to the ecclesial community.[18]

This survey of ecclesiastical documents demonstrates that the emphasis since Vatican II has been to strengthen priestly identity by emphasizing the difference between the common priesthood and the ministerial priesthood, by emphasizing the cultic nature of priesthood, by stressing the priest's configuration to Christ, and by stressing the state of life of the priest. Discussions of priestly ministry treat his sacramental ministry and pastoral care of individuals. More communal and ecclesial themes within pastoral leadership rarely occur.

Differences in theologies of the priesthood after Vatican II can be grouped around a number of themes in tension with each other. *Lumen Gentium* identifies the Christian faithful as a priestly people before it addresses the hierarchical priesthood. This emphasizes what all the people of God share in common before treating of specific groups within this people of God. It also situates the ordained priesthood in relationship to the common priesthood. The ordained priesthood exists to foster and nourish the common priesthood. Perhaps the most often quoted line is: "Though they differ from one another in essence and not only in degree, the common priesthood of the faithful and the ministerial or hierarchical priesthood are nonetheless interrelated" (*Lumen Gentium,* no. 10). This statement is subject to two interpretations, one positive with respect to the laity and the other more negative. On the one hand, since the two priesthoods are not a matter of degree, the ministerial priesthood cannot be interpreted as being "higher" and a priest a "super Christian." The ministerial priesthood is of an entirely different order and cannot be located on a scale of holiness with respect to the common priesthood.[19] On the other hand, in relation to a theology of lay ecclesial ministry, the phrase distances the ordained priesthood from the common priesthood lest the latter exceed its competencies.

Two fears seem to drive this distinction. First, some people fear a blurring of the two priesthoods, resulting in a weakened theology of the ministerial priesthood.[20] This accompanies a second fear that the priesthood will be considered as a delegation of the common priesthood along democratic lines where a local church may feel itself empowered to ordain its own minister on the basis of its common priesthood. Liturgical regulations emphasizing the distinction between the nave of a church and the sanctuary and movements of the nonordained in the sanctuary and their handling of sacred vessels further emphasize the distinction between the two priesthoods.[21]

David Power has identified three difficulties with this distinction: first, it rests on too sharp a distinction between the priesthood and the kingship of Christ; second, it gives priority to the nature of the Church as institution, with its different offices, while these are simply meant to support the life of the community as a body; and third, it seems to support a distinction between spiritual sacrifice and priesthood on the one hand and sacramental sacrifice and priesthood on the other hand.[22] Power suggests that institutions and roles, although necessary, be understood as relations and responsibilities within the context of the eucharistic and eschatological community rather than in terms of power and office.[23] This relational view would situate the priesthood more firmly in the context of the Christian community and move more in the direction of a relational ontology, thus avoiding the dichotomy between a functional and ontological view of the priesthood.

Current debates of priestly identity often split along more liberal lines espousing a functional view of priestly ministry and more conservative interpretations emphasizing an ontological change effected by the sacramental character of ordination.[24] A functional view presupposes that the priest is merely exercising a ministry derived from the common priesthood, which essentially any of the baptized could perform. A theology of an ontological difference emphasizes the distinction between the ordained priesthood and the laity. An ordained priest is essentially different from a lay person, a difference rooted in his very being.

Theologies that emphasize this difference may attract candidates to the priesthood for rather dubious reasons. A candidate may desire an exclusive relationship to Christ, a relationship not enjoyed by the lay faithful. He may seek sacred powers not possessed by the laity. The sacral priesthood exercises control over the dispensation of sacramental grace and even over the sacramental body of Christ.

The ministerial priest is therefore seen as "special," set apart, and as someone who does not share commerce with common men and women. Even while affirming this ontological difference, seminaries attempt to balance it with a theology of priesthood as service, priest as servant leader.

The choice between the two views is ultimately a false choice because function follows being, and being results in a corresponding function. The deeper theological question is to identify what the sacramental character actually effects. A review of the literature reveals a spectrum of views, from conformity of the priest to Christ, empowering him to confect the Eucharist, to a more ecclesial interpretation, according to which a new ecclesial relationship referred to as an "ecclesial repositioning" is effected and interpreted as a relational ontology. Within this latter interpretation sacramental power is not conferred on an individual apart from this ecclesial relationship, but the individual is empowered to act sacramentally because of that person's reconfiguration in a new ecclesial relationship.[25] This ecclesial repositioning enables a priest to act *in persona Christi capitis.*

A relational ontology neither reduces the ministerial priesthood to functionality nor does it define the priest apart from the priesthood of the baptized or set him above it. On the contrary, it defines the ministerial priesthood precisely in such a way that the ministerial priesthood has meaning only with reference to the community it serves. The ministerial priesthood is not a privatized relationship to Christ apart from the body of Christ which is the Church. Yet the ministerial priesthood remains distinct from the rest of the priesthood of the baptized since in occupying the relation of head of the community its locus within the community is specified, permanent, and distinct from that of other members of the community. One cannot in justice speak of a relational ontology as being "merely relational," for it is as ontological as it is relational, that is, being specified, constituted, and identified by its relation.

Does the priest represent the Church secondarily through his primary representation of Christ, or does he represent Christ immediately through his representation of the Church? From the twelfth century, through the instrumental causality articulated by the scholastic theologians, we have inherited the theology of the priest as the representative of Christ consecrating the Eucharist through his words spoken *in persona Christi*. In recent times, much theological ink has been spilt over the relationship of a priest acting *in persona Christi* and *in persona ecclesiae*.[26] Most of the discussion revolves around which relationship is primary, the priest's relationship with Christ or with the Church. Liturgically, there is evidence for both. While the eucharistic epiclesis recited by the priest is spoken in the first person plural, signifying that it is an act of the Church, he speaks the words of institution in the first person singular, signifying that it is an act of Christ.

Power finds that the debate may remain unpersuasive because the very terms of discussion and thought need to be refashioned.[27] Yves Congar notes that this theology became "isolated, hardened and material," suggesting that this theology is in danger of isolating the priest's identity and sacramental action from the identity and action of the Church. Insofar as the debate remains relevant, Congar's reminder that the categories *in persona Christi* and *in persona ecclesiae* are essentially sacramental categories indicating that a visible reality, here the priest, represents a spiritual reality, namely, Christ, is a helpful one. The category of sacrament prevents too close an identification of Christ and the priest because sacraments distance the sign and the referent at the same time as they identify them. He concludes that the relationship is mutually inclusive, although the West has prioritized the Christological relationship, while the East has affirmed the Christological in and through the ecclesial relationship.

> The true perspective of the *in persona Christi* is sacramental. The priest who celebrates the Church's act of worship is himself a sacramental reality, that is to say, he represents, at the level of what can be seen, a spiritual reality. He is that reality in accordance with the fullness that is realized by the Church's worship. That fullness is defined, for example, in the papal encyclical *Mediator Dei* of November 20, 1947, and in the Conciliar Constitution on the Liturgy, *Sacrosanctum Concilium*, [no.] 7, as the

"full public worship performed by the Mystical Body of Jesus Christ, that is, by the Head and his members." It is in accordance with this organic reality with its two aspects that the priest represents Christ. He represents not only Christ, the sovereign high priest, in whose person he acts, but also the *ecclesia,* the community of Christians, in whose person he acts also. He therefore acts *in persona Christi* and *in persona Ecclesiae.* One of these is contained within the other. An insistence on the Christological aspect — this has occurred in the West — means that the *in persona Ecclesiae* is situated within the *in persona Christi,* which is seen as the basis and the reason for the first. *Mediator Dei* presents the teaching in this way. If, on the other hand, the pneumatological aspect is emphasized, as the Eastern tradition loves to do, the *in persona Christi* is more easily seen as situated within the *in persona Ecclesiae.*[28]

Congar's analysis helpfully relativizes the debate, illustrating that we cannot pit *in persona Christi* against *in persona ecclesiae* any more than we can pit Christ against the Spirit. The reality is a relationship of mutual interiority. According to Congar, the East as well as the West affirms that the priest receives the "power" to consecrate the Eucharist. The nuance within the pneumatological interpretation is that he does not do so alone by virtue of a power which remains within his control but by a grace "for which he asks God and which is operative, and even ensured, through him *in the Church.*"[29]

The relationship between Christology and pneumatology in a theology of the priesthood is closely related to the relationship of a priest acting *in persona Christi* and *in persona ecclesia.* A Christological interpretation of the priesthood emphasizes a priest's identification with Christ and his role in taking the place of Christ in his recitation of the institution narrative in the Eucharist. This relationship in the priesthood is related to a theology of the Eucharist and interpretations of consecration as they relate to the words of institution and the epiclesis.

Not all eucharistic prayers recognized as valid have had an institution narrative. Early eucharistic prayers without the institution narrative include the Didache 9–10, the Papyrus Strasbourg 254, the Anaphora of Addai and Mari, and the Apostolic Constitutions 7:25–26. It is possible to have a valid Eucharist without the institution narrative. The West has stressed the words of institution said by the priest with the intention of "doing what Christ instituted and what the Church celebrates," while the East has stressed the consecratory action of the epiclesis. The more accurate response to the question of "what action consecrates" is that "the consecration of the sacred gifts is the act of Christ, the sovereign high priest who is active through his minister *and* the Holy Spirit."[30] The West has often neglected the role of the Holy Spirit. When this occurs, one result is an over-exaltation of the role of the priest, seeing the consecratory power as belonging to him personally in a sort of absolute way rather than the priest being a conduit of the action of the Holy Spirit. In the first instance, the theology of the priesthood is liable to a triumphalism. In the second, the priest is a servant, not only of the community, but of the Holy Spirit.

Although not the primary focus of this account of ministry forty years after Vatican II, an account of the ministry since Vatican II must necessarily include a brief discussion of lay ecclesial ministry. The development of a theology of lay ministry is often in some tension with a theology of the priesthood due to great concern that the two neither be conflated into the same thing nor confused. Thus, documents on lay ministry frequently cite the passage from *Lumen Gentium:* "Though they differ essentially and not only in degree, the common priesthood of the faithful and the ministerial or hierarchical priesthood are none the less interrelated; each in its own way shares in the one priesthood of Christ."

The term "ministry" was commonly applied to the laity only after Vatican II. The term the council used was "lay apostolate," and this referred to lay activity for mission that derived from baptism and confirmation. The apostolate of the laity belongs properly to the laity by virtue of their sacramental life and is no longer considered to be a participation in the apostolate of the hierarchy. The term "ministry" is now widely used to apply to the laity, although the Vatican document "Instruction on Some Aspects of the Collaboration of the Lay

Faithful with the Ministry of Priests" (1997) attempts to limit its use.[31] One notes an interesting parallel between the development of the notion of lay apostolate and the developing notion of lay ecclesial ministry. Before Vatican II, the lay apostolate was considered to be a collaboration in the apostolate of the hierarchy. After Vatican II, ministry is considered by this document to be a participation in the ministry of the ordained.

The use of the term "ministry" seems particularly apt for public, authorized service performed by laity in the name of the Church. However, the term has become so common that it and what it represents is in danger of being confused with the concept and fact of Christian discipleship. All Christians are called to discipleship, while only some are called to ministry. Discipleship, although service to the Church, is often not public, not officially authorized, nor in the name of the Church.

A certain tension exists in the documents of Vatican II, which assign the realm of the sacred to those in ordained ministry and the realm of the secular to the laity.[32] According to this view, clerics exercise ministry within the Church; the laity through their work and witness seek to infuse the world with Christian values. This dichotomy between the sacred and secular is not helpful, particularly when one understands the Church's mission to be essentially secular, that is, the transformation of the world according to the reign of God. The very term "lay ecclesial" points to the dichotomy of sacred and secular. Furthermore, the Decree on the Apostolate of the Laity, *Apostolicam Actuositatem,* affirms the role of the laity in both the temporal and spiritual orders: "The laity, carrying out this mission of the Church, exercise their apostolate therefore in the world as well as in the Church, in the temporal order as well as in the spiritual."[33]

A theological challenge requiring attention is to differentiate between lay ecclesial ministry and ordained ministry, to identify the essential difference between the common priesthood and ministerial priesthood mentioned by Vatican II. Functional answers along a division of labor and answers of power or office remain inadequate in and of themselves. Ministerial tasks have varied throughout history, and answers of power or office insufficiently attend to the responsibility for apostolicity or communion on the part of ordained ministers. The challenge is to identify which tasks are properly lay and which properly belong to the ordained because of the nature of baptism or ordination. For better or worse, pragmatism rather than theological distinctions has driven much of the change in the Church. Lay ministry cannot be a stop-gap measure in the absence of sufficient numbers of ordained ministers. Thus, a theological rationale for lay ministry must be developed that presumes lay ministry as a permanent phenomenon in the Church existing in a collaborative relationship to ordained ministry.

The Collegeville Ministry Seminar[34] suggested that, instead of speaking of lay ecclesial ministry, we use the term "ordered ministries," referring to the ministry itself rather than the minister. Ministry actually occurs on a continuum marked by whether one enters it through ordination, installation, or commissioning, by how stable it is, how fundamentally vocational it is in orienting the whole life of the minister, and by the formation and preparation required. This solution focuses on the ministry and the degree of permanence and authorization given to it rather than the status of the minister. It is not likely that this suggestion will be adopted any time soon, since the term "lay ecclesial ministry" seems to be here to stay, but it is one solution.

Both ecclesial lay ministry and ordained ministry are representative of Christ and the Church, although in different ways. Ordained ministry, unlike lay ecclesial ministry, represents and serves the ecclesial communion at the level of the parish, particular Church, or universal Church and has the responsibility of representing and serving the apostolicity of the Church either through participation in the episcopal college and through apostolic succession in the case of bishops, or by a relationship to the bishop in the case of presbyters and deacons. Round X of the U.S. Lutheran–Roman Catholic Dialogue, completed in April 2004, is an example of a theology that ties a theology of ministry to a theology of the Church as communion.[35]

Official magisterial documents on the priesthood still propose essentialist theologies of the priesthood that are universal for all

priests in all places. A more contextualized theology of the priesthood is needed.[36] This will necessarily account for parochial and
nonparochial priestly ministries as well as give an account of priesthood within religious communities, an area in which there has been
insufficient theological reflection.[37]

In emphasizing a priest's relationship to Christ, it is essential that
this not detract from every Christian's resemblance to Christ in baptism or that an emphasis on the cultic and sacramental role of the
priest in promoting the holiness of the Church not be divorced from
his work with the Church as a community in building up the Church
as the body of Christ, the people of God, and the temple of the
Spirit. As the council insisted, we are saved not as individuals, but
as a people (*Lumen Gentium*, no. 9). Finally, in the West we would
do well to balance the overwhelmingly Christological emphasis in
the theology of the priesthood by a more robust theology of the
Holy Spirit. This would necessarily place a theology of the priesthood firmly within the Church and the priest in solidarity with all of
the people of God.

Chapter 2

The Priest as Sacramental Minister

History and Theology

JOHN BALDOVIN, S.J.

Introduction

O N THE ONE HAND, the question of the relation between priesthood and sacramental ministry is so large and complex that it cannot be done justice in a single essay; on the other hand, it could not possibly be ignored in a study dealing with the future of priestly ministry. A caution is in order right from the start. The liturgical/sacramental aspect of priestly ministry and identity may be isolated as a subject for historical and theological reflection. In reality the sacramental activity of priests has never been so divorced from other aspects of the ministry (preaching, pastoral care) that priesthood could be adequately understood only on the basis of the cultic or liturgical nature of the priesthood. That insight has been clearly espoused by the Second Vatican Council's Dogmatic Constitution on the Church with its interpretation of the priesthood (i.e., both episcopate and presbyterate) in terms of the threefold office of Christ: prophet, priest, and king or shepherd.[1] Therefore, what follows should be understood as an attempt to understand one particular aspect of Christian ministerial priesthood, albeit a very important one.

First, I will very quickly sketch a number of key features in the historical development of the sacramental ministry of priests. On the basis of this history, I will briefly review what I understand to be some of the most sensitive issues and questions that arise in theology today. Second, I will deal somewhat more extensively with two areas of reflection: (1) validity together with the question of ministerial intention and (2) cultic purity. The third section will offer a theological understanding of the priest as sacramental minister today.

A preliminary comment about definitions is in order. The English word "priest" stands for the Latin word *sacerdos* and the Greek word *iereus* (*hiereus*). These Latin and Greek terms have cultic implications. "Priest" is a word that covers two of the sacramental orders of the Church: presbyters and bishops. At times there can be a confusion between the English word "priest" and the word from which it is derived — *presbyter.* The latter is not (in its origin at any rate) a cultic term but rather refers to an "elder" in the Church. The third sacramental order is that of deacon, but by common and universal agreement it has never been considered a priestly order.

Priesthood and Sacramental Ministry in History

Here are some commonly accepted historical factors in the development of priestly sacramental ministry.

1. The word "priest" is not applied to any particular individual in the New Testament — with the great exception of the High Priesthood of Christ in the Letter to the Hebrews. All of the baptized are referred to corporately as a priesthood in 1 Peter 2:9 and Revelation 1:6.

2. Priestly terminology begins to be used with regard to individuals, e.g., with references to sacrifice in the First Letter of Clement of the late first century and in the regulation of the Eucharist by the bishop in the Letters of Ignatius of Antioch.[2]

3. The first clear usage of priest, meaning bishop, as an individual occurs in Cyprian of Carthage during the third century, although just previous to him, Tertullian, also from Carthage, argues that any baptized person can preside at the Eucharist in an emergency.[3]

By the mid-third century eucharistic presidency is clearly reserved to bishops and presbyters. Even in the early fifth century, at least in the city of Rome, there is a question of whether presbyters were deputized to celebrate the Eucharist on Sundays.[4] Through the patristic period "priest" (*sacerdos, iereu*) is a term that is applied mainly to bishops, not presbyters, e.g., in John Chrysostom's *Sermons on the Priesthood* and Theodore of Mopsuestia's *Mystagogical Catecheses*.[5]

4. The fourth century begins to witness the vocabulary of awe, fear, and mystery applied to the liturgy and to liturgical ministers.[6] It is at this time that one can begin to trace the definitive qualitative distinction made between priests and laity and the notion that access to the altar means that priests belong to a higher realm. Bernard Cooke finds the rationale for this strictly hierarchical worldview represented in two enormously influential works: Augustine's *City of God* and the *Ecclesiastical Hierarchy* of Pseudo-Dionysius the Areopagite of sixth-century Syria.[7]

5. At the same time it becomes clear that sexual continence is expected or at least is the ideal for presbyters and bishops, who are to celebrate the Eucharist. Our first evidence of this as a regulation is found in the regional Spanish Synod of Elvira in the first decade of the fourth century. But the ideal of sexual abstinence was a feature of Christian piety from the second century. The ideal of clerical continence was by no means universal, as can be seen in the Christian East.[8] We shall consider this issue later in this essay.

6. In the late fourth and early fifth centuries, St. Augustine established one of the most fundamental principles of sacramental ministry. In his debate with the Donatists, who rejected the sacramental ministry of those who had been ordained by apostate bishops, Augustine insisted that the validity of the sacraments does not depend on the worthiness of the minister.

7. Although Old Testament images for Christian ministry had been employed as early as 1 Clement, the Carolingian period during the eighth and also the ninth century marks a significant development in the use of the priesthood as found in the Hebrew Bible as a model for Christian priests. This development accompanied the adoption of the Davidic kingship as a model for Carolingian royalty. During the Carolingian period, we begin to see evidence of a practice that would have been before then unthinkable — the private or solitary Mass, i.e., the celebration of the Eucharist without community participation. A number of factors were most likely involved in this development,

among them the increase of altars in churches, which miniaturized the great city liturgies with their use of multiple churches, and the increase of ordained monks.[9]

8. The increasing attention paid to penitential practice in the ninth to twelfth centuries was responsible for the association of the anointing of the sick with priests. Eventually lay persons were the sacramental ministers of marriage in the West and were allowed, at least in an emergency, to administer baptism. By the twelfth century it was clear that priests alone have the power to absolve sins. The perception of the sacramental system as significantly related to sin and forgiveness became a driving force in the development of eucharistic practice and one of the most sensitive issues of the Reformation debates.

9. As part of its increasing concern with organization and centralizing the legal system of the Church, the eleventh-century Gregorian reform introduced a new focus on the institution of the sacraments by Christ. Hereafter specific moments, e.g., the eucharistic words of Jesus, the post-Easter commission to forgive or retain sins, are identified with regard to the powers of priestly ministry.[10]

10. There was no developed tract on ecclesiology in Peter Lombard's *Sentences* and other scholastic treatises. The treatise on the sacraments followed immediately upon Christology. Moreover, the foundation for the sacraments was located in the Incarnation rather than in the Paschal Mystery, although St. Thomas does argue the redemptive death of Christ as the source of sacramental grace.[11]

For St. Thomas the priest is most priest when confecting the sacrament. He does this in the person of Christ (*in persona Christi*). That phrase has a long pedigree in patristic usage. What makes it crucially different for Thomas and subsequent theology is the identification of *in persona Christi* with the consecratory words of Christ. A number of modern Catholic theologians, as well as the contemporary magisterium, especially Pope John Paul II, have focused on this phrase as central to the relation between priesthood and sacrament and indeed central to the sacramentality of the priesthood itself. In his 1980 Holy Thursday Letter to Priests John Paul put it this way:

The priest offers the holy Sacrifice *in persona Christi;* this means more than offering "in the name of" or "in place of" Christ. *In persona* means in specific sacramental identification with "the eternal High Priest" (42) who is the author and principal subject of this sacrifice of His, a sacrifice in which, in truth, nobody can take His place. Only He — only Christ — was able and is always able to be the true and effective "expiation for our sins and...for the sins of the whole world." (43) Only His sacrifice — and no one else's — was able and is able to have a "propitiatory power" before God, the Trinity, and the transcendent holiness. Awareness of this reality throws a certain light on the character and significance of the priest celebrant who, by confecting the holy Sacrifice and acting *"in persona Christi,"* is sacramentally (and ineffably) brought into that most profound sacredness, and made part of it, spiritually linking with it in turn all those participating in the Eucharistic assembly.[12]

11. By the thirteenth century theologians clearly taught that the primary activity of the priesthood was the consecration of the Eucharist. This affirmation is related to a longstanding debate with regard to the episcopacy as a distinct order.[13] How could there be a significant difference between bishop and presbyter if the highest power that both possessed was precisely the same? Vatican II's *Lumen Gentium* marks a return to the theology of the first millennium by not only insisting on the distinction of presbyteral and episcopal orders, but also by emphasizing the role of bishop in the Church's constitution.[14]

12. A new stage in the association of priest and sacrament can be discerned in the work of Duns Scotus and others on the application of the fruits of the Mass.[15] The priest had a special role in assigning the fruit of the Mass. What had been a pious practice of praying for the dead, e.g., Monica on her deathbed asking Augustine to leave her body in Ostia but to remember her at the altar of the Lord,[16] now more and more took on the notion that the priest could offer the Mass for a specific intention. Thus, the practice of chantry chapels and priests who "made their living" from them became widespread.

13. Among the precursors of the sixteenth-century Reformation, John Wyclif reintroduced the question of the worthiness of the sacramental minister.[17] Despite Augustine's solution, this was an issue that would not disappear.

14. By identifying priesthood with the common priesthood of the faithful, as opposed to the priesthood of ordained ministers, Martin Luther broke the theological and sacramental connection between priesthood and ministry. Ministry was indeed necessary for Luther, and the good order of the Church required ordained ministers responsible for the proclamation of the Word and the right administration of the sacraments.[18] At the same time the Catholic notion of a priestly succession in ministry was rejected. The question of the break (temporary) in succession by the Anglican acceptance of this Lutheran approach in the form of ordination is central to the Roman Catholic rejection of the validity of Anglican orders.[19]

15. The synthesis of Christian doctrine achieved by the Council of Trent did little more than affirm the medieval consensus on the theology of the priesthood — thus perpetuating the notion of priest as primarily consecrator and sacrificer in the Eucharist.

16. The seventeenth-century French school of spirituality (Cardinal Pierre Bérulle, Vincent de Paul, Jean-Jacques Olier) proposed a theology and spirituality of the priesthood that centered on the ascetical identity of the priest as imitator of Christ's self-emptying.[20] In line with the Tridentine theological synthesis this spirituality found its focus in the priest as eucharistic person. This theology and spirituality has remained profoundly influential up to the present.

17. Finally, the decrees of Vatican II mark a significant development in the modern theology of the priesthood. In the first place the conciliar documents definitively consider the episcopacy to be an order distinct from the presbyterate.[21] Thus the "power to consecrate" which had been the prevalent notion of the unity of presbyter and bishop as priests is placed somewhat in the background, although of course not in any way denied. Second, every aspect of the Church is described in terms of a Christological model, one that relies on the threefold office of Christ as prophet, priest, and king or shepherd. The evangelical aspect of priesthood, i.e., priest as preacher, is given

a certain logical precedence since the gospel must be preached before it can be celebrated sacramentally.[22]

Here are several issues that recur in the history of the theology of priesthood:

- How precisely is the priest a representative of Jesus Christ, i.e., vis-à-vis the common priesthood shared by all of the baptized?

- How do we understand the nature of Christ's own priesthood being represented?

- What precisely is the difference of essence as opposed to degree between the ordained priests and the baptized?[23]

- Was Augustine correct in distinguishing the objective validity of the sacraments from the worthiness of the minister?

- How does the eucharistic focus of ministerial priesthood help the Church to grow into the Body of Christ? Does this traditional focus need nuance?

- Is the priest *qua* priest required to be more ascetical than other baptized members of the Body of Christ?

Reflection on Two Key Areas

Validity and Ministerial Worthiness

One of the questions just raised has to do with the complex issue of the objectivity of the Church's sacraments. Must one say that the sacraments are valid even when they are administered by an unworthy, perhaps even a schismatic, minister? St. Augustine attempted a solution to this Donatist criticism of sacraments. The Donatists denied the validity of sacraments administered by those ordained under questionable circumstances, as in the succession of Bishop Felix of Aptunga, who had been a *traditor* during the persecution of the emperor Diocletian. By emphasizing that it is Christ who baptizes, anoints, and celebrates the Eucharist, Augustine argued that even heretics and schismatics could celebrate valid sacraments.

The Council of Trent later affirmed this principle of the objective nature of the sacraments in a definitive way with its insistence on their *ex opere operato* character. In the popular understanding this principle can lead to a magical understanding of sacramental efficacy. It all depends on how one takes the council's statement that the sacraments bestow grace on those who do not close themselves off to them (*non ponentibus obicem*).[24] If one understands that a lack of faith, whether existential faith or intellectual belief, constitutes such a closing off, then clearly one can have no problem with the concept of *ex opere operato*. Sacramental activity is precisely participation in an act that engages the whole person, as opposed to the reception of something objective.

But Augustine's solution and its subsequent theological tradition were meant to deal with a different sort of problem. When the Church celebrates, can one be confident that God is indeed active in offering grace, i.e., God's own gift of self, even if the minister is unworthy? Augustine's answer gets the minister off the hook. Sacramental ministers do not act in their own person but rather as representatives of Christ, who is the true actor in the sacramental event. St. Thomas makes a similar move in his sacramental theology when he argues that God alone is the principal agent of the sacraments whereas human beings can be the instrumental agents.

Augustine's answer to the Donatists does indeed help to solve the problem of the objective nature of God's offer of grace to us in the sacraments. It places sacramental events where they belong — as ecclesial activities in which Christ is present. Vatican II's Constitution on the Liturgy and subsequent liturgical documents will locate that presence in a number of places: the assembled faithful, the proclamation of the Word, the minister and the consecrated gifts.[25] Augustine, however, leaves the question of the quality of priestly activity unresolved. Moreover, this is somewhat of a lowest common denominator solution. Assurance of the validity of the sacraments may be necessary, but it is a long way from appreciating what sacramental activity is meant to do. I am reminded of the priest who complained of liturgists: "I don't understand why they insist that I look at the people when I say 'The Lord be with you.' All I really need to do is to say the correct words over the correct matter and they will receive what they came to receive." For the sake of those to whom this priest ministers, I am happy to agree that he is correct in his affirmation of the *ex opere operato* principle. But statements like these encourage us to ask what sacramental activities are about in the first place. We must ask not only about the moral worthiness of the minister but also about his competence in liturgical leadership. The Episcopal New Testament scholar William Countryman represents a very balanced view of the issue:

> Even the sacramental priest who has sinned in some quite serious way can still preside at the Eucharist and perform a genuine sacrament of the body and blood of Christ. The alternative was to suppose that only the sacramental priest who had attained a certain level of perfection could legitimately perform the rites of religion. The consequences of that idea are too depressing to be seriously entertained. No one will ever be perfect enough to be beyond question.... There is, then, no adequate or even conceivable way to quantify degrees of perfection so that we could be entirely confident of the sufficient merit of any sacramental priest.... We must presume that only imperfect human beings are available to serve among us as sacramental priests.[26]

One very basic solution to the problems opened up by Augustine's solution is the notion of ministerial intention. Once again this is a lowest common denominator approach. The minister must have at least the intention of doing what the Church intends (*facere quod facit ecclesia*) in a sacramental activity. This principle was codified in the Council of Florence's Decree for the Armenians, in which the three necessary aspects of a sacrament were defined as matter, form, and ministerial intention.[27] To what extent, however, can ministerial intention be understood psychologically? Trent debated this issue. Except for a magisterial statement by Pope Alexander VIII (1690), which condemned a purely objective understanding of intention — one unrelated to the minister's subjective state of mind — it seems that the issue is unresolved.[28]

The question of ministerial intention deserves a far deeper reflection than we can give it here. Perhaps an anecdote will suffice. An

Anglican priest friend tells of an experience when his daughter was about four years old. Being brought up in a clerical household, she had rather religious sensibilities. One day while playing with one of her friends, who happened to be un-baptized, he heard her saying, "I baptize you in the name of the Father and of the Son and of the Holy Spirit" while pouring water over her head. She had valid matter and form and, at least psychologically, she had the intention of what the Church wishes to do. One might also think of the famous case of the Jewish boy, Edgardo Mortara, who was baptized by his nursemaid in Bologna in the mid-nineteenth century and subsequently taken from his parents by Church authorities.[29] In neither case, it seems to me, can we talk about valid sacramental activity. Ministerial intention cannot be psychological, since it would result in the same problem Augustine faced with the Donatists: a celebrating Church at the mercy of the worthiness and/or competence of its ministers. Doing externally what the Church requires must be sufficient for ministerial intention, as the Jesuit theologian, Alphonse Salmeron, argued at Trent.[30]

Purity

At the same time, it has always been clear that the Church has high expectations of its sacramental ministers. Though not clearly about liturgical ministry, 1 Timothy's charge to overseers (επισκοποι), elders (πρεσβυτεροι), and deacons reveals a very high standard of behavior for office-holders in the primitive Church. As I noted above, by the fourth century, at least in a number of places, that standard of behavior required sexual abstinence for those charged with presiding at Eucharist. A more positive evaluation of sexual intercourse could lead us to a different approach today. Paul Beaudette has argued that once the Church abandoned its reluctant acceptance of sexual intercourse a major factor in the argument for priestly celibacy disappeared. Sexual purity does not figure as an argument for priestly celibacy in more recent magisterial documents.[31]

And yet there remains a close relation between sexuality and dealing intimately with holy activities. I suspect that we have a long way to go before we understand the nuances of this relationship and the instinct that has kept these two very potent activities separate. Though such a psychological and cultural anthropological analysis is well outside the scope of my competence, I want to suggest that reflecting more deeply on the relationship between sexuality and priestly sacramental leadership may help us to find a way forward in questions of marital status and gender with regard to the priesthood. This is all the more the case given the increased attention to the spousal or marital imagery of the priestly representation of Christ by contemporary Roman Catholic theologians and the magisterium.[32]

In any case the consistent instinct of the Christian people has been to expect a high public standard of conduct from their priests. To some extent their manner of life needs to manifest a level of asceticism that leads to reverence and respect for the sacredness of the gifts that God wishes to offer human beings. This expectation helps to account for the scandal that Catholics have experienced when they have found some of their priests not only deficient but abusive. It is probably necessary to reinterpret our understanding of sacerdotal purity today, but it would be a grave mistake to abandon the ideal of priestly asceticism altogether.

Priest as Sacramental Minister

In his encyclopedic treatment of Christian ministry in history and theology Bernard Cooke summarizes a very characteristic and traditional approach to the Catholic theology of the priesthood in the post-Tridentine Jesuit theologian Francisco Suarez:

> The ordained minister of the new law offers sacrifice as the minister of Christ, through his power, and in terms of applying to those who need it the merits of Christ's propitiatory sacrifice. This he is able to do because of the consecration he received in ordination, a consecration that consists in the impression of the sacramental character. The primary function of the ordained is to worship God by offering sacrifice in the name of the whole people, and while this is definitively a representative role it seems

to have clear overtones of surrogate. Secondly, the ordained minister has the role of preparing the faithful for and leading them to the worship of God and the salvation of their souls. He is to do this by teaching, by governing, and by judging.[33]

This commonly held view of priestly ministry centers on the issue of a certain power given to the ordained. According to scholastic theology, the power to consecrate is fundamentally the power to offer sacrifice in the name of the Church, precisely since eucharistic sacrifice is being accomplished in consecration.

It seems to me that one starting point for dealing with this theology needs to be a consideration of *what* we mean by sacramental power. If Christ's exercise of divine power is most manifest in his giving of himself to others, his self-emptying (Phil. 2:5–11), then any exercise of power by his disciples must follow the same example. So notions like "power to consecrate" or "power to offer sacrifice" will necessarily be interpreted in Christological fashion. The post–Vatican II ordination rite for presbyters expresses this in the formula for the presentation of the gifts to the newly ordained. We must remember that the *traditio instrumentorum* was since St. Thomas until Pius XII considered the moment of priestly ordination: "Accept from the people of God the gifts to be offered to him. Know what you are doing, and imitate the mystery you celebrate: model your life on the mystery of the Lord's cross."

The clear implication here is that the high point, or at least the most visible and concentrated point, of priestly ministry in liturgical leadership is directly related to the priest's life as modeled on Christ. Here I think that Bérulle and the French School as well as much of traditional priestly training were right on target. A priest is meant to lead an exemplary life of imitating Christ's self-emptying. This sacramental life, since the sacrament of holy order like that of matrimony is primarily located in its being lived out rather than in its initiation, is empowered by God through the Church in order to help God's people to be priestly, i.e., to participate in Christ's life-giving, self-emptying activity. This is what I take to be the *Catechism*'s understanding of the qualitative distinction between ordained and common priesthood when it says:

> While "being ordered to one another," they differ essentially. In what sense? While the common priesthood of the faithful is exercised by the unfolding of baptismal grace — a life of faith, hope, and charity, a life according to the Spirit, the ministerial priesthood is at the service of the common priesthood. It is directed at the unfolding of the baptismal grace of all Christians. The ministerial priesthood is a *means* by which Christ unceasingly builds up and leads his Church. For this reason it is transmitted by its own sacrament, the sacrament of Holy Orders.[34]

It seems to me that the ordained priest's "conforming to the person of Christ" has to do fundamentally with service and therefore with love. In this way one can understand the nuptial imagery so frequently employed. In addition, this understanding helps us to see that one needs to interpret the role of the priest acting *in persona Christi* in the context of his acting *in persona Ecclesiae* and vice versa, as Edward Kilmartin has argued at some length.[35]

What then is the priestly sacrifice of Christ that the ordained priest imitates and whose participation the ordained priest facilitates? Christ's is clearly a priesthood of a different sort from that of the offering of animals or other things. Indeed some modern authors like René Girard, Raymund Schwager, and James Alison have argued that Christ's priestly act puts an end to ritual sacrifice.[36] Christ's sacrifice is the self-offering that leads to the full enjoyment of the Kingdom of God, the self-offering that Paul calls the true Christian sacrifice in Romans 12:1–2. Its essence is to be sought not in slaughter or destruction but in oblation, self-gift.

The liturgical activity of the Church must always be judged by how it is enabling this priestly activity of the People of God. The Letter to the Hebrews (Heb. 7:25) makes it clear that Christ continues to plead his sacrifice. What could this mean but that the Risen Lord is continually helping his Church to join in his self-offering, the life-giving source of the Kingdom?

Conclusion

And so, as I noted at the beginning, we can isolate the question of the priest as sacramental minister for the sake of reflection, but in the final analysis the Christian ministerial priesthood can only be understood in a Christological context which takes account of the threefold office of Christ — as *Lumen Gentium* made clear for bishops and presbyters alike. Ordained priesthood should not be understood as a cultic activity in any way abstracted from the evangelical (preaching) and service (leadership) aspects of ministry any more than one should try to understand the priestly role of Jesus Christ without taking into account his preaching and healing activity. Christ serves as the sole model for Christian ministerial priesthood — in all of its aspects.

Chapter 3

Reflection

Amy Strickland

T HE PRESENTATIONS MADE by John Baldovin and by Susan Wood both seem to raise a central, foundational question: *What does it mean to be a priest?* As Wood rightly observed, there is a crisis today in priestly *identity*. Only when this critical question resolves itself can there be any fruitful discussion of what constitutes priestly *ministry*.

I must admit that my first impression, when listening to both speakers, was a feeling of being horribly old-fashioned in my own thoughts about the nature of priesthood. Perhaps it is merely the legacy of a Dominican theological education, but I remain quite comfortable thinking in terms of the ontological change effected at ordination as a significant distinguishing factor between the ministerial priesthood and the common priesthood. I am also not distressed by so-called "private Masses," given the desirability of a priest celebrating the Eucharist daily, both for the benefit to the Church and to his own soul.[1] In fact, since the celebration of the Eucharist is the "source and summit of the Christian life,"[2] the description by Pope John Paul II of a priest as, "above all, a man of the Eucharist"[3] rings true to my ears.

Yet while I still firmly embrace these traditional notions, I still see the very real dangers of not only a stifling clericalism but also a certain functionalism creeping into this understanding of priestly identity. For all the value the Church places upon the celebration of the sacraments, we do not want priests to be viewed as (or feel like) mere sacramental vending machines. In these days of declining vocations, many priests are charged with trying to pastor numerous communities of the faithful — a virtually impossible task. The faithful in these communities do not interact with these priests as shepherds in the fullest sense, but only as priest-celebrants of the Eucharist.

I fear the same dynamic often plays itself out under the guise of empowering the laity. I see this most clearly in my teaching work with graduate students preparing for lay ministry, many of whom do not hesitate to share their firm conviction that their parishes and institutions only need — or want — the service of priests in those cases in which the Church demands it, e.g., the administration of the sacraments. Many priests themselves foster this type of thinking by, for example, choosing to appear at nuptial Masses and requiem Masses without ever having once met any of the people about to celebrate the sacrament. Oddly enough, these priests, who absolutely only materialize when needed for Masses, are often the same ones who would roundly reject the cultic model of priesthood.

In thinking of a priest primarily in terms of the *munus sanctificandi,* there is also the threat of reductionism, as if being a "good priest" can be measured simply in terms of the number of weddings, baptisms, and Masses at which he presides. We are all familiar with priests who are constantly busy in such ways but nevertheless fail to give the impression of truly being men of prayer. It is rather like the man who insists that he loves his family so much that he must work all hours to provide a better life for them, to the extent that he never spends time with his wife and children. We know that this is an unhealthy dynamic in a marriage, but we often neglect to encourage our priests to make their annual retreat or to allow enough time in the day for personal prayer. Instead, we often want the priest to be constantly available, as one can clearly see by looking at not only the schedule of sacramental celebrations, but also the schedule of meetings in an average parish.

Both priests and laypeople alike need to remember that a fundamental part of being a Christian is falling in love with Christ so passionately that one's relationship with him sets the course for every other. The person who loves cannot help but want to be united as closely as possible with the beloved, and it is this desire that compels us to seek God in prayer. If we turn a deaf ear to this longing, even if it is ostensibly so we can focus on our ministries, there is the temptation to make our work a god unto itself or to convince ourselves we are indispensable. When a priest falls into this trap, he often permits his community to develop a "cult of personality" around him as an individual, which is clearly detrimental both to him and to the faithful. Even worse, when the priest recognizes that constant activity alone is not staving off what Pope John Paul II referred to as "spiritual atrophy,"[4] he may try to fill this emptiness at his center, or at least try to be distracted from it, in other ways, which invariably leads to trouble.

As to other critical issues in the life of the priest today, I would concur with Baldovin that there needs to be a reexamination of the issue of clerical celibacy in the Church. However, I strongly believe the question needs to be framed not as "celibacy: yes or no?" but as "celibacy: what and why?" At a time when married Protestant ministers are permitted to become Catholic priests and retain their spouses, and when widowed permanent deacons may remarry under certain circumstances, it is necessary to consider whether we are succumbing to what T. S. Eliot referred to as "the greatest treason...to do the right thing for the wrong reason."

First, celibacy cannot be seen as a continuation of some antiquated idea of ritual purity, as if sexual intercourse somehow defiled a person. Second, celibacy cannot be construed as the mere obligation to refrain from sexual intercourse, as if a person who engages in other sexual activity, e.g., viewing porn on the Internet, can be truly considered to be living a chaste life. Third, celibacy cannot be blamed for the appalling abuse of children by some members of the clergy, any more than the burden of this abuse can be placed solely upon homosexual priests. It is imperative for the Church to make it clear that being a celibate does not liberate a person from the human condition; celibates are not exempted from either the desire or the need for intimate human relationships.

The Church, however, still guards against seminarians forming personal attachments, those dangerous "particular friendships." It should worry instead about those who seem incapable of forming, or of sustaining, genuine human love. Priests must be encouraged to cultivate healthy friendships with other priests, as well as with laypeople of both sexes. They must be prepared also for the nearly inevitable romantic experience of "falling in love," so that they do not view this as a sign of a weak faith or an incorrect vocational decision. Instead, they should welcome these feelings as an opportunity to deeply engage in the very language of love, which articulates itself in self-sacrifice.

Since fragmentation already pervades many quarters of the Church, we need today a theology of priestly identity that appropriately integrates priestly consecration with priestly mission. As Wood so eloquently asserted, function follows being, but being requires its corresponding function. To place the two in unnecessary conflict with each other creates a false dichotomy. Only with this schism healed can our priests firmly take hold of their own identity and fully realize their great value in the life of the Church.

Part Two

UNDERSTANDING PRIESTHOOD TODAY

Chapter 4

The Priest as Pastor

Rooted in Christ, the Holy Spirit, and the Church

JAMES BACIK

❦

Introduction

THIS CHAPTER examines the history and theology of the priest as pastor, from the perspectives of Christology, pneumatology, and ecclesiology.[1] It will not attempt a comprehensive history of pastoral ministry or a fully developed theology of the priesthood, but it will present a few representative snapshots of priestly ministry, from significant historical periods, and some theological perspectives for exploring the nature and function of the priest-pastor.

In terms of the common threefold description of the ordained minister as priest, prophet, and king or shepherd, this exploration centers on the shepherding ministry of the priest. Our interest is in the pastoral task of forming, guiding, building up, and empowering the baptismal community. From my vantage point of over forty years of pastoral ministry, however, it is clear that the ministerial functions of priest, prophet, and shepherd cannot be neatly separated. They are, in fact, intertwined in the daily life of the priest-pastor. The pastoral task of shepherding the flock is intimately connected with the priestly function of presiding at the Eucharist, which symbolizes and nourishes pastoral ministry, the prophetic work of preaching, and teaching the word of God, which also guides and informs pastoral leadership. We can isolate ordained pastoral ministry for the sake of analysis, but an integrated understanding of the priesthood must also include the ministry of word and sacrament.

The Christological Dimension

A theology of ordained ministry must take into account the public life of Jesus and the ongoing activity of the risen Christ. Priest-pastors are called to put on the mind of Christ, to carry on his work in the world, to learn from his style of ministry, and to appropriate his message. Many pastorally relevant images of Jesus emerge from the New Testament and witness to his public life: the master teacher, who proclaims the kingdom, especially through his provocative parables; the exorcist and healer, who cures the ills of body and soul; the definitive prophet, who proclaims the word of God; and, the savior, who freely hands over his life for the cause of God and humanity. Especially significant for pastors is the image of the Good Shepherd, who gathers the flock, calls the sheep by name, and pursues the strays.

Jesus the Community Builder

Gerhard Lohfink provides a valuable summary of the way Jesus functioned as a community builder throughout his public life.[2] He identified himself at his baptism with the ministry of John the Baptist to reform the community of Israel and to prepare for the end time. His choice of the Twelve was a "symbolic prophetic action," which represented his mission to constitute Israel as a true light to the nations. Lohfink suggests that Jesus chose the Twelve from different regions and different factions within Judaism in order to make clear his desire to gather together the entire nation of Israel. The mighty works of Jesus, including the healing miracles, are signs of the kingdom and an integral part of the eschatological project of restoring Israel. When Jesus cures the ten lepers, for example, he tells them to go and show themselves to the priests, who will authenticate the cure and admit them back into the community life (Luke 17:11–19). The healing miracles generally signal that no one, including the sick, is excluded from the reign of God.

The community-building aspect of the ministry of Jesus is also found in the special prayer he taught his disciples. The prophet Ezekiel had proclaimed that God would bring Israel back from exile, so that God's holy name would be honored (Ezek. 36:22–24). In the

Lord's Prayer, the phrase "hallowed be thy name" recalls this divine promise to restore Israel. The next phrase, "thy kingdom come," suggests that God's reign will be established through the restoration of Israel. For Jesus, this restoration is not an end in itself but is for the sake of gathering together the entire human family. Israel must be a genuine community of faith in order to attract the other nations and to be a compelling example of a reconciled humanity.

Jesus saw himself as the Suffering Servant who would take on the sins of Israel and offer his death for their redemption and that of the world. When Israel as a whole refused to accept his message, Jesus concentrated his attention on a small circle of disciples, which symbolized his salvific intention for Israel and all people. In Matthew's Gospel, the Sermon on the Mount is directed to the disciples and the crowds, but applies to all human beings (Matt. 5:1, 7:28). The disciples who left their families in order to follow Jesus became a new family based not on blood relationships but on their commitment to Jesus. They shared regularly in table fellowship with him, which set the stage for the Last Supper, where he broke tradition by washing the feet of his disciples (John 13:1–20). Jesus had indeed come to serve and not to be served (Mark 10:45).

In the new community established by Jesus, there is a fundamental equality. Patriarchal domination is no longer permissible. The disciples are to call no one on earth "father" (Matt. 23:9). Those who aspire to be great among them must be servants (Mark 10:42–45), and the greatest shall be as the youngest (Luke 22:26). There is to be no violence; they are to respond to brutality with kindness, to turn the other cheek, and to go the extra mile (Matt. 5:38–42). The counter-cultural community formed by Jesus is charged with the task of transforming humanity through its good example. The whole community functions as the salt of the earth, as the light of the world, and as a city on a mountain, which cannot be hidden (Matt. 13–16). The disciples of Jesus represent the whole of Israel and serve as a sign and instrument of the universal reign of God.

Lohfink summarizes: "Jesus did not speak of the church. But he did gather around himself, in the midst of Israel and for Israel, people who were for him the new family of God, the true Israel, and the eschatological city of God. For Jesus, the reign of God shone already in these people; the future kingdom was already symbolically present in them."[3]

The historical Jesus and his public life of self-giving service provide an inexhaustible resource for reflection on the nature and function of ordained ministry in the Church.[4] Pastors have the primary responsibility for forming a local community of faith which functions as a credible sign and effective instrument of the kingdom. Compassionate pastors follow the example of the Good Shepherd in gathering the flock and reaching out to those who have strayed. They are especially attentive to the sick and the needy, as was the Master. Their love for the flock is inclusive, as was his. Pastors are to follow the example of Jesus by washing feet and not seeking power or prestige. Ordained ministers are called to a life of service by God and sent on a mission, as was the Word made flesh. The amount of energy Jesus devoted to forming community provides continuing motivation for pastors involved in the day-to-day work of serving parishioners, maintaining the unity of the parish, and enhancing its vitality. Reflection on the failures Jesus experienced in his ministry, e.g., the desertion of his inner circle, can help pastors face the inevitable disappointments built into pastoral ministry.

The Risen Christ

Pastors not only gain inspiration and guidance from the example of the historical Jesus, they also participate in the power and energy of the risen Christ at work in the Church. In tune with Augustine, we can say that it is Christ who shepherds the flock, just as he baptizes and consecrates it. The risen Lord continues the pastoral tasks of nourishing, leading, guiding, purifying, governing, unifying, and empowering the faith community. Pastors are representatives of Christ, who is the head of the Church. They are configured to Christ and serve as his co-workers in building up the baptismal community. The risen Lord empowers pastors to carry on his work.

Given the rich material in the New Testament, it is quite remarkable how little the public life of Jesus has influenced theological reflection on ordained ministry throughout Christian history. For example, Gregory the Great's book *Pastoral Care,* which shaped the understanding of the priesthood and its practice for almost half a millennium, makes only a few references to Christ and says little or nothing about the pastoral ministry of Jesus. The great medieval theologians, Aquinas, Bonaventure, and Scotus, did not write much about Jesus as the example for pastoral ministers, probably because they saw the essence of the priesthood in the power to consecrate at Mass.[5] The Council of Trent also neglected the historical Jesus in its treatment of the priesthood.

The Second Vatican Council

The Second Vatican Council retrieved elements of the Christological dimension of the priesthood which highlight the pastoral role of ordained ministers. Walter Kasper argues that the notion of the priest as representative of Christ is the fundamental theme running through the conciliar documents on the priesthood.[6] *Presbyterorum Ordinis,* for example, notes that "priests exercise the function of Christ as Pastor and Head in proportion to their authority" (no. 6). It is significant that in the original Latin text of this document the bishops chose to use the broader biblical term "presbyter," which encompasses the pastoral function, rather than *sacerdos,* which emphasizes the priestly cultic role. The decree goes on to say: "By the Sacrament of Order priests are configured to Christ the priest as servants of the Head, so that as his co-workers with the episcopal order they may build up the Body of Christ, the Church" (no. 12). Priests do not take on the pastoral role themselves, nor are they simply deputized by the community. They are called by Christ to share in his saving work. The Decree on the Training of Priests, *Optatam Totius,* admonishes priests "who are to take on the likeness of Christ" to form "the habit of drawing close to him as friends in every detail of their lives" (no. 8). They should "live his paschal mystery" in such a way that they will know "how to initiate into it the people committed to their charge" (no. 8). Seminary training should make them "true shepherds of souls after the example of our Lord Jesus Christ,

teacher, priest and shepherd" (no. 4). Priests should conduct themselves among the flock "after the example of the Master," who came
not to be served but to serve (no. 9). They should be "more intimately
united with Christ the teacher" and be "guided by his spirit in the
very act of teaching the word" (no. 13). Priests can achieve greater
unity and harmony in their lives by "following in the fulfillment of
their ministry the example of Christ the Lord," who did the will of
him who sent him (no. 14).

The Virtue of Humble Confidence

Presbyterorum Ordinis highly recommends the virtue of humility for
priests who are representing Christ the head of the Church, who are
taking on a task that "transcends all human strength and human wisdom" (no. 15). God chose weak human beings in the world to shame
the strong (1 Cor. 1:27); the "true minister of Christ is conscious of
his own weakness and labors in humility" (no. 15). Priests are called
upon to "conform themselves to Christ," who emptied himself and
took the form of the servant, becoming obedient unto death (Phil.
2:7–9).

   Given the unprecedented problems facing the priesthood in the
United States today, priests are experiencing a crisis of confidence.
Dwindling numbers, the sex-abuse scandal, and polarization in the
Church have hurt the morale of many priests. In this situation, it
seems wise to speak not only about humility but also about the dialectical virtue of humble-confidence. Paradoxically, true humility leads
to confidence. Humility prompts priests to recognize our personal
limitations and complete dependence on God. It is the power of divine grace that works through us to help spread the kingdom. We are
ambassadors of Christ, who strengthens us for the task of sharing the
good news. The Holy Spirit can transform our weakness and limitations into instruments of healing and spiritual growth for others. We
do not need to be perfect or have all the answers to minister effectively. Humility, rooted in truth, bolsters our confidence and deepens
our trust in God. We priests are public representatives of the rich
Catholic tradition, which possesses valuable resources for counter-
ing some of the most destructive trends in contemporary culture. We

can confidently draw on our communal sense of human existence, which challenges rugged individualism; our tradition of asceticism, which counters consumerism; our natural law ethic, which opposes total relativism; and our rich spiritual tradition, which exposes the superficiality of materialism.

Furthermore, pastors bring the gospel to crucial moments in the lives of individuals and families, ranging from the baptism of babies through preparation for marriage to the burial of the dead. People allow us to enter into their lives at times of deep spiritual need. We can be confident that we are bearers of good news for people with genuine needs.

Events have pushed priests off the pedestal into a more humble posture, where we know the cross in a new way. From this position, it becomes clearer that our confidence comes not from ourselves but from our relationship to Christ the head of the Church. Humility and confidence are mutually reinforcing. They form a dialectical virtue with the accent today on confidence. When we look at ordained ministry from a Christological perspective, we learn from the example of the historical Jesus witnessed in the Gospels; we gain strength and confidence from the risen Christ, who continues to shepherd the flock and guide the community of faith.

The Pneumatological Dimension

Spirit in the New Testament

The New Testament indicates that the movement begun by Jesus was guided by the Holy Spirit from the very beginning.[7] This is especially clear in the two-volume work of Luke. In his Gospel, the Holy Spirit overshadows Mary, who conceives a son named Jesus (Luke 1:35). The Spirit comes upon Jesus at his baptism, anointing him for his role as the Servant of Yahweh (Luke 3:31–22) and empowering him for his teaching ministry starting in Galilee (Luke 4:14–15). In the beginning of the Acts of the Apostles, Jesus instructs the disciples to wait in Jerusalem for "the promise of the Father," which is their baptism with the Holy Spirit (Acts 1:4–5). On the Jewish feast of Pentecost, the promised Spirit descends upon the Apostles, enabling them to proclaim the mighty deeds of God in different tongues understood by people from every nation under heaven (Acts 2:1–13). Peter interprets this remarkable event as the outpouring of the Spirit of God promised by Joel, which would bring salvation to all who call upon the name of the Lord (Acts 2:14–21). Indeed, all those who were converted and baptized received the gift of the Holy Spirit (Acts 2:38). This Spirit continues to guide leaders of the baptismal community. Led by the Spirit, Peter preaches the word to the household of Cornelius, a Gentile (Acts 10:19). The Council of Jerusalem announces its open policy for Gentile converts as "a decision of the Holy Spirit and us" (Acts 15:28). For Luke, the Church is born in the power of the Holy Spirit. The Spirit continues to energize and guide both the community and its leaders. The whole Church is a sacrament of the Spirit.

The Apostle Paul turned the kingdom image of Jesus into spirit language. His first Letter to the Corinthians highlights the power of the Spirit at work in their community. His ministry to them draws its strength not from his own talents but from spirit and power (1 Cor. 2:4–5). The Corinthians received the Spirit, who enables them to understand the things of God and to have the mind of Christ (1 Cor. 2:12–16). Paul invokes their relationship to the Spirit to warn them against factions which harm the community: "Do you not know that you are the temple of God and that the Spirit of God dwells in you?" (1 Cor. 3:16). In the Christian community, there are many charisms or spiritual gifts, such as wisdom, healing, and prophecy, but all flow from the same Spirit (1 Cor. 12:4–11). Paul urges them to use their charisms to build up the body of Christ (1 Cor. 12:12–26) and to serve the common good (1 Cor. 12:7) — an admonition that strikes at the root of all individualistic piety and reveals the practical thrust of his pneumatology.

In the Gospel of John, Jesus promises that the Father will send the Paraclete, the Spirit of Truth, who will remind them of everything Jesus taught them (John 14:16–17). This Advocate will empower the disciples to testify to Jesus (John 15:26–27) and will guide them to all truth by declaring what Jesus had taught them (John 16:12–15).

These brief references to the Paraclete remind us of the Johannine conviction that the Spirit is at work here and now in the whole community of faith.

During the New Testament period, leaders who were guided by the Spirit carried out pastoral ministry in local communities of faith. Paul admonishes followers of Jesus to esteem "those who are over you in the Lord" (1 Thess. 5:12). The Acts of the Apostles mentions setting up presbyters in every church (Acts 14:23). There was, however, no normative structure of leadership, no clear delineation of roles, and no common terminology to name the pastoral leaders. Jesus did not leave a blueprint or flow chart for leaders in the Church. Forms of oversight leadership developed gradually, in response to the needs of the faith community and social influences, under the inspiration of the Spirit.

We know little about the actual functions of the pastoral leaders in the primitive Church. Clearly, they did not take to themselves all the ministerial functions of community life, and they did not claim all the charisms of the individual members. They were not called priests; their duties were not confined to cultic matters. The pastoral leaders in the New Testament period did not separate themselves from the people and form a privileged class. Presumably, they were called by God, with the consent and collaboration of the local community, to positions of leadership and received the gift of the Spirit to carry out their ministry. The whole baptismal community had the task of keeping alive the memory of Jesus and carrying on his mission. All the members constituted a chosen race, a royal priesthood, a holy nation (1 Pet. 2:1–10). Judging by the Corinthian experience, those charged with oversight had the difficult task of maintaining unity and reconciling differences. They had to coordinate the charismatic gifts of the baptized in their charge. Paul's general admonition not to quench the Spirit (1 Thess. 5:19) surely applied in a special way to the pastoral leaders. So did his great emphasis on the freedom of Christians who partake in the paschal mystery of Christ: "For freedom Christ has set us free" (Gal. 5:1). The warnings of Paul suggest that even in the original charismatic communities, overseers knew the temptation to control the Spirit.

The Clericalization of Ministry

Edward Schillebeeckx portrays the history of ordained ministry in the Church as a gradual process of clericalization, which placed the diverse functions shared by all the baptized in the early Church into the hands of the bishops and the clergy assisting them.[8] The development of a mono-episcopate is already evident early in the second century in the churches addressed by Ignatius of Antioch in his letters. After Constantine and Theodosius gave official status to Christianity, senior clergy began to take on imperial trappings. During the patristic period, the clergy gradually appropriated for themselves the responsibilities of the community. This process was sanctioned legally and theologically in the Middle Ages. The clergy controlled the sacraments and their spiritual power. The New Testament ideal of servant leadership was often lost in this accumulation of power by the ordained leaders.

According to Schillebeeckx, theology played a role in this process of clericalization. The position of Aquinas and other medieval theologians that the essence of the priesthood is rooted in the power to consecrate the bread and wine at Mass gave further prominence to the clergy and disassociated them from the community and its pastoral care. The theological distinction between the power to consecrate conferred by the sacrament of order and the power of jurisdiction, which extends to pastoral oversight, separated the priestly and pastoral functions and contributed to the clericalization process. Furthermore, the Christology developed from the seventeenth century onward, which rooted the priestly work of Jesus in his divinity rather than his humanity, tended to sacralize the priesthood and to divorce the sacrament of holy orders from its foundation in baptism. Priests were seen as other Christs, given a new ontological reality through the character imparted by ordination.[9] As a result of all these developments, priests and laity alike tended to identify the Church with the ordained leaders and to relegate lay persons to a passive role. It should be noted that there are exceptions to this broad generalization. For example, in the United States during the nineteenth century, lay people exercised great power in their parishes.[10]

Typically, the Catholic immigrants clustered together in national groups, bought land, built a Church, and hired a pastor. Lay trustees controlled the finances of the parish and much of the decision-making process. Pastors were often forced to comply with the wishes of the lay leaders who represented the parish. Only gradually did the bishops of the United States gain control of the parishes, setting up the heavily clericalized Church of twentieth-century America.

The Second Vatican Council

The clericalization of the Church, which gave great power and prestige to the pastor, was challenged in various ways by the Second Vatican Council, including its emphasis on the role of the Holy Spirit in all the members of the Church, both laity and clergy. *Lumen Gentium* underscored the power of the Holy Spirit, which "dwells in the Church and in the hearts of the faithful." The Spirit guides the Church, bestowing on her "hierarchical and charismatic gifts." Through baptism lay people are full members of the Church, sharing in the priesthood of Christ and the gifts of the Holy Spirit. They are co-responsible for creating a vital parish community. They participate in the mission of the parish not by delegation of the pastor but by virtue of their baptism. The task of the ordained minister is to empower parishioners to use their own individual gifts to build up the Body of Christ and to contribute to the common good.

The Decree on the Ministry and Life of Priests recognizes that ordained ministers are disciples of the Lord along with all the faithful. They too received the Spirit in the sacraments of initiation. Holy orders direct their baptismal gifts to the role of oversight in the Church. They act not only as representatives of Christ but also as representatives of the Church. In this role priests are to promote the dignity of lay people and their vital role in the Church's mission. In one of its most significant statements, the decree insists that pastors "must discover with faith, recognize with joy, and foster with diligence the many charismatic gifts of the laity, whether these be of a humble or more exalted kind." In other words, the pastor's task is to spot talent and to help individuals to develop their particular gifts, which they then can use to enhance parish life and to humanize society. To accomplish this, a pastor needs to know his parishioners and deal with them as unique individuals. He should make sure they get proper training through parish and diocesan programs. The priest functions like a conductor of an orchestra, who elicits the best from each musician, or like the coach of a basketball team, who convinces players based on their particular skills to play their proper role on the team. The pastor helps the parish become a genuine sacrament of the Spirit, a community where the gifts of all the members are encouraged and celebrated. A Spirit-filled community celebrates the liturgy with joy and enthusiasm, ready to take on the responsibilities of humanizing the world and spreading the reign of God. A parish fully alive is the glory of God. It serves as a credible sign of the presence of the Spirit in the world and of the unity of the human family.

A Collaborative Style

Effective pastors today employ a collaborative style of leadership which involves parishioners in decision making and fosters team approaches to ministry. They encourage the formation of various interest groups and bring parishioners together to work on particular projects. Collaboration helps to multiply the energy centers within the community and enables more people to respond to the Spirit, who produces and distributes special gifts to all the members of the parish (1 Cor. 12:11). We can imagine a parish with so many distinct energy centers, so much creative activity, so many groups praying and serving that the pastor could not control it all even if he were tempted to do so.

The Virtue of Committed Openness

Priests who have developed the virtue of committed openness are better able to lead a parish which functions as a sacrament of the Spirit. Committed openness is best thought of as a dialectical virtue in which two apparently opposed values interact in a fruitful tension. At its best, commitment to the vision, values, and ideals of the Christian heritage leads to a more receptive spirit which is open

to truth, goodness, and beauty wherever they are encountered. Ordained ministers who cultivate this virtue find their lives are enriched
as they drink in the experience of those they serve. Their own commitments will, in turn, encourage others to take greater responsibility
for the well-being of the faith community. This virtue enables pastors
to avoid both a weak, vacillating leadership style that leads to mind-
less relativism and a rigid approach that leads to authoritarianism.
The ideal of committed openness encourages pastors to be so rooted
in their faith, so knowledgeable of their Christian tradition, so confident about their own identity that they are open to the constructive
contributions, helpful initiatives, good ideas, and valid criticisms of
others in the faith community. With this open spirit they can share
themselves and their vision of the parish without embarrassment or
coercion, while at the same time receiving from the community praise
and criticism without being puffed up or threatened. Pastors who
develop this virtue do not need to control everything. They can re-
joice in the successes and accomplishments of the other members of
the parish. They can encourage their parishioners to greater involvement without getting strident or forgetting that lay persons have other
commitments to their families and jobs.

The Ecclesial Dimension

Pastoral Ministry

Priest-pastors are not only empowered by the Spirit to represent
Christ, but are also ordained by their bishop to minister within a
local parish. In other words, pastoral ministry has an ecclesial, as
well as Christological and pneumatological, dimension. The ecclesial
perspective brings into sharper focus the concrete relational character of ordained ministry. Pastors relate to their bishops, their fellow
priests, their neighbors, and their parishioners. All these relationships
are significant and raise important questions. I want to concentrate,
however, on the connection between the pastor and his parishioners.
These parishioners inhabit a particular social, economic, political,

and cultural milieu, all of which influence pastoral practice. Parishes have their own history and exist in a particular neighborhood or geographical area. As Susan Wood has pointed out, we can do a rather abstract, ahistorical analysis of the cultic priesthood, but an examination of the priest as pastor demands a more concrete historical approach.[11]

There are, of course, constants in pastoral ministry. Pastors must attend to the flock, preach the word, and preside at liturgy. They have the common responsibilities of caring for the sick, reaching out to the needy, preparing couples for marriage, encouraging the works of justice and peace, burying the dead, and consoling the grieving. The precise shape of pastoral ministry, however, has varied, according to the concrete needs of parishioners and the historical development of parishes, throughout Christian history.

A Theology of the Parish

Karl Rahner has argued persuasively that there is a proper theology of the parish.[12] "The parish is, in a very definite sense, the representative actuality of the Church: the Church appears and manifests itself in the central life of the parish."[13] The premise of his position is that "the Church, as event, is necessarily a local and localized community; the Church must always again and again become event."[14] The Church is the graced but sinful community which carries on the work of the incarnate Word of God in the world. It becomes event most intensively in the celebration of the Eucharist, which always occurs in a particular place. It is in the parish that most Catholics celebrate the Eucharist and thus experience the Church as event. The liturgical ideal may be the Eucharist celebrated with the bishop in the cathedral surrounded by his presbyters, but in actuality most people experience the Eucharist in the local parish. The parish Church is not simply a division of the larger universal Church; it is rather "the highest degree of actuality of the total Church."[15] Moreover, it is the primary realization of the Church as event. A proper understanding of the local church calls for a theology of the priest-pastor which is rooted in the concrete history of parish life.

The Relationship of Pastor and Parish

In the early centuries of the Jesus movement, bishops served as oversight leaders of the churches in the major cities. After the time of Constantine, the growing number of Christians in both rural areas and the cities made it necessary for bishops to ordain presbyters to help carry on their pastoral work.[16] These ordained ministers, who served as leaders in local Christian communities, are the real forerunners of modern pastors. The presbyters, or priests, as they came to be called, clearly functioned as representatives of the bishop in providing pastoral care to a particular community. They were chosen or accepted by the local church and were ordained by the bishop, generally through a liturgical laying on of hands. Their pastoral work of building up the Body of Christ was organically connected with their liturgical ministry of presiding at the Eucharist. The essential connection between priest and congregation was mandated by the Council of Chalcedon in 451: "no one can be ordained priest or deacon in an absolute manner... unless a local community is clearly assigned to him."[17] In general, the Church followed this legislation throughout the first millennium.

During the second millennium, another understanding of the nature and the role of the priest, which undercut the original normative pattern, emerged. The local community lost its right to choose or accept its pastoral leader. The practice of absolute ordinations forbidden by Chalcedon became common. Monks were ordained as priests although they did no pastoral work and said private Masses without a congregation. Reflecting and supporting this change in practice, theologians located the essence of the priesthood in the power to consecrate the Eucharist and to forgive sins. This shift reduced the importance of pastoral ministry. Since priests already possessed the fullness of the power conferred by holy orders, historical circumstances reduced the episcopacy to a position of dignity and jurisdictional power.

Historical Snapshots

Even without an adequate theology of the priesthood, pastors continued to minister in local congregations in various historical circumstances. Unfortunately, there is no comprehensive history of Christian parishes and the priests who led them.[18] We can, however, gain a better understanding of the functions of priest-pastors by examining selected segments of church history that are better documented. These five historical snapshots offer only a very limited view of a complex reality in one geographical area of the large universal Church. Nevertheless, they do indicate some significant changes in the practice and theory of the priesthood.

Cyprian's Carthage

In the middle of the third century the Church in Carthage, North Africa, was suffering under the persecution of the emperor Decius. Many Christians renounced their faith, and disputes arose about readmitting them to the Church.[19] Cyprian, a convert to Christianity, was elected bishop of his native city, Carthage, in 249 and provided vigorous leadership until he was martyred in 258. His voluminous writings provide the most detailed knowledge we have of pastoral ministry in the pre-Constantinian period. He describes the role of the preeminent pastoral figure, who is called "bishop" but who functions in some ways like a priest-pastor, in the Church. Each Christian community had one bishop who served for life. He was elected by the community or by neighboring bishops and was installed by other bishops with the consent of the community. His ministry of oversight included control over the church finances. He was the principal judge in the Church, instructing his people in the moral demands of the gospel and punishing those who failed to live up to them. He presided at the Eucharist, administrated the sacrament of baptism, and received sinners back into the community. Caring for the poor was an important part of his pastoral duties, as was maintaining the unity of the Church. The bishop, like Peter, was the rock upon which the local church was founded. He helped provide a stable community, a place to belong, a bulwark against the idolatry of the Roman Empire. In carrying out his pastoral duties, he consulted with the presbyters, the confessors, and the laity, especially on important matters, such as readmitting lapsed Christians back into the Church. The other ministers in the faith community worked under his supervision.

In this snapshot of Cyprian's Church, we note that the ordained leader was chosen or accepted by the local community and maintained a close relationship with his flock. His pastoral oversight extended to all aspects of community life and included priestly and prophetic functions. He presided at the Eucharist and other sacraments; he spoke out against division in the Church. Finally, he enlisted others in his ministry and coordinated their efforts.

Europe in the Tenth Century

Pastoral ministry near the end of the first millennium reflected the disarray of the times as well as the continuing influence of the book *Pastoral Care,* written centuries earlier, in 591, by Pope Gregory the Great. After the death of Charlemagne in 816, Europe continued falling into a state of decline and disintegration. Islam posed an ongoing threat. Popes were political pawns and guilty of scandalous behavior. Bishops exercised temporal power as well as the spiritual oversight of the local church. Feudal lords had control of many local congregations, known as proprietary churches, and hired priests to carry out the pastoral ministry.[20] These pastors were often poorly educated and lacked training for ministry. The most important resource available for training priests was Gregory's *Pastoral Care,* which advocated a more paternalistic style of ministerial leadership than found under Cyprian. Pope Gregory stressed that the priest provided important services for the people, especially at Mass when he consecrated the bread and wine, offered the sacrifice of Christ to the Father, and distributed the Body of Christ to the faithful.[21] Pastors served the spiritual needs of the people by preaching sermons which described the Christian life as a fierce warfare against evil and admonished sinners to repent. Gregory's advice that preaching is more effective if reinforced by a priestly life of virtue and good example was often ignored. As the ordinary ministers of sacramental reconciliation, pastors made the healing power of divine mercy available to the people. In general, priests acting in Christ's name served as ministers of salvation for the people in their care, who were expected to obey the clergy.

We see in this snapshot a different style of pastoral leadership compared to Cyprian's approach in third-century North Africa. Pastors were more paternalistic and did less consulting with ordinary parishioners. They were appointed or hired without the consent of the people. Lay persons were more passive and less involved. Preaching was more moralistic and less uplifting. The priest's main function was liturgical, rather than pastoral.

Europe in the Fourteenth Century

In fourteenth-century Europe, people were preoccupied with the mystery of death. In less than two decades, the Black Death wiped out almost three-quarters of the European population. Parish priests, especially in the remote villages, were poorly educated and not well trained for their pastoral role. Some of the clergy were celibate, but many others entered common law marriages or were involved in sexual relationships with parishioners.[22]

Given the devastating effects of the plague, pastors had to provide important services surrounding death, i.e., caring for the sick, burying the dead, and comforting those who mourned their loss.[23] They frequently celebrated Masses of the dead and promoted All Souls as a major feast. Their sermons often dealt with the four last things, death, judgment, heaven, and hell, along with strong admonitions to go to confession for the forgiveness of sins. Lay people valued priests for their power to consecrate the bread and wine at Mass. Eucharistic piety put great emphasis on seeing the consecrated bread elevated at Mass. Exposition of the Blessed Sacrament provided parishioners with another opportunity to see the host and adore Christ. Benediction became a popular devotion, especially the blessing imparted by the priest with a consecrated host visible in a monstrance. The piety of the times was more interested in seeing Jesus in the host than in receiving him in communion.

Pastors in this period were influenced by a manual entitled *Instructions for Parish Priests,* which encouraged priests to study and to lead virtuous lives, so that their preaching and teaching would be more effective.[24] According to the manual, the pastor should dress like a cleric and avoid worldly pursuits. He was to prepare people for marriage, instructing them on the duties of husband and wife. One of his major responsibilities, to make sure the Eucharist was celebrated properly, was instructing his parishioners on the real presence, on the proper way to receive communion, and on the benefits of seeing the host. He had to teach the people the Our Father, the Hail Mary, and the Creed and had to explain to them the seven sacraments. The manual gave the greatest attention to confession and the process of leading penitents through a complete examination of conscience and then assigning them a penance to fit the severity of their sin.[25] During this period, the complex relationship between priests and their flock did have positive elements. Some pastors in towns and rural areas were very close to their people, sharing a harsh common life with them and functioning as physicians of the soul for them in a time shadowed by suffering, sickness, and death.

This snapshot reminds us that pastors are always called to respond to the historically conditioned needs of the people they serve. The effectiveness of pastoral ministry is organically related to the personal qualities and lifestyle of the ordained ministers. Clergy education is essential for effective ministry. In the late Middle Ages, priests were clearly seen as cultic figures, esteemed for their power to make Jesus present in the host, more to be seen and adored than received as spiritual food. The ministry of the word was heavily moralistic, stressing personal sinfulness and the need for confession. This was a low point in European society and in the Church. Pastors could not easily rise above the disintegration and immorality that surrounded them.

The United States in the 1920s

The Council of Trent (1545–1563) with its many reforms set the tone for pastoral ministry for the next four centuries, all the way up to the time of the Second Vatican Council.[26] Practically, Trent had to respond to the decadence of the clergy, as well as the challenges to the theory and practice of the priesthood, as presented by the Reformers, especially Luther and Calvin. The council mandated that the parish priest preach on every Sunday and Holy Day and offer catechetical, sacramental, and moral education for his people. Pastors must live within the boundaries of their parish. Bishops should make sure that worthy pastors are assigned immediately to vacated parishes. Priests entrusted with care of the sheep have multiple responsibilities: to offer sacrifice for their parishioners; to nourish them by preaching God's word, by administering the sacraments, and by providing good example; and, to care for the poor and those in need. Pastors in tune with the spirit of Trent encouraged Benediction and processions of the Blessed Sacrament as well as various Marian devotions. Over a period of time, the reforms of Trent produced a better-educated clergy and a greater uniformity in pastoral ministry and parish life. Cumulatively, however, the reforms put the clergy in such a strong leadership position that lay members of the Church often assumed a purely passive role.

Theologically, Trent simply accepted the standard scholastic understanding of the priesthood and left in place the cultic model.[27] The council said little about the public ministry of Jesus as a model for priests and their pastoral tasks. The bishops did insist, against Luther and Calvin, that holy orders is a sacrament that imprints an indelible character, although they left open the question of how to define it. Bishops are superior to priests, possessing the power to ordain and to confer confirmation. Priests are defined by their power to consecrate and offer the body and blood of the Lord and remit or retain sins. Bishops can assign priests to parishes without the consent of the parishioners.

The reforms of the Council of Trent helped shape ordained ministry in Catholic parishes throughout the whole history of the United States, including the 1920s, known as the golden age of Catholic parish life.[28] By 1920, the congregational model, which gave the laity great influence in parishes during the nineteenth century, had disappeared, and clerical dominance had prevailed. It was common for a priest to enjoy a long tenure as the pastor of a parish, which reinforced his authority. Pastors functioned like the pope in their parish. Catholic culture celebrated the "brick and mortar pastor" who built the church, the school, the rectory, and the convent. As we saw in previous snapshots, lay people held priests in high esteem because of their power to celebrate Mass and to forgive sins.

Pastors earned the respect of the Catholic immigrants, when thirty million of them came to the United States between 1820 and 1920, by meeting their spiritual needs and helping them gradually move into the mainstream of American life. Parishes functioned like Catholic ghettos, where lower-class working people could renew their religious identity and find refuge from a culture that attacked their values and degraded their religion. Anti-Catholic nativism was a harsh reality for immigrants trying to survive in a new country. Pastors helped meet the spiritual needs of their parishioners by administering the sacraments and providing many devotional opportunities, such as Benediction and Sorrowful Mother Novenas. Sermons often emphasized the horror of sin and the need to go to confession as a sign of repentance. Preachers presented God both as stern Judge and as kind Father.

The pastor was not only in charge of the parish; he also, with the help of assistant priests in larger parishes, did most of the ministerial work. He celebrated Mass every day, administered the sacraments, preached at the Sunday Masses, led devotions, prepared couples for marriage, instructed converts individually, took communion to the sick, visited homes, and taught religion in the parish school. The St. Vincent de Paul Society helped care for the poor and needy. The Altar and Rosary Society kept the church looking good and sponsored social events. The Holy Name Society helped raise money and sponsored public expressions of the faith, such as parades and processions. For the most part, however, the pastor was a Lone Ranger, carrying out the pastoral tasks by himself.

We see in this snapshot a reformed clergy at work. The priests were better trained and, for the most part, committed to meeting the needs of their parishioners. The pastor had total control of all aspects of parish life, and his many pastoral tasks consumed his time and energy. There was truth in the old saying that the parishioners' job was to pay, pray, and obey. Priests formed a special clerical caste and generally enjoyed the respect of their people. Their ministry, while heavily cultic, did include pastoral and prophetic aspects. The parishes they ran were collectively a remarkable institutional achievement, offering much-needed service to a growing immigrant population. Parishes helped pass on the faith to succeeding generations of Catholics and provided a protective and nourishing spiritual home for them. The priests who helped provide these services earned the respect and affection extended to them by generations of Catholic immigrants.

Parishes in the United States Today

The Second Vatican Council (1962–1965) set the stage for a new approach to pastoral ministry and the role of the ordained priest. By 1960, most Catholics had entered the mainstream of American life. The election of John Kennedy that year as the first Catholic president signaled this new status. The GI Bill played a major role in the upward mobility of Catholics by enabling many veterans of World War II to go to college, get better jobs, and move to the suburbs. New parishes were established to serve this growing population. The more educated lay persons wanted a greater voice in the life of the parish and presented new challenges to the clergy. At the same time, about one-fourth of the Catholic population, predominately Hispanic, still had not made it into the economic mainstream and required a different type of pastoral care.

In this situation, the reforms of Vatican II were welcomed by many American Catholics. The council prompted a great resurgence of lay ministry rooted in the baptismal call of all Christians. This ministry included service to the world as well as greater participation in the internal life of the parish. The council also presented a broader notion of the priesthood by linking it to the threefold office of Christ as priest, prophet, and king or shepherd. This effectively put greater emphasis on the pastoral role of ordained ministers. As we have seen, it also highlighted the Christological dimension of the priesthood as well as the task of identifying and encouraging the gifts and talents of all the parishioners. Vatican II did not produce a new comprehensive theology of the priesthood, but its points of emphasis did contribute to dramatic changes in the practice of pastoral ministry.

Priests who have appropriated the spirit of Vatican II function quite differently from the typical pre-conciliar pastor. These pastors see themselves as servants of the community rather than as authority figures who run everything in the parish. They employ a more collaborative style of ministry than the Lone Ranger style in the preconciliar Church. Today, lay persons perform many of the ministerial duties formerly done by priests. Much of the work is done by groups or committees. The parish council helps set policy; the finance committee is in charge of raising money; the liturgy committee helps plan weekend Masses; the social justice committee organizes activities to help the poor and work for social change. Individuals also perform important ministerial tasks: the religious education director runs the catechetical programs for all age levels; the RCIA coordinator organizes the program to prepare people to be received into the Church at the Easter Vigil; married couples prepare engaged couples for marriage; the youth minister coordinates activities for young people; and the deacon handles annulment cases, leads wake services, and periodically preaches at weekend Masses. Vital parishes are blessed with many people who use their gifts for the sake of the Church.

Today a pastor needs a new and different set of skills than he would have needed in the past. He must find the right people to do all of these ministries and provide them with proper training, plus give them regular encouragement. He mediates disputes and promotes harmony among the many people ministering in the parish. Much of his time is spent going to meetings and interacting with the various groups. He does less hands-on ministry since his staff and parishioners do much of that. The pastor ministers to the ministers.

All of this ministerial activity finds sacramental focus in the weekend liturgies. A wise pastor puts a great deal of energy into presiding at the liturgy and preaching the homily. In his preaching task, he functions as a mystagogue who helps evoke a sense of mystery in the assembly and shows how the Scripture readings illumine the spiritual journey. His homilies are designed not to pour new knowledge and inspiration into empty minds and hearts, but rather to enable people to become more aware of the God within who calls each of us to responsible action on behalf of the kingdom. This approach to preaching is also evident in his teaching and counseling.

Part of the role of the Vatican II pastor is to make sure the parish does not get turned in on itself. He must remind parishioners that they are part of the larger diocesan Church that links them to the universal Church. As a priest, he is a member of the diocesan presbyterate and participates in the oversight ministry of the bishop. His leadership role in the parish represents the essential connection between the parish and the diocese. The pastor encourages parishioners to spread the kingdom in the world and to meet the needs of the poor. Drawing on the social teaching of the Church, he guides the effort to overcome social sin and transform unjust structures into more humane instruments of good. He calls the parish to be a leaven in society, a model for how human relationships work best. Effective pastors keep this prophetic vision before their people as a constant reminder that parishes exist not for their own sake but for the cause of God and humanity.

This last snapshot presents one idealized version of contemporary pastoral ministry. Not all parishes today are vibrant, well-organized communities with wise leadership and many active parishioners. Not all pastors buy into the Vatican II pastoral model. Some priests today see themselves primarily as liturgical presiders and only secondarily as pastoral leaders. Even among those guided by the spirit of the council, there are different operative theologies of the priesthood and diverse leadership styles. Nevertheless, the contrast between a vibrant Vatican II parish today and a pre-conciliar parish is remarkable, as those of us who have ministered in both types can attest.

The contemporary pastor has less direct contact with parishioners than priests in the past. The pre-conciliar pastor, for example, gave individual instructions to each convert and knew the people entering the Church better than today's priest, who teaches a few classes in the RCIA program and encounters the catechumens mainly in the liturgical rites. Although lay persons do much of the hands-on ministry today, pastors still set the tone for the whole parish and provide crucial leadership: enunciating a gospel-inspired vision for the parish; motivating parishioners to participate in the life of the parish and service to the world; coordinating and encouraging the gifts and activities of the various ministers and groups; presiding at liturgical celebrations; preaching homilies that relate the Scripture passages to the existential concerns of the parishioners; and speaking prophetically on behalf of justice and peace. He is the servant leader of a community, which, as a whole, carries on the ministry of Christ.

Snapshots Compared

Our historical investigation reveals both continuities and discontinuities in the relationship between a pastor and his flock. Christian communities have always had leaders in charge of oversight. They have always provided pastoral care and presided at liturgical celebrations. However, the balance between the pastoral role and the priestly liturgical role has shifted throughout the centuries, ranging from the New Testament period, which is silent on the cultic role, to the Middle Ages, which celebrated the power of the priest to make Christ present at Mass. The style of leadership has also varied, from the collaborative approach of Cyprian to the authoritarian mode of pre–Vatican II pastors in the United States. The shape of pastoral ministry has been influenced by the needs of the people: those suffering from the plague in the fourteenth century needed solace; educated Catholics today need a greater voice in the life of the Church. Parishes at the end of the first millennium tried to provide stability in a disintegrated world; at the beginning of the third millennium, pastors are urging their people to get more involved in evangelizing culture. Our selective examination of the history of pastoral ministry has highlighted the discontinuities.

Hopeful Realism

A realistic assessment of the ecclesial dimension of ordained ministry brings to mind many current problems and challenges. Most pastors in the United States today find significant pluralism among their parishioners, often described in terms of more liberal or conservative tendencies. Sometimes a healthy pluralism devolves into a destructive polarization that weakens the parish and puts extra stress on the pastor. Some priests feel that the sex abuse scandal has weakened their relationship to the parish and impeded their natural openness with parishioners. The shrinking number of priests hurts clergy morale and leaves pastors with more ministerial work to do. Their frustrations grow when the hierarchy refuses even to discuss possible ways of expanding the pool of potential candidates for the priesthood.

Faced with these serious problems, pastors struggle to maintain a hopeful spirit. Hope, which is distinguished from optimism, is ultimately based on the fidelity of God and the promise of Jesus to remain with the Church. Hope is nourished by prayer and reflection. It can flourish even when problems threaten to overwhelm us and solutions elude us. Hope enables us to sustain our ministry even in the midst of misunderstandings and failures. Christian hope strengthens us to face our problems in all their harsh reality without escaping into utopian fantasies or repressing our anger and frustration. A hopeful attitude helps us appreciate the positive developments in the Church today, especially the tremendous growth in lay ministry and the vitality of good parishes. The dialectical virtue of hopeful realism enables us to hold together in a fruitful synthesis both trust in God and a realistic approach to church problems. The severity of our current crisis moves us to put our hope in God rather than in ourselves. This ultimate hope opens our eyes to the hopeful signs in the Church today. Pastors who live and minister in a spirit of hopeful realism perform a great service for their parishioners.

Conclusion

We have looked at three dimensions of ordained ministry: Christological, pneumatological, and ecclesial. In each case, our survey took us up to the Second Vatican Council. The teachings of the council on the priesthood, reinforced by social and cultural factors, have had a remarkable impact on the pastoral practice of ordained ministers, as our comparison of parishes today and during the 1920s clearly indicates. Although Vatican II did not produce a new theology of the priesthood, certain points of emphasis have helped create a new model out of traditional principles. Jesus in his life of service sets the example for pastors. The risen Christ empowers priests to act in his name. The Church as a whole carries on the memory and the mission of Jesus. Priests are servant leaders within the community of faith, representing Christ in his role as priest, prophet, and shepherd. Pastors have the responsibility to identify and coordinate the charisms of their parishioners, who share in the priesthood of Christ. They preside at the liturgy and preach the word. Priests are called to holiness and to the development of human virtues esteemed by the community. When pastors put into practice these principles, which are now normative for the Catholic community, the parish community flourishes.

Chapter 5

The Priest Preaching
in a World of Grace

THOMAS O'MEARA, O.P.

CONSIDER FOR A MOMENT: how frequently preaching appears in the Church today; how numerous the homilies in their daily delivery; how tireless the effort that every week thousands put into preaching; and just how much faith claims that preaching is for speaking the Word of God.[1] Since Vatican II there are so many resources — newsletters, workshops, books, journals — to assist in the writing of a sermon. Nonetheless, Catholics often complain about preaching; some preachers and their delivery are boring, even annoying. Sociologists tell us that poor preaching (not doubts over the perdurance of the human existence of Jesus in a hypostatic union with the Logos or over the salvific value of Hindu rites in Bombay) is a main reason that Catholics stop attending Church and join the fourth largest religious group in the United States, nonpracticing Catholics.

Personal Experiences

Although I have spent my life teaching and writing, I have and do preach often, usually at Masses in university contexts, and less frequently in parishes. The following observations come from a theologian thinking about preaching. The advice I received during courses on homiletics from 1956 to 1962 was to write a sermon with a beginning, a middle, and an end. The future preacher for America, I was told, would be assisted by reading the sermons of great preachers of the past. Experts argue that Thomas Aquinas, in comparison to his contemporaries, gave a concrete and pictorial presentation in his sermons, but the abbreviated reports we have could not serve as a model for preaching, either in the United States during the 1950s or even now fifty years later.[2] I searched Bossuet for an exciting approach but found none; Lacordaire seemed long, convoluted, and empty of examples, although it was said that a few of his hearers in the Cathedral of Notre Dame fainted from excitement during his sermons. There was one successful contemporary Catholic preacher, Fulton Sheen, but he was inaccessible to us young Friars Preachers, for he was on television; we were not permitted to watch television. The sermons I heard prior to 1962 were so abstract, so bland as to lead one to conclude that it was beneficial that many Masses had no sermon. Later during Vatican II, I discovered that great theologians could be good preachers. Romano Guardini attracted large crowds throughout his life; the texts of Karl Rahner's sermons remain today insightful and original.[3] Aristotle's philosophy, Aquinas's content, and Bossuet's rhetoric were of little help.

Approaching Preaching

There are obviously different ways to approach preaching. Some touch on structure and composition; others treat the technique in delivery. I wrote an article recently on the need to have one conclusion to a sermon, one clear ending, in "The End!" I mentioned the anxiety before the abyss of nothingness, e.g., as analyzed by Martin Heidegger or Paul Tillich, as one reason that preachers went through three endings. The end of the sermon might be a form of "Nichts."[4] There can also be an analysis of who is preaching, of the person's theological education, worldview, orientation, specific ministry, and spirituality. Here, one could ponder, who today in the Church is preaching and who is not preaching, and why? The reductive control of preaching is a serious issue, for the denial of baptism's empowerment to preach is an impoverishment of the human means offered to the Word.[5] A confusion of preaching as the charismatic gift of empowerment and as the organization of the local church can hold back Christians from hearing others' voices. It is hard to think of a single argument supporting the exclusion of baptized men and women from sometime proclaiming their faith to other Christians. The exclusion of the baptized is a facet of older theologies of the priesthood drawn from patristic neo-Platonic hierarchy, where the lower never enlightens the higher, and from French Baroque spiritualities, where every act of every priest is sacred, and where every lay enterprise is secular.

If technique and structure are important, preaching, however, has other aspects. It is verbal, social, intellectual, and emotional, even as it seeks to mediate between the human person and divine grace. Rahner says that the preached word "is the bodyliness of grace."[6] One can look also at the content of a sermon. What is being preached in terms of the biblical critique of religion, power, and wealth? How does one make traditional theologies of liturgy and Eucharist interesting? Are new issues of bioethics, sexuality, and family life presented with positive information and respect, or are they, in fact, too novel and too complicated to be addressed? Does preaching remain an ideology of rules, a journey into guilt, an exercise in devotional clichés, a gospel of authoritarianism?[7]

Preaching is an art, not a science. Preaching is somewhat like playing the piano or tennis; if you do it well, it is not because of a theory or a book; if you ponder too much what you are doing, you stumble. As an art, preaching depends upon the imagination and experience of the preacher. It is difficult to preach in an interesting way if the preacher is not interested in people and culture, in the colors of art and film.

Today, in the United States, poor preaching appears often in one of three forms: dogmatic clichés, personal self-help, or simply retelling the Gospel story without explaining its historical context and theological meaning. For Trinity Sunday, an attempt at a sermon might choose either the tack of "what a great mystery, three in one, one in three" or "wondering what to preach about, I saw three robins fly up into the sky."

For a theology of preaching, I would look not at technique or content, but at the human hearer of the Word and at the preacher speaking to the world. I would for a few moments turn our attention away from the preacher, away from the topic of the priest's sacramental power or spirituality. I want to highlight preaching by paying attention to the broader human and social horizons in which people exist.

Preaching Resources

Before I pursue my own ideas, I would like to mention a valuable resource, unfortunately existing only in German, a kind of psychological-philosophical *summa* or *System* on preaching, Wilfried Engemann's *Einführung in die Homiletik*.[8] While Engemann stresses the general homiletic misdirection of ignoring the differences among hearers and of ignoring the fact that they are Christians, the first of the book's five parts is about "homiletic misconceptions" and is a striking list of misdirections compromising or injuring the sermon. The author mentions the metamorphosis of the gospel into law, obsession with grammar and concepts, preaching sin in a moralistic way, exegesis without focus, vague examples, adopting the style of speculative theology, the format of an artificial dialogue, and, finally, an ill-defined use of the subjectivity of the preacher vitiated by jargon, sarcasm, and references to embarrassing feelings. The second part develops a theology of preaching as a precise task, as a communication-event; the third treats three aspects in preaching, which are an understanding of the text, the act of the preacher, and an interpretation of Scripture in language adapted to a particular kind of person in the context of the liturgy. The next section looks at the point of departure of preaching from six different perspectives, which are content, pastoral theology, psychological perspectives, language, rhetoric, and semantics. The book concludes with pages on how to compose a sermon.

Another new book worth noting is Andrew Wisdom's *Preaching to a Multi-Generational Assembly*.[9] A sermon comes to several generations on Sunday morning. Subcultures of age, ethnicity, and race should be seriously considered in preparation. There can be a limited generational segmentation for the Sunday assembly. Other new considerations of preaching have also emerged. Guerric DeBona in *Fulfilled in Our Hearing: History and Method of Christian Preaching* focuses on sermons and liturgy; James Bacik and Kevin Anderson in

The Preaching Ministry: Theological Perspectives and Practical Advice concentrate on the hearers of sermons.[10] I would turn preachers' attention to the depth or the background of those hearing preaching. The sermon's words come first to the lives of those hearing it. The Word enters first the broader and deeper horizons of the lives of American Catholics.

The World

The preacher needs to be open to the world of those to whom he preaches, to learn a little about their world. "World" in the modern sense means not the weather report, the stock market, or traffic reports for the day, but the broad, highly influential currents in our psyches that come from culture, society, personality, and language that relate preaching and faith to experience. Such an approach is not presumed to be secular or sinful but to be the atmosphere of economics, work, family, education, culture, and entertainment, which a person breathes. What drives people's lives, what forms their personalities, and what ultimately shapes their human world is simply not noticed, not studied, not pondered. Preaching needs links to the various psychological and social levels of life.

The attention to the concrete world counters the idea that all people and all Catholics think and live in the same way. Their minds would still be the tabula rasa of Aristotle's perennial philosophy, without any aspects of their languages of Zulu or Spanish. To deny that people, liturgies, and theologies are the same leads to "relativism." Dismissing people in terms of relativism, however, gives the preacher permission not to study or to work to get to know people.

Today social and ecclesial communities face processes of personal independence, aloneness.[11] In American society, and around the world, the people who sit quietly in a congregation, the people in front of the preacher, are being made individualized by technology. The cell-phone provides a universal communications connection apart from home or business or even place. I know to whom I am talking, but I do not know where they are; I am talking to someone, but that person does not know where I am. The iPod offers a personalized selection of music, lectures, information, in which I do not share. An attention to the broad backgrounds of sin and grace — whether in Norway or South Africa — accepts that the people existing in the congregation to be touched by word and sacrament are increasingly individualized. Hence the metamorphosis today of moral and dogmatic theology into spirituality.[12] Preaching is the verbal expression of spirituality, where faith and doctrine have been made personal.

The World of Grace

Catholics live in a sacramental world, a world of the immanence of grace, a world of circles of dynamics of the Incarnation. They do not confuse creation with grace, but they also do not replace grace with sinfulness. Some preachers (spatially removed from the people and dressed in odd clothes) may give the impression that most of the baptized are sinners or, at best, morally lazy. They presume that people, whose lives have been evaluated as formless, also know nothing about their faith, about the Bible, about theologizing.

For Christianity, the human person and the course of salvation history do not have as their paradigm a neutral person attracted equally by sin and salvation. God's grace is everywhere as an aspect of life; God does not retreat in the course of history to be an angry judge or a failed repairperson, who tries to rescue only a small remnant. After the Resurrection, the divine plan, though faced with evil, courses ahead to be triumphant. We live in a world of grace, as Aquinas and Rahner, each in his own way, point out.

American Catholics discuss with unease their faith in public worship, but that does not mean that they do not have convictions and reflections. Everyone lives on the boundary between life and grace, and more or less frequently this unthematized interplay surfaces in ideas; everyone is at times a theologian. God's presence reveals itself in individual life. There is above all the quest for "the more." The preacher is a voice, a word proclaiming, illuminating, picturing the dialogue between God and adult men and women. The goal of a sermon is not to list moral rules or to repeat dogmas set aside as "mysteries." The goal is to describe the real world, an invisibly graced world. The hearer and the preacher are not patient and agent, but members of a conversation. The goal of the preacher is not to move the will or to impart data to the mind, but to serve God's grace already at work in this human existence and experience. When preaching takes seriously the human lives and the Christian lives of its hearers, it engages people in their individuality, in the variety and uncertainty of their jobs and families. Rahner observed that faith and life need to be integrated. "The human person strives for a fully structured world-view in which every object of individual experiences has a definite place and in which all details are reciprocally explained and rendered intelligible, in which no contradictions appear. Because of the unity of consciousness it is understandable that the realities of secular experience and those of the Christian faith should be integrated together into one world-vision."[13] A preacher can almost see the atmospheres of sin and grace, of temporality and society moving through the congregation. Seeing this is not an extrasensory experience, but the gift of belief, according to the eighth chapter of Paul's Letter to the Romans, in the ongoing incarnation of the Spirit in people.

This perspective counters the idea that people live in a mono-form secularity. The importance and inevitability of a Christian's world counter the idea that all that does not happen inside a church or in religious clothing is secular. The aspects of people's worlds have their own proximate goals and forms. If one's world is not immediately religious, still one's world whether in Malawi or Iceland is not secular, materialistic, or modern in a negative sense. Creation and grace fashion their lives.

The complaint that people have little basic Catholic information is sometimes an excuse for the preacher to speak at a simple level, because he is unprepared to preach at exegetical, ecclesial, and theological levels. We must also recognize that today, of course, there is difficulty talking about the organization of the Catholic Church and its hierarchy because of the issues of sexual misconduct, financial mismanagement, and the practices of a rigid, autocratic hierarchy.

At the same time, there is very much a need to explain how episcopal and papal authorities might really exercise authority at different degrees of importance without being always correct, much less infallible. Dedication to the magisterium often involves an avoidance of theological and doctrinal preaching altogether, as it asserts Vatican positions and unconvincingly raises the old guilt-spectrums of materialism and secularity. The subject of preaching is not ultimately rituals and Church, but faith and the reign of God.

A World That Is Mystery

Rahner employed the distinction between the things of religion and the broader horizons of the kingdom to help us understand the Christian message today; this remains unavoidable. Grace and revelation in the things and ideas of religion is a Kantian "categorical" presence of grace and revelation, while the initial, primal, and universal special presence of God (active and real) awaiting articulation in religion is a "transcendental" presence. The word refers not to God's transcendence, but to horizons of human life.

Is this not a goal of Jesus' teaching, to move people's attention from religious things and rules to what lies beneath, to the reign of God? Have not great mystics, theologians, and prophets generally tried to lead men and women to see that religious things, rites, and creeds must be grounded in something deeper, something holy and healthy, in an unthematic but deeply real mode of divine presence? Jesus advocated the reversal from the things, rituals, and observances of religion to life in the kingdom. Aquinas did this by his identification of the New Law as, first and foremost, the Holy Spirit.[14] A person searches for an identity out of and amid a silent, always-offered grace. Nonetheless, in an incarnational faith, the concrete is not disdained but affirmed, understood as necessary, renewed, and re-presented.

This distinction between grace and religious things counters the spirit of fundamentalism, which finds some phrase, some thing, some person, in which to locate the divine on an absolute basis. American society furthers sects and fundamentalisms, desperate parades of the miraculous, of a new Pelagianism, of political and religious externals.

The point of a sermon is not to multiply religious objects, to discover more Marian apparitions, bizarre miracles, or papal privileges, to decide who is and who is not brain-dead. Credulity in eccentric religion is far removed from faith in the Holy Spirit. The faith needed is broader, deeper. It accepts the reality of the reign of God within the world of creation and human social struggles.

Jesus as Preacher

A sermon can learn from Jesus' way of teaching; he meets various people — state bureaucrats, religious leaders, soldiers, foreigners, the sick — searching for identity amid the competing atmospheres of sin and grace. Implicitly, the hearer is learning how to think more maturely about a divine presence which is intimately present but elusive of control and isolation, the Spirit — the underlying topic of religion and revelation.

The parables of Jesus, experts tell us, are not about new information or changes in rituals and sacral objects, not about a shift from an old to a new covenant. He teaches about the deepest issues in religion, foundationally present in God's relationship to us. We learn of how God sees us and how he wishes to be understood by us. The stories are not about arbitrary customs or the clothing of human religion but about the intersection of human and divine worlds.

Jesus preaches first and foremost the kingdom of God. This "realm" is not a metaphor for the soul or cloister, but it is a special atmosphere surrounding human life, a gift of God. The parables seek to describe this reality, which will forever elude laboratory machines. Every sermon, like all of the occasions of Jesus' teaching, takes place against the background of the kingdom of God, not as a set of metaphors, but as a reality which speaks to believers through inadequate metaphors. The reign of God is always drawing us forward, promising forgiveness and divine help, criticizing human institutions, warning against the abuse of religion.

Preaching about the parables — they are read often on Sundays — should explore a horizon of human activity before God, before a higher Truth and Life. The parables do not recommend an occasional good deed, but a conviction, for instance, of being forgiven and of forgiving. Love of neighbor occurs not because it is a tough commandment from God, but because the Incarnation states how much God has loved us, because the Word consecrated human nature in life and reality. John Donahue argues that

> preaching should also embody some of the paradoxical, upsetting, and shocking quality of the teaching of Jesus. Religion in our society often has been a bastion of the expected, often serving to enforce the values of the dominant majority. People do not want to be either surprised or upset on Sunday.... Metaphorical and open-ended parabolic preaching are related. Much Christian preaching has become so moralistic that there is little doubt at the end of a sermon what should be done, even if it will not be done. Metaphorical preaching points beyond the sermon to engagement with the mystery of God, and God's relation to the world. It does not hesitate to point to deeper problems and fears which lie below the surface.[15]

Preaching, then, does not begin with Sunday-morning parishioners as blank pages upon which some dogma or moral imperative is to be written, whatever the readings might say. The sermon unfolds within the horizon of the rich, if simple, complexity of Jesus' teaching about the kingdom of God and against the background of the profound messages of the great parables. The sermon articulates what is real and active at a deeper level. "God is not one 'object' beside others, either objectively speaking or in the subjective knowledge and free action and their unity in a man or woman.... God is given indirectly in a kind of boundary experience as the origin and destination of our actions."[16]

Contemporary Issues

Today's issues — the expansion of diversified ministries drawn from primal ministry, central authority and local church, ephemeral devotions and virtual sacramentalities, Christ in a history of religions amid a world of grace, bioethics — are concrete and momentous in their own ways, although each refers to what is most basic: the Spirit and the community in history. The preacher speaks to someone who exists, who hears, who believes, who is living and changing. The sermon with the help of exegesis and theology leads hearers to accept the unseen but real vision of a faith that is incarnational and sacramental. The preacher may preach on concrete topics, but he does not lose sight of imagining the horizons or picturing the worlds in which the audience moves and has its being — or, at least, some of them. These are the cultures and societies in which human beings exist, the atmospheres of sin from which sins come, as well as the horizons and worlds of grace and faith.

Jesus uses metaphors of light and seeing. Still, as we know well, those who live in faith do not see. We should try to see the presence and activity of grace in a modest and respectful way and not in a controlling and triumphant assertion. Paradoxically, the visual and concrete nourish the horizons of personal life, while the rational and dogmatic may shut them down. The goal of the sermon is not so much for the hearer to say "I know" something new, or to say "I believe" something more firmly, but to recognize calmly that, even in the darkness of faith, a person can say about some facet of the Spirit's plan for him, and for all of humanity, "I see."

Chapter 6

The Moral Rights of Priests

James Keenan, S.J.

⟨≈⟩

About two years ago I began asking questions about the moral rights of priests. Since I am not a canonist, I am not speaking about canonical rights. Rather I use the word "rights" as moral theologians and Christian social ethicists do when speaking of the right to food, or work, or health care, that is, as a moral right. I propose these rights with the hope that they may eventually be articulated into canonical precepts. But I do not claim that they have canonical force today. Why do I ask about moral rights?

Lately we have seen priests writing and signing a variety of statements. For instance, on December 9, 2002, fifty-eight Boston priests signed a letter calling for the resignation of Cardinal Bernard Law. In a letter of October 1, 2003, priests of Rockville Centre called for a meeting with Bishop William Murphy over "widespread dissatisfaction" with his leadership. The priests of Chicago wrote an open letter to the hierarchy about the tone and content of Church leaders' remarks about gay and lesbian persons, a letter subsequently adopted by priests from Rochester, New York, and from Boston. Then there was the letter of August 2004 signed by over 160 priests in Milwaukee calling for a married clergy. More recently 84 priests from Milwaukee wrote to Archbishop Timothy Dolan protesting his "Clergy Support Initiative," which would compel priests to relinquish basic American privacy rights and allow for unannounced searches of their property based on reports of suspicious activity.

These actions are amazing inasmuch as many cannot remember during the 1980s or 1990s any other letters written by priests. Yet as a theological ethicist I believe I have a responsibility to ask: Do priests have a moral right to do this? Elsewhere, I have examined related questions, such as how interested are priests in these rights and how appropriate is rights language for speaking about the priesthood?[1] There I also began discussing four of the rights that I am developing here. But, as I begin, I want to propose an important corollary between rights language and personhood.

I do not see rights as voluntaristic assertions of power over and against others; rather, I see rights language as springing from a community of faith looking to see how best its members can protect the good of the whole Church and of its specific members. Following Brian Tierney I believe that rights were originally recognized by eleventh- and twelfth-century theologians and canonists who tried to articulate those that belonged to popes, bishops, clergy, and other church members, not as inimical to the life of the Church, but as constitutive of the Church.[2] In other words, way before the use of rights language appeared in modern liberal democracies, they were first expressed as intrinsic to the good of the Church.

Rights language developed in the twelfth century precisely as the Church became more interested in the nature of the person. Caroline Bynum points to the privileging of the spiritual experiences of members of charismatic movements of the twelfth century, which eventually led in the next century to the founding of the great religious orders by Dominic, Francis, and Clare. In the twelfth century mystics saw themselves in union with God and understood God as triune, that is, as three persons in one God. Bynum asks the very relevant question, "Did the Twelfth Century Discover the Individual?"[3] Her question is pivotal, since much of twelfth-century spirituality was an appreciation of God's love for the human in God's image. As that image was not predominately Christological but Trinitarian, the Christian saw herself/himself more and more like the Trinity, that is, as a person constitutively related to other persons.

Rights are for persons. The more we recognize rights, the more we recognize personhood, and the more we recognize personhood, the more we recognize others as related to ourselves. Rights language, therefore, does not alienate or individuate, divide or polarize; rights language rather incorporates into the human community those who are persons. Upholding one's rights is an act of upholding one's own participation in the goods of the community.

Over the past fifty years we have seen the language of rights being used precisely to build up the community by asserting particular rights to particular groups of people. First, the civil rights movement grew from asserting moral rights to articulating legal and constitutional ones so as to break down the predominant American mentality that kept African Americans segregated, that is, outside of the body politic. Leaders in the movement asserted their rightful places on buses, at lunch counters, in schools, and, finally, in neighborhoods. Second, in the pro-life movement we find vigorous attempts to restore to fetuses the rights that earlier court decisions suppressed. Whenever we see the human fetus being protected by the state, we see the community's growing recognition of the personal status of the fetus. Finally, in the gay/lesbian rights movement, we see the search for parity with regard to property, housing, health care, and other issues as steps toward gays/lesbians being treated more as persons, being more fully incorporated into the body politic.

Thus, as Aristotle taught us, ethics is for the community, and asserting the moral rights of priests is certainly not at the cost of the community, but rather for its benefit. To the extent that these rights are not respected, then, to that extent not only priests but the community of the Church, its own very *communio*, suffers. Correlatively, to the extent that we withhold these rights, to that extent we exclude priests from being incorporated into the community and relegate them to a second-class status.

I am convinced that the process of recognizing, articulating, and asserting the rights of priests is a deeply humanizing process for a group of men who have suffered a great deal these years. I believe that this work of rights helps restore to priests not only their incorporation into the community, but also occasions the possible restoration of much of their humanity that has been disregarded. Thus, we need to see these six rights that I am proposing as related to one another; taken together they more fully comprehend the man in his humanity and in his priesthood.

The Moral Rights of Priests

Book II of the *Code of Canon Law* outlines the obligations and rights of all the Christian Faithful (204–223). The first set of rights and obligations belong to the laity (224–231). Eventually, the *Code* turns to the rights and obligations of clergy (273–289). Here we find three canonical rights: of association, to a vacation, and to fitting and decent remuneration. Instead of these three canonical rights, I propose six "moral" ones: the right to share in the episcopal ministry of the local ordinary; the right of association; the right to discern the proper exercise of our ministry; the right to our personal development; the right to privacy; and the right to fair treatment.

The Right to Share in the Episcopal Ministry of the Local Ordinary

The first right echoes one that had been discussed in the revision of the *Code of Canon Law:* "the right of cooperating with the bishop in the exercise of his ministry." Similarly this is the right implicitly invoked and exercised by priests in their recent letters to bishops and bishops' conferences. John Lynch, a canon lawyer who has written on the rights of priests, frequently asserts that the "cleric shares in the Episcopal ministry." Interestingly, he roots his claim precisely in the first canon in the section on rights and obligations, canon 273: "Clerics are bound by a special obligation to show reverence and obedience to the Supreme Pontiff and their own ordinary."

Lynch's claim is derived from three Vatican II documents. The Decree on the Ministry and Life of Priests reads: "Priestly obedience, inspired through and through by the spirit of cooperation, is based on the sharing of the Episcopal ministry which is conferred by the sacrament of order and the canonical mission." Similarly, the Bishops' Pastoral Office states: "All priests, whether diocesan or religious, share and exercise with the bishop the one priesthood of Christ." Finally, the Dogmatic Constitution on the Church declares: "The Bishop is to regard his priests, who are his co-workers, as sons and friends, just as Christ called his disciples no longer servants but friends."

The foundation for the moral right is found not only in the *Code,* its commentary, and Vatican II documents. It is also found in the rite of ordination. The first question the bishop asks the ordinand is: "Are you resolved, with the help of the Holy Spirit, to discharge without fail the office of priesthood in the presbyteral order as a conscientious fellow worker with the bishops in caring for the Lord's flock?" Then, in the prayer of consecration we hear the bishop say:

> Lord, grant also to us such fellow workers,
> for we are weak and our need is greater.
> Almighty Father, grant to this servant of yours the dignity of
>   the priesthood.
> Renew within him the Spirit of holiness.
> As a co-worker with the order of bishops
> may he be faithful to the ministry
> that he receives from you, Lord God,
> and be to others a model of right conduct.

When we hear of repeated unsuccessful attempts by clergy to meet with their ordinary, we become aware of the fact that this right is not adequately recognized. In fact, when we consider the phenomena of public letters by clerics, we ought to see this not so much as an indication of that right being exercised, but rather as expressing frustration that the presumed right has been ignored.

The Right of Association

The right of sharing in the ministry of the bishop leads to fostering right relations among the clergy through association. The *Code,* in canon 275.1, asserts, "Since clerics all work for the same purpose, namely, the building up of the Body of Christ, they are to be united among themselves by a bond of brotherhood and prayer and strive for cooperation among themselves according to the prescripts of particular law." Immediately after this paragraph, the *Code* adds, "Clerics are to acknowledge and promote the mission which the laity, each for his or her part, exercises in the Church and in the world." Associations among the clergy are intimately tied to promoting the laity's own involvement in the life of the Church. In fact, in the earlier draft of the *Code*, the clergy were only called to recognize the laity's mission; according to the promulgated code, they must promote it.

Though canon 215 defines the right of all the Christian Faithful to form associations, that is, both lay and clergy, canon 278 establishes it as the first canonical right for priests. The *Code* reads: "Secular clerics have the right to associate with others to pursue purposes in keeping with the clerical state." This is the first time that canon law recognized this moral right. In developing the revised code, the commission rejected a proposal that placed associations of priests under the local ordinary. To do so would be to infringe on the exercise of the very right that was being promulgated.

The *Code* derives its inspiration from the natural law and from the writings of previous pontiffs. For instance, in his encyclical *Pacem in Terris,* Pope John XXIII upholds the natural right to assemble and says that people "have also the right to give the societies of which they are members the form they consider most suitable for the aim they have in view." He adds, "It is most necessary that a wide variety of societies or intermediate bodies be established equal to the task of accomplishing what the individual cannot by himself efficiently achieve. These societies . . . are to be regarded as an indispensable means in safeguarding the dignity and liberty of the human person, without harm to his sense of responsibility."

Thus, from the natural law, our own experience, papal teaching, and the *Code* itself, we recognize the moral right of priests to form associations so that we can achieve what only solidarity can afford. Throughout the United States, we have seen in the past few years free-standing priests' associations emerge, for example, the Boston Priests Forum, the Milwaukee Archdiocese Priest Alliance, or New York's Voice of the Ordained. This moral right validates these groups. The recent innovations by priests to form local groups are congruent with good thinking within the Church. Moreover, these organizations do not replace presbyteral councils but represent a few of what Pope John XXIII referred to as the "wide varieties" of gatherings necessary for human flourishment.

The Right to Discern the Proper Exercise of Our Ministry

While there is an obligation to exercise one's priestly ministry, there is also a right to exercise that ministry according to one's particular judgment. Here I think of pastors who must discern a variety of issues on a weekly basis: whether this particular couple is actually ready to get married in the Church, whether they should preach about the way the gospel applies to this particular local issue, or how these children in this parish should be prepared for confirmation. Sometimes this right might engage the right of the local ordinary to teach. This question was raised last year by the Boston Priests Forum regarding preaching. They wanted to reflect on the conflict that arises when the bishop is engaged in defending one particular value and the local priest believes he needs both to teach what the bishop teaches and to address another possibly competitive value that has been addressed by his local parish.

In the USCCB document on Sunday homilies *Fulfilled in Your Hearing,* we find the bishops calling the pastor to listen to the Scriptures and to the congregation and to respond to that listening. Is there something that happens existentially in that listening that could prompt the pastor to hear the needs of the laity of his parish in some way that the bishop has not yet addressed? If the priest in all his listening is also obliged "to foster peace and harmony based on justice," as canon 287 states, he may find himself needing to obey his conscience as a preacher of the Word to the particular congregation he serves.

This is not advocacy for rebel priests. Rather it recognizes both the context in which a priest exercises his ministry and the process by which he comes to preach the sermon and exercise other forms of ministry. Though by his faculties a priest exercises his ministry at the bishop's pleasure, there seems to be another claim on the priest that comes not from the bishop directly but from the people whom the priest serves. If the priest is truly to promote peace and justice and *communio,* it seems that in order to discern how to do so, he needs to rely on something in addition to the bishop's particular perspective. Like other expressions of his ministry that he shares with the bishop

and with the laity, a priest's preaching calls for a conscientious integrity to witness to the gospel as he sees it expressed in his midst.
This too follows from the insight of Thomas Aquinas that as we de-
scend into a situation, we need to attend to more and more specific
circumstances in order to rightly discern what is actually required.

Putting the right of the bishop to teach and the right of the priest to
discern the proper exercise of his ministry in tandem with one another
is very important, for together they achieve a balance. For example,
imagine that a diocese is rocked by urban riots due to police racism.
The bishop asks all priests to address racism in their Sunday homily
but a priest in a predominantly white, gated community discerns that
this would only upset his GOP-dominated congregation. Whether he
should conclude his discernment solely by listening to his parishioners
misses the needed tension to heed the bishop's summons as well.

The Right to Our Own Personal Development

While the previous right affirms the relevance of a priest's personal,
though professional, experience with his congregation and encourages him to trust the development of a professional fealty with
his parishioners that couples the fealty he enjoys with his ordinary through the orders which unite them, this right encourages the
community and the priest to appreciate the priest as an embodied,
personal relational agent. In many ways it expresses the insight that
the priest must learn not only about his parish and his chancery, but
also about himself. If the previous right is about him developing himself into a professional, this right recognizes that a professional needs
to be a person first in order to be a true professional.

Because of clericalism, many priests' personal affective experiences
were measured not with mature adult self-understanding and responsible affective conduct based on mutual respect, but rather on
an intuited sense of what constituted "proper discretion." In other
words, so long as a priest manifested decorum, he stayed within the
boundary lines of acceptable clerical conduct.[4] By this right, however,
we see that affective experiences are good and necessary for personal
growth and wisdom; this right recognizes what clericalism shadows.
It proposes to say that priests need and have a right to the forms

of friendship and affective relations that make a person a mature adult, and that he has a right to invoke these experiences as sources of wisdom.

The range of the right is broader than simply the development of responsible affective relationships, since it includes intellectual and spiritual development as well. Thus, priests have a right to continuing education, leisure, sabbaticals, retreats, adequate time for daily prayer, etc. In other words, priests have duties in these areas and thereby should have rights as well. A more inclusive right to human development embraces responsible affective experience (intimacy, friendship, etc.), while also calling for needed intellectual and spiritual development and their related goods as well.

Rightly understood, these spiritual and intellectual developments happen within an affective context. Thus, the right could be expressed as I heard it from a fellow priest and friend: the right to our own affective experience and the wisdom that derives from it. Bernard of Clairvaux supports the claim, *"Instructio doctos reddit, affectio sapientes."*[5] Instruction renders us learned, experience renders us wise. In my own life as a priest, I have received much wisdom about myself, God, and those whom I serve, precisely through the affective relationships that challenged, sustained, and nurtured me.

This right then sustains some of the others. For instance, the more a priest has responsible affective relationships and the more he trusts the wisdom he derives from them, the more he should trust his own ministerial competency with his parishioners and the more he should confidently see his bishop not simply as a father but as a leader inviting him into collaborative leadership. This right, in turn, is sustained by the right to associations, wherein priests could nurture the humanity of one another by encouraging them to affectively face and articulate the challenges of priesthood.

The Right to Privacy

This right turns inevitably to the right to privacy. Though this right is found in *Gaudium et Spes,* which argues that privacy should be protected, the right has a distinctively American relevance. In earlier American judicial rulings, we find the real meaning and relevance of this right. In 1890 Samuel Warren and Louis Brandeis defended privacy by declaring it a general principle that protects one from defamation of character, breach of confidentiality, and invasion of property. In 1891 a citizen refused a medical examination and in *Union Pacific v. Botsford,* the Court ruled in favor of the citizen that "no right is held more sacred . . . than the right of every individual to the possession and control of his own person."[6] Later in *Olmstead v. United States,* Brandeis ruled that privacy "is the right to be let alone — the most comprehensive of rights and the right most valued by civilized men."[7]

More recently, the noted Roman moral theologian Brian Johnstone proposed privacy as the protected zone wherein a person can exercise self-determination, pursuing ends in a shared moral climate wherein the individual and society respect the claims of one another, that is, the individual's personal good and society's common good.[8] This right stands as a vanguard against the suppression of a priest's own civil liberties, which were dramatically threatened recently by a proposed policy in Milwaukee.[9] That policy had two documents. The "Clergy Advocacy and Monitoring Program" specifically dealt with monitoring priests involved in sexual misconduct with minors. The "Clerical Support Initiative" pertained to any priest, but gave the archbishop ambiguously broad invasive powers on two points: that any action by a priest could make him subject to the initiative ("any . . . act or illness involving a cleric that is deemed inappropriate by the archbishop"); and that the archbishop solely determines whatever restrictions he wishes to impose on the priest ("The archbishop retains the right to review, add to, or remove any of the restrictions . . . at any time he deems necessary."). Moreover, the list of "potential restrictions" for the monitoring program was the same as the Clerical Support Initiative. Finally, the initiative claims that "the restrictions are not to be seen as punitive in nature"; "rather they are designed to support the individual in his desire to live according to the example of Jesus Christ, the Gospels, the teaching of the Church and the demands of his vocation." Still, as the archdiocesan spokesperson for communications noted, "The monitoring protocols are modeled after those used in the criminal justice system for sex offenders on probation or parole."

This policy was not the result of a simple indiscretion, error, or oversight. It required forethought, planning, drafting, recruiting personnel and coordinators, compelling priests, mailing, taking the media questions, etc. Moreover, no one can look at this policy and not wonder whether other ordinaries have entertained similar procedures. Fortunately, a variety of voices, but most especially the priests of Milwaukee, persuaded the archbishop to abandon the policy.

Though this action occasioned me to think of the need for the right to privacy, quite apart from that incident the right sustains both a priest's personal welfare and the diocese's own common good. That is, the right to privacy is the right to exercise personal responsibilities and decisions. It is the right to be self-determinative, the right to be a mature adult whose movements are not subject to suspicion or intrusion without civil warrant. The right protects a person to be a person. In short, it allows a priest to have a place he calls his home, a circle of acquaintances to be called friends, and a conversation to be called confidential. The assertion of the right to privacy not only shoulders the earlier rights stated above, but it also prompts us to recognize the relevance of the final right.

The Right to Fair Treatment

To appreciate this right we need to turn to the zero-tolerance policy as it appears (paragraphs 56–60) in the *Report on the Crisis in the Catholic Church in the United States by the National Review Board for the Protection of Children and Young People*. There the ten lay authors note that the policy "was deemed necessary because some bishops and religious superiors in their assessment of sexual abuse of minors by priests under their authority badly underestimated the seriousness of the misconduct and harm to victim, and allowed wrongdoers to continue in positions of ministry, from which they went on to harm others." They conclude: "To prevent any recurrence of such situations, the Charter and Essential Norms remove any further discretion on the part of bishops and religious superiors in this regard."

But what then is the net effect on an offending priest? Here the *Report* notes: "Accordingly, the zero-tolerance policy applies without regard to any assessment of the degree of culpability of an offending priest based upon such factors as (1) the nature of the sexual act (e.g., the improper touching of a fully clothed teenager versus the sodomization of a child), (2) the frequency of abuse (e.g., an isolated event versus a protracted history), or (3) efforts to address the problem (e.g., successful treatment of a problem that had led to an act of abuse years ago versus untreated problems that manifested themselves more recently.). The policy also applies with equal force to a priest who reports himself as having engaged in an act of abuse in an effort to obtain help with his problem."

Fair treatment usually observes some form of due proportionality. Though the Review Board acknowledges objections from a variety of observers about the fairness and effectiveness of the policy, and though they write "the zero-tolerance policy may seem to be too blunt an instrument for universal application," nonetheless, they believe "that for the immediate future the zero-tolerance policy is essential to the restoration of the trust of the laity in the leadership of the Church, provided that it is appropriately applied. In assessing individual cases in order to determine whether the priest engaged in an act of sexual abuse of a minor, the bishops must consult with the diocesan lay review board, so that they might strive for individualized justice in light of their developing experience and expertise."

The *Report*'s caveat with regard to appropriate procedures and diocesan lay review could serve, then, as a witness to the fair treatment of priests, but that witness needs to be guaranteed by the National Review Committee as it endorses the zero-tolerance policy. Inasmuch as they recognize disparity regarding the role of these review boards as well as the application of appropriate procedures, they need to witness to priests' rights as well as to the rights of the laity, especially children. Finally, they acknowledge that any discussion of the Charter's zero-tolerance provision would be incomplete without noting that there is no equivalent policy of zero tolerance for bishops or provincials who allowed a predator priest to remain in or return to ministry despite knowledge of the risks. In fact, in the minds of some priests, the impression was created that the Dallas Charter and the Essential Norms were the bishops' attempt to deflect criticism from themselves and onto individual priests. Priests, who now stand uneasily under a sword of Damocles with their every action scrutinized, understandably may ask why the bishops do not face such consequences if they fail to abide by the Charter. This distinction has deteriorated the relationship between priests and bishop. The *Report* concludes its section by stating that the bishops "must show that they are willing to accept responsibility and consequences for poor leadership."

Fairness, then, cuts two ways. Due proportionality in the treatment of accused and offending priests ought to emerge somehow; priests cannot and should not bear the weight of the scandal alone. If a zero-tolerance policy is applied to priests, where is an analogous policy for the scandalous bishops? The scandal will only come to rest when justice has been served, but an inequitable justice is not justice. The National Review Board has, then, two more responsibilities: they must somehow guarantee that due process and due proportionality are granted to priests, and they must hold proportionally accountable both the offending priests and the offending bishops. As we attempt to discern the rights of priests, it is this right more than any other that demands that a priest accused deserves to be treated as a human being, that is, as a person, a point that Cardinal Avery Dulles addressed in his essay on the rights of priests to due process.[10]

Throughout these recent years, when priests occasionally, though not at all often enough, address the harm and shame attached to the abuse of children or the rights of the laity and bishops, it has been done so most frequently from the place that they are called to be: the parish pulpit. I suggest that if priests begin to recognize the rights due them — especially at a time when many find themselves, as the *Report* states, demoralized — they might in turn be more vocal from that pulpit in recognizing the rights of others and in fostering the *communio* that the Church so desperately needs. I propose these six rights — one of participatory leadership, another of the right to associate, a third of ministerial vocation, the fourth of personal growth, the fifth of basic civil liberties, and the sixth of fairness — with the hope that these may further encourage the voice of the clergy.

Chapter 7

Reflection

Elizabeth Donnelly

❦

A s I attended the conference and prepared this reflection, my thoughts were of many priests whose friendship my husband and I have enjoyed over the years. With particular affection I remembered four Maryknoll priests with whom I had the privilege of working in the early 1980s. Our parish served over a hundred thousand people in a sprawling shantytown on the sand dunes south of Lima, Peru. Due to the economic crisis at the time, most people were unemployed or underemployed, usually as street vendors, who made the equivalent of a few dollars a day. Infant malnutrition and tuberculosis were rampant, and the pastoral challenges considerable.

Each of the four priests fully embodied the model of the ideal pastor that James Bacik so eloquently draws; they animated a faith community, which functioned as a credible sign and effective instrument of God's reign amid extreme poverty. In addition to presiding at moving liturgies and administering the sacraments, the four priests — two middle-aged and two older — took on other ministries. Tom, a vigorous leader of the deanery's human rights commission, set up a booth (like Lucy in *Peanuts*) in the local market, so that people working and buying food there could consult him during the day. Pete, a charismatic theology professor at Lima's Catholic University, led a committed group of neighborhood women who ran vital soup kitchens. Jim, perpetually smiling and upbeat, was thoroughly beloved by young catechists, whose ministry he supervised. Charlie, the quietest, enjoyed warm friendships with the couples for whom he directed marriage encounters. Each was a servant leader who recognized and nourished charisms present in the community. Each entrusted people to exercise their ministries responsibly. Each in his own way helped to foster a dynamic parish with over one hundred active lay leaders.

The Maryknollers consciously eschewed the Lone Ranger approach to ministry. They also had a healthy attitude about attending to their own needs for down-time and community. Most Sunday evenings, the priests, another lay missioner, and I would gather at the parish's main church to wait for whoever had the last Mass. We would then pile into a couple of beat-up VW Beetles and bounce down the sanded tracks to the highway and over to a neighboring café for pizza and beers. In addition to exchanging views on Peruvian and U.S. politics, we would chuckle over stories from their seminary days and mull over which student and which professor had inspired ex-Maryknoller Eugene Kennedy to craft which character in his popular novel, *Father's Day*. All too aware of the degree to which such generous, committed priests have been demoralized by the sex-abuse scandal and their own dwindling numbers, I realize that too many U.S. Catholics have not enjoyed such dynamic parish leadership.

Bacik calls for a renewed commitment to a servant leader model of priesthood, which is Christ-centered, Spirit-led, humbly confident, open, and collaborative. He reminds us that St. Paul urges all to use their charisms to build up the Body of Christ and to serve the common good. He contrasts this Vatican II understanding of the priest as presbyter with the narrower cultic model of the priest as set apart from the people. Some of the Vatican's recent liturgical changes favor the cultic model, which gained ascendancy in the Church's second millennium.

Thomas O'Meara also calls for renewed commitment to that which is sorely missing in too many liturgies, i.e., effective preaching that helps people to be more attentive to the reality that the reign of God surrounds us, that the world is graced. He urges the preacher to engage the "world" of his, the preacher's, hearers, their lived psychological and social experience, and to respect their intelligence as well as their understanding of their faith. This, by the way, should include children and teens; preachers should consider whether some part of their sermon is accessible to and animates younger listeners. As O'Meara points out, hearers' lived experiences are diverse and increasingly individualized in an age of cell-phones and iPods. Catholic preaching by definition should encourage listeners to expand their sense of what constitutes their "world" and to redefine to whom they have moral obligations. Catholics should regularly hear themes from the Church's social teaching, which would help them make concepts like social sin, a preferential option for the poor, and solidarity a regular part of the vocabulary that they draw on when making daily decisions.

The Church's current approach assumes that all priests and deacons have a gift for preaching. Only priests and deacons may formally use that gift during the celebration of the Eucharist. As O'Meara observes, this denial of baptism's empowerment to preach is an impoverishment of the human means offered to the Word. My husband's high school chaplain, a diocesan priest who is a much sought after retreat leader, told us recently what a pleasure it had been at one retreat to hear a black, female Episcopalian priest break open the Word. My husband sighed, "We're starving ourselves, and food is in the pantry." There should be a process at the diocesan and parish level by which interested laywomen and laymen with theological training could be certified to preach at Mass.

While sociological research cited in this volume indicates that U.S. priests believe that they are overworked and face unrealistic demands and expectations from lay people, the primary concern of these priests, in particular of the older priests, is the way in which the Church exercises authority. James Keenan cites the recent spate of letters by priests questioning the leadership of and positions taken by their bishops, as well as the frustration of some priests unable to obtain meetings with their ordinary. It is primarily bishops, then, who need to recognize priests' rights and treat them as adult colleagues.

Space prevents analysis of each of the six rights proposed, but brief comments can be made on their foundation and concomitant duties. In making his case, Keenan grounds the source of priests' rights in their personhood, beginning with the work of late medieval theologians and canonists who came to see the individual Christian, like the three persons of the Trinity, as constitutively related to other persons. He draws on historical examples to argue that respecting rights builds up and extends communities, and that to recognize priests' dignity benefits not only them but the entire Church. He grounds the six moral rights he proposes in natural law, papal encyclicals, canon law, the rite of ordination, the priests' own experiences, and Vatican II documents. Nevertheless, like the *ressourcement* which animated Vatican II, he might have drawn more extensively on Jesus' own example of recognizing the dignity of his disciples and co-workers. How does Jesus' witness of regularly eating with his disciples and of washing their feet challenge those bishops who avoid meeting with their priests?

Keenan does suggest that a priest's rights are conditioned by fidelity to the gospel and accountability to both his bishop and the people he serves. He points out the possible tensions that may be caused when these claims are in conflict. In the wake of the widely publicized sexual abuse crisis and cases of financial mismanagement, wary parishioners usually support their priests and share the frustration that bishops do not seem to be held to the same standard of accountability as priests. However, people do expect priests to exercise their rights to privacy and to discern the proper course of their ministry, and people have called for greater lay participation in more effective diocesan and parish structures to prevent future abuses.

The three papers mention frustrations surrounding the priest shortage, but are not intended to address the theological rationale for excluding those women and married men who could serve just as ably as much-needed, dynamic presbyters. Bacik does argue, drawing on Gerhard Lohfink's scholarship, that Jesus chose the Twelve from different regions and factions within Judaism as a "symbolic prophetic action" *to gather together* all of Israel as a light to the nations. It is ironic, then, that Jesus' choice of the Twelve is used as a rationale for excluding women from the priesthood. If the Church, like Israel, is to be a compelling example of a reconciled humanity, that prospect is fundamentally impeded when women — and married men — are excluded from priestly ordination.

While the focus of these papers and indeed the conference itself is on the parish-based role of the priest, many Catholic priests play a broader role in society and the Church. Like the nonordained, they serve as professors, social service providers, and policy advocates. By virtue of their ordination and status as full-time employees in the Church, they are in doing so more public representatives of the rich Catholic tradition. In such positions, as in parish work, they spot talent and encourage lay people to use their own gifts to build up the Body of Christ and contribute to the common good. Within the Church, it must be acknowledged that priesthood is the necessary stepping stone to formal leadership; it is priests who are considered as candidates for bishop, cardinal, and pope. Many have asked whether the Body of Christ and the common good are best served by excluding women and married men from the priesthood and thereby the Church's leadership. On so many issues, the Church's credibility (particularly in the eyes of younger people) and the efficacy of its public policy ministry are thereby undermined. The Church's leadership currently places a much higher value on mandatory celibacy and the exclusion of women than on ministry and ensuring that we remain a Church centered in the celebration of the Eucharist.

Part Three

IN UNION
WITH BISHOP AND LAITY

Chapter 8

The Priest's Relationship to the Bishop

John Strynkowski

I WANT TO OFFER a theological reflection on the relationship between bishops and diocesan priests. I emphasize the word "theological" because I do not intend to review the vast literature of recent years on the actual state of that relationship. Regarding that literature, I would only offer two comments by way of caution.

First, I do believe that we have to be careful not to presume that the situation is the same in every diocese. That would be unfair to many bishops and priests who work hard to maintain a genuinely collegial and collaborative spirit and style of pastoral ministry. Second, it would also be unfair to assume that there was some golden age, in which this relationship was perfect. I have an axiom that where two or three are gathered, even in the Lord's name, there will be misunderstanding and conflict. I am reminded of St. Bernard of Clairvaux's warning to his monks (granted that they were not priests) in his twelfth sermon on the *Song of Songs* against the temptation "to covet the fame of a bishop's status, and to pass rash judgment on his excesses."[1] A historian would provide us with a helpful perspective on the relationship between bishops and priests over the course of the centuries.

My focus will be on the relationship between the bishop and diocesan priests, not the priests of a religious order or congregation. While much of what I say can be applied to them, insofar as they are engaged in pastoral ministry in a particular diocese and thus are related to the bishop and the priests of the diocese, the charisms of their particular institutes remain the dominant characteristic of their identity and service.

I will also want to insist in this paper that we cannot look at the relationship between bishops and priests in abstraction from the priesthood of all the baptized. The mission of bishops and priests is defined not only by their relationship to each other, but also by their joint relationship to the entire people of God. Indeed, it is my hope to show how the latter relationship can and should enrich the former.

An essential starting point for theological reflection on the relationship between bishops and priests is that through the sacrament of orders they share in a special way in the priesthood of Christ, though on different levels. "The priests...constitute, together with their bishop, one presbyterate" (*Lumen Gentium*, no. 28).[2] The unity of the bishop and priests in the priesthood of Christ through the sacrament of orders, forming them into one presbyterate, means that the one cannot be thought of without the other. Their bond is inextricable and necessarily shapes their action. They must take one another into account.

From the side of the bishop, Pope John Paul II spelled out some implications of this relationship in his address to the bishops of Region IX on the occasion of their "ad limina" visit in November of 2004: "Together with fostering mutual trust and confidence, dialogue, a spirit of unity and a common missionary spirit in his relationship with his priests, the bishop is also responsible for cultivating within the presbyterate a sense of *coresponsibility for the governance of the local Church*."[3] This seems to point to a close involvement of priests in the decisions that affect the pastoral directions of a diocese.

From the side of priests, their relationship to their bishop is shaped by their promise of respect and obedience at ordination. The bishop's primary responsibility is the proclamation of the gospel in fidelity to the tradition of the Church. The more that the bishop's teaching and governance patently reflects the tradition of the Church, the greater his claim to that respect and obedience becomes. A bishop's participation in a national conference of bishops can assist him in achieving a deeper awareness of that tradition as it has unfolded through the centuries and as it is being lived out today by the Church locally and universally.

None of this can be achieved in a fruitful and effective way without what Pope John Paul II called the "spirituality of communion," as he described it in *Novo Millennio Ineunte*.[4] Among other aspects of this spirituality, he noted that it "implies also the ability to see what is positive in others, to welcome it and prize it as a gift from God."[5] He wrote that this spirituality of communion must be the underlying principle for all relationships and structures in the Church: "the spirituality of communion, by prompting a trust and openness wholly in accord with the dignity and responsibility of every member of the people of God, supplies institutional reality with a soul."[6]

A spirituality of communion is not possible without humility. Contemporary theology has helped us significantly to appreciate again the humility of God in creating the universe and in redeeming us. In a homily given at the Good Friday Liturgy of 2002, with Pope John Paul II presiding, Fr. Raniero Cantalamessa, O.F.M. Cap., preacher of the papal household, said: "The greatest wonder at the moment of passing from faith to vision will not be to discover the omnipotence of God, but his humility."[7] A Christian's humility, which flows from God's very own humility, makes possible the welcoming of the other as a gift from God. Christian humility, founded on divine humility, makes possible that true dialogue that is essential to the spirituality of communion.

Dialogue fosters the spirituality of communion, as well as reconciliation, within the Church. In his post-synodal apostolic exhortation *Reconciliatio et Paenitentia* (1984), Pope John Paul II placed dialogue as the first of the means for reconciliation.[8] He wrote: "Authentic dialogue, therefore, is aimed at the rebirth of individuals, through interior conversion and repentance, but always with profound respect for consciences and with patience and at the step-by-step pace indispensable for modern conditions."[9] I think it is legitimate to add that the "rebirth" brought about by dialogue includes not only moral but also intellectual conversion. It is also legitimate to conclude that the relationship of bishops and priests should be shaped by an authentic dialogue, which should lead through moral and intellectual conversion to a "rebirth" for both sides. In other words, both bishops and priests should find in each other sources of holiness and insight.

This is all the more necessary because of their particular sharing in the priesthood and mission of Christ through the sacrament of orders. The actualization of that priesthood and mission, while already set in determined sacramental and structural forms, is still being played out in the myriad of concrete pastoral situations and is far from being exhausted. There is an unceasing refraction of the priesthood and mission of Christ within the contingencies of historical circumstances. To use the words of Gerard Manley Hopkins, "Christ plays in ten thousand places." Bishops and priests can learn from each other, by their dialogue with one another, where the priesthood and the mission of Christ want to lead them today.

There are many possible settings for such dialogue. Perhaps the most effective would be the parish itself, since, as Pope John Paul II pointed out in his post-synodal apostolic exhortation *Pastores Gregis* (2003), it "is pre-eminent among all the other communities in his diocese for which the bishop has primary responsibility: it is with the parishes above all that he must be concerned."[10] In this context, the pope reminded bishops of the canonical obligation of the pastoral visit. Canon 396 reads: "The bishop is obliged to visit his diocese annually, either in its entirety or in part, in such a way that the entire diocese is visited at least every five years."[11] Quoting a classic pastoral manual, the pope described the pastoral visit *quasi anima episcopalis regiminis.*[12]

John Paul II had a particular fondness for parish visitation, as was evident from his practice in Cracow and Rome and from the chapter he dedicates to it in his autobiographical *Rise, Let Us Be On Our Way.*[13] He writes that his parish visits were "rather long." He had separate meetings with the clergy: "I wanted to give an opportunity to each of them to confide in me. . . . I greatly valued these meetings; they enabled me to learn from the treasury of wisdom accumulated over many years of apostolic labor."[14]

The recently published *Directory for the Pastoral Ministry of Bishops* (2004) from the Congregation for Bishops gives considerable detail for the pastoral visit, noting that it is based on centuries of experience.[15] The bishop is to celebrate Mass, preach, confirm, meet with the clergy and with pastoral and finance councils, visit all those being catechized, and also visit the sick. In all of this, he is to present himself "clothed in humility and goodness, always interested in the individual person and capable of listening and making himself understood."[16]

Through such visits a bishop can learn how the ministerial priesthood and baptismal priesthood are being lived out in concrete circumstances. This should be for him a source of holiness and insight. But the relationship is reciprocal, because the people and priests should also be enriched by the faith and wisdom of their bishop. It is important to recognize that the Church is not at the end of its effort to understand, or to live according to, the gospel. At the Liturgy for the Feast of Pentecost, the priest prays over the gifts as follows: "Lord, may the Spirit you promised lead us into all truth and reveal to us the full meaning of this sacrifice." The concrete life of the people of God is a step in that direction. We remain on our way to that fullness of truth and to that consummate understanding of the Paschal Mystery.

The Lord Jesus himself, in his humility, gives an example in this regard. When asked by a Canaanite woman to heal her daughter, Jesus refuses: "My mission is only to the lost sheep of the house of Israel." But when she responds that "even the dogs eat the leavings that fall from their masters' tables," Jesus recognizes her "great faith" and heals the girl (Matt. 15:21–28). Jesus extends his mission and gives it a new shape in light of his experience of the woman's faith. The well-being and future direction of the Church hinge on a dialogue which embodies Christian humility, which in turn fosters the spirituality of communion among bishops, priests, and the people of God.

Chapter 9

One Priestly People

Ordained and Lay Ministries in the Church

E D W A R D   H A H N E N B E R G

Introduction

A VOLUME on the Catholic priesthood in the twenty-first century
is a great place to talk about lay ministry. Or, to put it more
strongly: a volume on the priesthood in the twenty-first century would
be misguided if it did not talk about lay ministry. The post-conciliar
expansion of ministries in the Church has pushed us past the time
when the priesthood could be considered in isolation. The impact of
these new ministries on the way we think about ordained ministry
can no longer be ignored.

We see quite clearly the pastoral impact of lay ministry on the
priest. Parishes today witness a variety of volunteers and active laypeople offering many of the services once reserved exclusively to
the ordained. And full-time lay ecclesial ministers — lay directors
of religious education, pastoral associates, youth ministers, liturgical coordinators, and others — have become some of the pastor's
most important collaborators. The ministerial team that now constitutes most parish staffs has without a doubt enriched and expanded
the ministerial base of the contemporary Church. But this same team
also poses a challenge for today's pastor. For in order to delegate,
the pastor must also manage; to collaborate, he must also coordinate. More ministers mean more meetings, greater responsibility for
oversight and leadership, even as the pastor's weekly schedule bulges
with the demands and expectations of today's active churches. Lay

ministry has changed the ministry of the priest in ways he experiences every day.

But what about the theological implications? How has the changing shape of parish ministry changed the way we think about the priesthood? What direction does the rise of lay ministry suggest for a twenty-first-century theology of ordained priesthood? The following pages take up these questions by exploring three distinctions that are too often hardened into problematic dichotomies: ministry vs. apostolate, sacred vs. secular and ordained priesthood vs. priesthood of the faithful. Each of these pairs invites reflection on the theological relationships among various ministries, and each opens out to a distinct challenge for the priest. By moving beyond dichotomies, we move beyond an approach to identity rooted in contrast and toward a vision of the ordained priesthood grounded in the one priestly people of God.

Minister among Ministers

It comes as a surprise to some that the documents of Vatican II never use the phrase "lay ministry." By and large, "ministry" in the council texts is something the clergy do. Laypeople have an "apostolate." This distinction of terms, though not entirely consistent in the documents, reflected the actual distinction at the time of the council between the well-defined ministry of the ordained and the still developing general apostolate of the laity.[1] A few voices in the Church today suggest a return to this distinction, claiming that the language of ministry has been extended too broadly. At first, this seems merely a question of semantics. But behind the discussion of language lie important assumptions about ministry and a certain claim to ownership of the Church's mission.

Expanding Ministry and the Language of Ministry

Vatican II's reluctance to apply the term "ministry" to the laity soon gave way to an expansive use. In the years following the council, the language of the lay apostolate, which had dominated theological

treatments of the laity since the early twentieth century, all but disappeared. In its place came "lay ministry." This terminological shift
followed an appropriation by Catholics of the ministry language then
current among Protestant theologians.[2] It had some papal support,
particularly in Paul VI's letter *Ministeria Quaedam* (1972), which established the lay "ministries" of lector and acolyte.[3] But what fueled
the rapid and wide embrace of lay ministry language was a changing reality; lay Catholics began to take up activities in liturgy and
in education that had until then been reserved to priests or nuns.
Parishioners were proclaiming the Scriptures, planning liturgies, visiting the sick as part of parish teams, distributing communion, and
coordinating education programs and other projects alongside the
priest. New roles in religious education, liturgy, and outreach soon
became positions of leadership on the parish staff. Schools developed
degree programs and national associations promoted professional-
ization, giving credence to the notion of a career in lay ministry. In
the last decade, the term "lay ecclesial ministry" has emerged to emphasize the preparation, stable commitment, and responsibility for
ministerial leadership that characterize many of these ministers.

If this history blurred the neat distinction that had held between
clergy and laity, it was because more and more Catholics were active
in the Church and its communities. Those who saw in this movement
the work of the Spirit and who sought to encourage such activity did
not draw on the language of the lay apostolate, which still evoked the
pre-conciliar world of marginal, clergy-controlled activities. Instead
they pointed to the broader ecclesiological themes of Vatican II: the
Church as the whole people of God, baptism as an initiation into the
community and its mission, a sense of the laity as appointed directly
by Christ, and an expectation of active participation as the norm.
A broad and inclusive appeal to "ministry" captured these themes
in a forceful and positive way. And in using the term, lay Catholics claimed their ownership of the Church's mission that had been
recognized by the council.

In a perceptive early essay, John Coleman pointed out that by the
end of the 1970s the term "ministry" had become a pervasive catch
phrase among Catholic religious professionals. He underlined the fact

that the term was already so taken for granted that it was rarely defined; he noted that it is precisely those things that are taken for granted that constitute the existing theological culture. "What we do not need to define itself defines our world and charts our view of reality. It is our prevailing ideology, our map of expectations."[4] Coleman called the term ministry a "motivational symbol" for active laity. Its use reflected a shifting view of life in the Church and new expectations on the part of many American Catholics. "To speak of ministry is to evoke this whole gestalt of the priority of baptism, charism, competence and collegiality over ordination, office, status and hierarchy."[5] For Coleman, this ideological shift is ultimately in the best interest of the Church. But it is not without repercussions, particularly for the ordained. Before the council, the ministerial priesthood was taken for granted, and the difficult questions concerned the residual category, laity. After the council, ministry emerged as the generic term, and the ordained became the problematic subset within this broader category. In this world of ministry, "it is precisely and increasingly priesthood that seems a residual category whose essence is difficult to discern."[6]

Reaction: Limit the Language

This linguistic and ideological shift has not gone unnoticed by those concerned about the identity of the ordained priesthood. And, in certain quarters, it has fed an attempt to retract ministry language. This is particularly clear in the 1997 Vatican instruction "On Certain Questions Regarding the Collaboration of the Nonordained Faithful in the Sacred Ministry of Priests." After briefly laying out theological principles intended to "safeguard the nature and mission of sacred ministry and the vocation and secular character of the lay faithful," the instruction turns to terminology.[7] The document recognizes that for some time the word "ministries" has been used not only for activities of the ordained, but also for activities of the lay faithful. But it insists that only in the most general sense is this appropriate, namely, insofar as the term affirms the laity's reference to the ministry of Christ. Indeed, it is only in virtue of sacred ordination that the term ministry takes on that "full, univocal meaning that tradition has attributed to it."[8]

The most sustained theological critique of a broad and inclusive use of the word "ministry" is that of John Collins.[9] Collins claims that the modern view of ministry as generic service is unprecedented in the tradition. He traces this modern interpretation to early twentieth-century German biblical scholarship, which he blames for the mistaken assumption that "ministry" (*diakonia*) in the New Testament is a word borrowed from secular Greek life. This assumption led to an interpretation of *diakonia* as lowly service, specifically, service at table. According to Collins, this interpretation, propped up in part by H. W. Beyer's 1935 entry on *diakonia* in Kittel's *Theological Dictionary of the New Testament*, infected a generation of Protestant scholars, colored the early discussions of the World Council of Churches, and even contributed to the confusion of ministerial language at Vatican II.[10] Collins's own exegesis argues that the New Testament meaning of *diakonia* was drawn not from secular life, but from the world of ancient religion, where it evoked a sense of divine authorization or representation. To be a minister in this sense was to be one sent or commissioned to act for another, usually a god. Thus when Paul or the author of Acts employed the word "ministry" (*diakonia*), they did so precisely to evoke this religious meaning and to emphasize that the minister (*diakonos*) was commissioned, either by the community or by the Lord himself, to present the word of God. This diaconal activity was restricted to a few in the early Church. Collins concludes that ministry today is not for everyone, nor is its meaning broad and undifferentiated. Ministry is rooted in the word of God and limited to those commissioned for it.[11]

The Challenge to Be Priest among Many Ministers

Only the most superficial theology of priesthood would pin identity to titles or rely on the assertion that ministry belongs exclusively to the priest. The 1997 instruction and Collins's presentation are more nuanced than this. But they both veer toward a nominalism that seeks words to control reality; in fact, the reality of a new experience of Church has so far overwhelmed any attempt to restrict vocabulary. We could limit the title "ministry" to the ordained or those officially commissioned, but we would still have to contend with the tens of thousands of laypersons who fill important leadership roles in the community, who seem more than just exceptions to the formal ministerial structure, and the millions of Catholics who assume they are called to contribute, in some way, to the mission of the Church. Words cannot hold back the tide of this paradigm shift.

But on a deeper level, what these alternative voices are calling for deserves some attention. How are we to talk about being a priest among so many ministers? And what can we learn from ministry's biblical roots? Collins defines ministry in light of Paul's sense of himself and his colleagues as having been commissioned to preach the word of God. This link between ministry and word, suggested by many post-conciliar voices, offers one way to reflect on the meaning of the ordained priesthood today. In his Letter to the Romans, Paul described service to the word as a priestly act because the word serves to foster among all who hear it the "acceptable sacrifice" that consists in offering up one's life to Christ,[12] not because it is a cultic function reserved to a specialist. This sense of the sacerdotal nature of preaching shapes the opening paragraphs of Vatican II's Decree on the Ministry and Life of Priests (*Presbyterorum Ordinis*), which in turn encourages a broad understanding of what it means to serve the word. Responsibility for the gospel extends beyond formal preaching to encompass the evangelization that is one with the mission of the Church. True, ministry is not reducible to service, if service is understood simply as humble or menial servitude, social work, or Christian charity. But if service is seen as that help to others or to the Church that contributes to its mission of spreading the good news in order to draw the whole world into communion with God, then surely ministry is service. This broad sense of service to the word is the basis for all ministry in the Church, especially that of the ordained priest.

Presbyterorum Ordinis goes on to state that preaching the gospel of God is the first task (*primum officium*) of the priest.[13] Many commentators since the council have taken this as the key to priestly identity. Karl Rahner placed sacrament in the context of word, presenting the seven sacraments as the highest or most intense actualization of the Church's primary ministry of the word. Thus he turned to the ministry of the word as the starting point for a definition of priesthood.[14] In the American context, Donald Cozzens invites the priest to see himself as "tender of the word." In calling for greater attention to a priestly identity rooted in the word, Cozzens does not burden the priest with the guilt of having to get better at preaching. Instead, he offers a spirituality rooted more in listening than in speaking. He warns of the perennial temptation for the preacher: "Too often, it seems to me, the priest dares to preach alone."[15]

One challenge for the priest today is to be minister of the word in the context of many ministers. Much of the daily ministry of the word in the parish is now being done by others. Lay ministers run religious education programs and provide sacramental preparation; they lead Bible studies and organize faith-sharing groups. The homily remains a central feature of the priest's ministry. But to locate his service to the word in the homily alone leads to a theology of leftovers, in which the identity of the priest is built around those things the laity cannot do. The challenge is to understand the priest's ministry of the word as comprehensive but not exclusive.

Several things are needed in order to meet this challenge. There is *the need of the priest to listen to Church past.* Effectively tending the word requires being tended by it. This begins with time to contemplate Scripture, time to be "washed in the word," as Michael Downey puts it.[16] This is the need for meditation, prayer, reflection, but also the need for continuing education, the need for study. To speak one should have something to say. And one cannot pass on a tradition that one does not know. The introduction to the tradition that seminary provides cannot sustain a lifetime of ministering to the word of God. Rather, a lifetime of study begins to introduce the minister to the depth and breath of a tradition that hands on to us God's revelation. There is also *the need to listen to Church present.* Cozzens underscores the mistake many preachers make in offering answers to questions no one has asked. "Something serious is lost if this dialectic between existential question (the human condition) and essential answer (the word of God) is not sustained in our preaching and religious education."[17] Ministering to the word of God requires recognizing that this word is addressed first and foremost to the whole people of God, and that further insight into this word occurs — thanks to the work of the Spirit — in and through the experiences, questions, and conversations of ordinary believers.[18] This recognition prompts *the need to let others speak*. According to the Second Vatican Council, the whole Church preaches the gospel; and its documents name multiple agents of the Church's preaching — presbyters and bishops, but also deacons, laity, missionaries, the faithful, parents, and many others.[19] The priest's ministry of the word aims at promoting a community of witnesses to the resurrection. But this ministry is also exercised in providing more opportunities for formal preaching by competent lay ministers. Such encouragement does not detract from the priest's responsibility. It is simply one way of exercising this responsibility for a word that he does not own.

Servant in the World

The participants at the Second Vatican Council wanted to affirm the Christian vocation of the layperson and to encourage a more active role for the laity in the Church's mission. They did this by describing the Church as the whole people of God, by speaking of the universal call to holiness, by stressing baptism as a participation in Christ's threefold work of priest, prophet, and king, and, finally, by underlining the secular character of the laity. If the ministry-apostolate distinction has proved an inadequate way of naming the relationship between ordained and lay activity today, the distinction between the sacred ministry of the ordained and the secular role of the laity raises more basic theological difficulties.

A Theology of the Laity

Chapter 4 of *Lumen Gentium* and *Apostolicam Actuositatem* (Decree on the Apostolate of the Laity) were shaped by an evolving positive view of the secular world. These texts affirm the laity's full place within the Church and, at the same time, assert that the layperson's proper activity lies in the transformation of the temporal. *Apostolicam Actuositatem* reflects on the many ways laywomen and laymen, through their influence on family, society, and nation, can contribute to the Church's mission — describing a variety of tasks open to laity working in the secular sphere. But the positive impetus this theology of the laity gave toward engagement with the world came with a certain ambiguity. For certain of these texts give the impression that there exist two different realms of responsibility: clergy are *primarily* responsible for the Church; laity are *primarily* responsible for the world. Some post-conciliar interpretations have hardened this tension into a distinction between a secular laity and a sacred clergy.

In his apostolic exhortation following the synod in 1987 on the laity, John Paul II said of Vatican II that "it opened itself to a decidedly positive vision and displayed a basic intention of asserting *the full belonging of the lay faithful to the Church and to its mystery. At the same time it insisted on the unique character of their vocation* which is, in a special way, to 'seek the Kingdom of God' by engaging in temporal affairs and ordering them according to the plan of God."[20] And then the pope went beyond the council by arguing that "for the lay faithful, to be present and active in the world is not only an anthropological and sociological reality, but in a specific way, a theological and ecclesiological reality as well."[21] This emphasis on the secular dimension offered a strong foundation for the pope's exhortation to lay people to bring their Christian faith to bear in politics, culture, and family — a positive message of encouragement, whose goal is the transformation of the world in the light of Christ.

But this appeal to the secular vocation of the laity does not always serve to exhort or encourage. At times it emerges as a caution, or a way of constraining certain lay activities in and on behalf of the Church. In warning against what he sees as the dangers of an over-reliance on lay ministry, the pope wrote: "The various ministries, offices and roles that the lay faithful can legitimately fulfill in the liturgy, in the transmission of the faith, and in the pastoral structure of the Church, ought to be exercised *in conformity to their specific lay vocation* which is different from that of the sacred ministry."[22] Here the notion of a secular vocation becomes a kind of limit. And this limiting of lay activity is pronounced in the 1997 instruction described above. The instruction tends toward an earlier church-world dualism when it speaks of safeguarding "the nature and mission of sacred ministry and the vocation and secular character of the lay faithful."[23]

An explanatory note accompanying the document underlines the distinction: "The laity, by virtue of the holiness of their baptism, have an urgent duty toward the material and spiritual world, but what is purely lay — that is, the consecration of the world — is different from what is concerned by ministeriality."[24]

Avoiding a Church versus World Dualism

But must we separate ministry from the world? Returning to the discussion at the council surrounding article 31 of *Lumen Gentium*, we note, first of all, that the drafters of this text did not intend to define the laity in terms of this secular characteristic. Rather, they set out to provide a description of the layperson as compared to clerics and religious. The *relatio* by Cardinal John Wright introducing this article to the full body of bishops noted that the text should not be read as an "ontological definition" of the layperson but rather as a "typological description."[25] In other words, the drafters did not intend to define the essence of the lay condition in their secular orientation, but rather offered "a description of a type, that is, of what typifies a layperson's situation and activity. A layperson typically is married, has a job, lives in the world, etc."[26] Thus, later attempts to absolutize the secular dimension of the layperson, or to elevate it into an essential definition are in fact advances on the council's more modest intent. Looking around, as it were, at the contemporary situation of lay Catholics, the council participants attempted to articulate a theology that would reflect this reality.[27] The question we might ask today is whether this reality has changed.

Moreover, the documents of Vatican II reflect a larger theological shift away from a dualistic view of the Church/world relationship to a view that places the Church within the world. The description of the laity in terms of a secular characteristic was worked out early on in *Lumen Gentium* and drafts of *Apostolicam Actuositatem*. But over the course of the conciliar debates — particularly in the emergence and eventual acceptance of the Pastoral Constitution on the Church in the Modern World (*Gaudium et Spes*) — a broader vision appeared, one that saw the *whole Church* with a mission to transform the world. While not devaluing the traditional activities of liturgy and devotions, preaching and teaching, *Gaudium et Spes* challenged an isolation from the world and any simplistic attempt to set Church and world over and against one another. The Church is *in* the world. A separation of the two realms is impossible, for the Church itself is to be "a leaven and, as it were, the soul of human society in its renewal by Christ and transformation into the family of God."[28] Richard Gaillardetz points out an important shift in this metaphor of leaven. In *Lumen Gentium* and *Apostolicam Actuositatem,* the metaphor of leaven applies specifically to the laity. But by *Gaudium et Spes,* it is the *whole* Church that is to be leaven in the world.[29]

Giovanni Magnani underscores the fact that in *Gaudium et Spes* — a document dedicated to the place of the Church in the temporal world — the term "layman" appears only six times, and not at all until article 43.[30] In fact, Magnani argues that the council texts cannot be used to justify a contrastive approach, one that would posit a secular laity over against a sacred clergy. For Magnani, what the texts offer is an "intensive" theology of the laity. That is, in describing the laity as secular, the council is presenting the laity as an intensive, or fuller, realization of the situation of the entire Church. The whole Church is in the world; the laity realizes this in a more intense way.[31] In the end, then, the history of the council suggests a growing realization that the call to transform the created world is a call that marks the whole Church, and not just the laity: "The church, then, believes that through each of its members and its community as a whole it can help to make the human family and its history still more human."[32]

The Challenge to Be Priest in the World

It seems we can no longer rely on the notion of "sacred ministry" to identify or distinguish the priest, if by "sacred ministry" we imply activity in a realm separate from the secular, a Church apart from the world. To link identity to separation, to rest alone as "a man set apart" for the things of God is, at best, a return to a French baroque spirituality and, at worst, a drift into clericalism. Every priest today is not called to be an agent for social reform, a spokesman for political causes, or a worker-priest one with the people, but disengagement from the world in which we live is not an option. The rise of certain disciplinary requirements and the migration of the monastic lifestyle to all of the ordained may have given the impression that such separation defined the priest. But given the reality of a Church in, but not of, the world, "separation from worldly obligations, however much they may be justified in the prudential order, cannot enter into the *essential* character of ordained ministry."[33]

What does it mean for a priest to be secular? What does it mean to be in the world, or rather, to be a part of and serving this Church which is in the world? Perhaps *Gaudium et Spes* offers some direction here. In that document, the council called on all the Christian faithful, clergy and laity, to work to make the human community more fully human. It is the human person, "each individual human person in her or his totality, body and soul, heart and conscience, mind and will," that is the key to this discussion.[34] The human person provides a common language that allows the Church to dialogue with the modern world, a vocabulary for the Church to articulate and advance its mission in a society where the religious is not taken for granted. The challenge to be priest in the world is the challenge to serve human life, to be *for* human life in all its dimensions. Thus, to borrow the language of *Gaudium et Spes,* the priest takes a leading role through a life and a ministry that heals and elevates the dignity of the human person, that works to draw society and people more closely together, and that strives to endow people's daily activity with a deeper sense and meaning.[35]

The Latin American liberation theologian Jon Sobrino calls this challenge to be *for* human life the "pro-existential" nature of priestly existence.[36] He locates the finality or goal of priesthood in salvation, understood concretely as God's drawing near to human beings. In a way that can never be earned or demanded, God comes close to us for our good. It is a saving approach that fosters bodily and spiritual life, particularly among the weak and oppressed. "In these terms, at the theological level, priestly service is anything that helps to express, concretely and historically, that coming of God's."[37] But we learn this definition of priestly service from Jesus, the personal expression of God's coming. For Jesus' "obsession, if we may call it that, was with an approach to human beings, in whatever manner and whatever area that approach might be possible."[38] Sobrino's reflections point to an understanding of priestly service extending beyond the sacristy and broader than administering the sacraments, since God approaches people where they are. If the priest serves God's good coming, then the field of priestly service must be determined by the field of God's saving activity, which is coextensive with the world itself. "At least, it ought to be clear that one is not more priestly the less one ventures into the world. One is not holier the less one is willing to face the dangers of the world. One is not closer to God the less one is contaminated by the world." Sobrino cites the forceful words of Charles Péguy as an indictment against the indifferent priest: "Because they have not the courage to be of the world, they believe that they are of God . . . because they love no one, they believe that they love God."[39]

Leaving behind the misleading dichotomy of a secular laity and a sacred ministry, the priest faces the challenge of being a priest in the world and of being *for* human life. But what does this mean in the context of today's American parish? Perhaps too obvious are the many threats, which are often politically orchestrated spectacles, to the dignity of the human person, to human life itself, which we see regularly in the media and in social commentary in this country. Beyond these examples are more subtle, but no less anti-human, forces shaping the very way we understand our existence and orient our lives. We live in a world obsessively interconnected, but deeply fractured. Sitting at my computer in Cincinnati, I can order tennis shoes from a company with offices in Rochester, warehouses in Houston, and factories in Manila. And yet I can so easily ignore the impact this purchase has on human beings scattered around the globe. We live with a culture that seems to have replaced discernment with purchasing power. Concern about the common good is overrun by niche marketing, where even churches study ways to increase brand loyalty.[40]

One pressing challenge for the priest in the world is to proclaim, in the way he ministers and in the way he lives, the truth that the person is higher than the product, and that my identity is greater than what I buy. Here the disciplinary requirements that have "freed" the priest from certain worldly cares can help facilitate a prophetic witness against the consumerism of our times. But it also complicates this witness, for the celibate priest may find it difficult to speak credibly to families about money. Thus, his cannot be the only voice, the only example. Fortunately, around most pastors today moves a group of laypeople who live out this prophetic witness. They work for small salaries and sacrifice a great deal of family and leisure time in order to run important ministries for the parish. The fact of their existence suggests a vision of success defined in terms of service. These lay ecclesial ministers are indispensable collaborators in the Church's mission to transform the world in the light of Christ. And the priest risks too much in ignoring their wisdom or in failing to lift up these dedicated disciples as examples of that full human life to which Christ calls each of us.

Priest for a Priestly People

Discussions at the Second Vatican Council surrounding what would become *Lumen Gentium,* no. 10, reveal that the council participants wanted to do two things: first, clearly and positively affirm the priesthood of the faithful; and second, distinguish this common priesthood from the priesthood of the ordained. Thus the final text grounds both in the one priesthood of Christ and asserts that the priesthood of the faithful and the ministerial priesthood "differ essentially and not only in degree." Since the council, many pastoral leaders and some theologians highlight this essential difference as the key to distinguishing lay and ordained ministries. But in this, the essential difference is imagined as if two groups of priests — that of the laity and that of the clergy — are set side-by-side. This was not the intention behind *Lumen Gentium.* Moving beyond this faulty reading allows for a more fruitful appeal to the category of priesthood in describing ministry today.

The Return of the Priesthood of the Faithful

The priesthood of the faithful, held suspect among Catholics since the Protestant Reformation, made something of a comeback in the first half of the twentieth century. This scriptural category found its way into Catholic theological conversations not primarily through studies of the New Testament or by way of ecumenical conversations. Instead, Catholics rediscovered it in Thomas Aquinas.

It was in Aquinas's sacramental theology, in particular, his teaching on the sacramental "character," that the baptismal priesthood appeared. Neoscholastic theologians understood character to be the effect on the soul produced by the sacraments of baptism, confirmation, and holy orders, a kind of permanent spiritual mark, which helped explain why these three sacraments could not be repeated. But Aquinas had a richer understanding. He described the sacramental character as a participation in the priesthood of Christ. Thus these three sacraments, in distinct ways, make their recipients priests or instruments and ministers of Christ's one priesthood.

Catholics involved in the liturgical movement of the late nineteenth and early twentieth century saw rich possibilities in Aquinas's view. One of the driving forces of this movement was the call for the active participation of the laity in the liturgy. The lay faithful were being called not only to be present at Mass but also to be attentive; they were invited to receive communion, but also to give of themselves in active prayer. Initial and hesitant participatory responses were added; missals with vernacular translations appeared; a few roles for laity in the service were tried. All of these initiatives eventually led to the full-scale reforms encouraged by Vatican II.

In the early days of the movement, theologians pointed to Aquinas's view that baptism initiates both a spiritual priesthood, entailing the inward offering of a spiritual sacrifice that marks the Christian life, and an external priesthood that is shared by all and that is directly related to the Church's public worship.[41] For Aquinas, the reception of character in baptism, confirmation, and orders empowers Christians in different ways to participate in the worship of the Church. Orders empower those who *give* the sacraments. Baptism and confirmation empower those who *receive* the sacraments. But for Aquinas, even the reception of the sacraments involves an active profession of faith. It is a true priestly act. The theological recovery of this insight made its way into official papal teaching in Pius XII's 1947 encyclical *Mediator Dei*. Encouraging within certain limits the participation of the laity in the liturgy, Pius XII stated: "By the waters of baptism, as by common right, Christians are made members of the Mystical Body of Christ the Priest, and by the 'character' which is imprinted on their souls, they are appointed to give worship to God. Thus they participate, according to their condition, in the priesthood of Christ."[42]

By the time John XXIII announced the Second Vatican Council, both Catholic theology and the teaching magisterium had reconciled itself to the notion of the priesthood of all the faithful. But the priesthood of the faithful remained heavily qualified and was seen in terms of and subordinated to the hierarchical priesthood. The category also remained individualistic. Reflection on the common priesthood began with the sacramental character imprinted on the soul of an individual, rather than being seen as an entrance into the priestly people described in 1 Peter. These tendencies shaped the initial presentation of the priesthood of the faithful at Vatican II. But important developments during the council broadened and reoriented this category.

The Priesthood of the Faithful and the People of God

The development that the Dogmatic Constitution on the Church went through over the course of the council is well known. The initial draft, presented by the preparatory commission at the first session of the council, reflected the neoscholastic approach that dominated Catholic ecclesiology prior to the council. This draft was roundly rejected by the council participants for its clericalism, juridicism, and triumphalism.[43] It was replaced by a second, and finally, a third draft that approached the Church less juridically, drawing instead on Scripture and the rich resources of the tradition to speak of the Church as mystery, as the people of God, and as the body of Christ. This development through the drafts would have important implications for the council's teaching on the priesthood of the faithful.

The first draft of what would become *Lumen Gentium* included a statement on the universal priesthood in its sixth chapter, titled "The Laity." This placement suggested that the universal priesthood is in some way peculiar to the laity. Even though the text itself notes that the universal priesthood includes both the hierarchy and the laity, it still functions in this context to support the chapter's call on the *laity in particular* to a more active participation in the Church's apostolate. The text reflects the basic orientation of *Mediator Dei* and cites a 1954 address by Pius XII in which he clarified that the ministerial priesthood and the universal priesthood "differ not only in degree but also in essence."[44] Thus we see the efforts of the text both to say something positive about the universal priesthood in relation to the laity and to maintain distinctions. However, the distinction undercuts the full reality of the universal priesthood. For after tracing the scriptural basis of the universal priesthood, the chapter speaks of ministerial priests as "priests properly so-called." And the commentary provided at the time by the Theological Commission explained this phrase as an attempt to present the universal priesthood as "metaphorical or analogical" relative to the ministerial priesthood.[45] Thus, the universal priesthood is presented in terms of and subordinate to the priesthood of the ordained.

This bias against the full reality of the universal priesthood of the faithful was not lost on the council participants. Several bishops and groups of bishops took exception to this language, and, after the draft on the Church was sent back for a complete rewrite, the phrase "properly so-called" dropped out.[46] In the second draft of the Constitution on the Church, both the common and the ministerial priesthood are affirmed as real, different from each other, but both derived from the one priesthood of Christ.

The real change came with the third and final draft of *Lumen Gentium*. In draft two, the chapter on "The People of God, Especially the Laity" followed chapters on the mystery of the Church and the hierarchy, giving the impression that the hierarchy preceded the people of God. A suggestion was made by the drafting committee that this third chapter be divided and that the material on the people of God be placed before the chapter on the hierarchy. Such an arrangement would have the effect of affirming that the unity of the whole people of God is prior to any distinctions among roles in the Church. The suggestion was followed and the final draft included the first four chapters in this order: Church as mystery, people of God, hierarchy, laity. Within this new arrangement, the article on the universal priesthood of the faithful was moved to chapter 2 on the people of God. And for the first time in the council debates, the common priesthood was separated structurally from the laity as a particular group within the Church. Thus two points were clearly made: first, the common priesthood encompasses the whole people of God, clergy and laity; and second, the ministerial or hierarchical priesthood is to be understood in light of this common priesthood, and not vice versa. The common priesthood and the hierarchical priesthood are not side-by-side categories; the hierarchical priesthood exists within and in order to serve the common priesthood.

Despite this helpful corrective, an ambiguity remains in the way in which *Lumen Gentium,* no. 10, has been interpreted. The ambiguity follows from a failure to recognize that the word "priesthood" is used here equivocally.[47] In describing the common priesthood, the passage speaks of the spiritual sacrifices of daily life, prayer and praise, offering the Eucharist, witness, and the reception of the sacraments. In describing the "ministerial or hierarchical priesthood," the passage speaks of the power to form and lead the Church and to celebrate the Eucharist. The first "priesthood" describes the life of holiness that ought to mark a disciple of Christ. The second "priesthood" describes the activities of one group of ministers that serve to support this life of holiness. The common priesthood refers to discipleship; the hierarchical priesthood refers to a particular ministry. Thus, the common priesthood and the ministerial priesthood do not "differ essentially" because there exists an ontological wall of separation between the ordained and the nonordained. Rather, these two priesthoods differ essentially because they refer to two different dimensions of the Christian life, i.e., the discipleship of all and the ministry of the ordained. While they certainly have a proper relationship to one another, these are very different things.[48]

The Challenge to Be Priest for the Priesthood of the Faithful

On this reading of *Lumen Gentium,* no. 10, we should be cautious about attempting to distinguish lay and ordained ministries based on

a distinction of priesthoods, i.e., lay ministry flows from the priesthood of the faithful, ordained ministry flows from the ministerial
priesthood. To say the common priesthood is the source and ground
of lay ministry is true, but not because it offers to the layperson an
analogous priesthood that is modeled on and thus somehow less than
the priesthood of the ordained. The common priesthood of all the
faithful is simply discipleship, the life of holiness lived in union with
Christ, the high priest. Thus the common priesthood grounds the
work of the lay minister just as it grounds the work of the ordained
minister. For the common priesthood is a facet of every baptized
Christian's place within the community of Christ called to be the
people of God.

What then does the ministerial priesthood add to the ordained
membership within the priestly people of God? *Lumen Gentium* answers that it adds a certain power and responsibility to serve the
universal priesthood.[49] The ministerial priesthood helps the priesthood of all the faithful exercise its priesthood. But what might this
mean for ministry today? It is often repeated that the Second Vatican
Council abandoned a phenomenological, exclusively cultic model of
ministry, one that stressed the role of the priest as a mediator between
God and the community, an individual who is ritually set apart from
the people in order to offer sacrifice on their behalf. But in displacing
this model, which had dominated the Church for centuries, the council did not abandon the language of priesthood altogether. Rather,
it sought to recognize and incorporate a broader pastoral ministry
within its definition of priestly service. And it resituated the eucharistic sacrifice within the wider context of that sacrifice of life lived in
imitation of Christ's sacrifice. To serve the priesthood of all the faithful, the ordained priest faces the challenge to celebrate and recall
Christ's own priesthood, so that the community may participate in
it. It is in imitating Christ's priesthood that we as a Church exercise
our own priesthood that embodies that discipleship that constitutes
the "acceptable sacrifice" of praise.

To put it another way, the challenge to be priest for the priesthood
of the faithful is the challenge to serve the memory of Christ.[50] According to the Letter to the Hebrews, Christ is the high priest who

is also the sacrifice. The cross does not exhaust this sacrificial action; rather, the cross is the culmination of an entire life of self-gift, enacted through the concrete acts of love for God and God's children that constituted Jesus' life. His priesthood was simply his life, lived as a total response to God. His actions did not install a caste of religious professionals, but invited all of his followers into his vision and example of self-gift. When the author of 1 Peter and other early Christians spoke of priesthood, they meant the whole community. The sacrifices of the temple were replaced with the sacrifice of praise embodied in lives of self-offering and holiness. But to imitate Christ, the faith community continually needs to be reminded of and made present to his life of faith. This is the crux of ministry; human beings serve the work of the Holy Spirit through acts of ministry that remind the community of Christ. All ministers, in one way or another, serve the memory of Christ by continuing his mission.

But the ordained priest accomplishes this ministry of memory in a distinctive way, symbolized in the eucharistic celebration. Through the eucharistic anamnesis, in which the saving deeds of Jesus are recalled, the priest repeats the words and gestures of Christ in a public act that points to the climax of Jesus' life for us. In that act, it is not that the priest himself reminds us of Christ. Instead, he helps us remember Christ by pointing beyond himself and his actions to the life of Jesus.[51] The eucharistic anamnesis is the highpoint of the priest's ministry of calling to mind Christ for the community. But his ministry of memory extends beyond this moment to include the whole eucharistic prayer, the whole eucharistic celebration, indeed, the whole life of ministry of the priest. For the various acts of teaching and preaching, prayer and presiding, service, leadership, coordination, and prophetic witness all serve to remind the community of Christ's own priesthood. And in doing so, these actions draw us into the dynamic of Jesus' own response to the Father, pushing us toward an active participation in this response, a participation in Jesus' own priesthood. By calling the community to discipleship in imitation of Jesus, the ministerial priest helps the priesthood of all the faithful exercise its priesthood.

Conclusion

In my introductory course in ecclesiology, I often begin by asking my students: What is essential to Catholicism? What is essential to being Catholic? They shoot back a familiar litany: following the pope, belief in transubstantiation, Mary, the saints, having seven sacraments. I push them: What about the law of love? What about recognition of God's saving presence in the world? What about commitment to Jesus Christ? "Yes, yes, yes," they respond, "but those things aren't *essential.*"

Like my students, too often we confuse what is *essential* to a thing with what is *distinctive* about it. We seek identity by way of contrast. Bored with the genus, we are more interested in the specific differences. Much of the discussion about lay and ordained ministries in the Church today operates in a contrastive mode; it is preoccupied with safeguarding and strengthening the distinctive identity of this or that ministry.[52] And the best way to do this, it seems to some, is to draw a dark line between my ministry and your ministry, between categories or realms of activity. And so we assume as true false dichotomies. The pairs of ministry and the apostolate, of the sacred and the secular, and of the ministerial priesthood and the priesthood of the faithful are set side-by-side in a contrastive way. The truth, however, is that the first term in these pairs is always found within the context of the second. Ministry serves mission; the sacred permeates the secular; the ordained priesthood exists within and for the priesthood of all the faithful. Over thirty years ago, Yves Congar noticed a shift that continues today to direct the reality of ministry in the Church: the shift away from a dividing-line model pitting clergy against laity to a model of concentric circles of diverse ministries within the community.[53]

This shift in models does not leave behind distinctions among ministries. But it does challenge the assumption that distinction implies separation, that the act of affirming any one ministry necessarily detracts from another. Perhaps Magnani's description of "contrastive" and "intensive" approaches to the laity might be applied to the ordained priest in a different way. Rather than begin our theology of the priesthood with what is unique, exclusive, or reserved to the priest (contrastive approach), what if we turn instead to those realities and relations that the ordained priest shares with the whole people of God, but in which the priest serves as a fuller, more intense realization (intensive approach)? Proclaiming, serving, and celebrating the reign of God are not unique to the priest, but they are essential to the ministerial priesthood. And the priest realizes these in a particularly intensive way. He has a special responsibility for the word of God, for sharing the tradition that has come down from the apostles. He is a presence in the world of the humanizing power of love. He offers the Eucharist within and on behalf of the community, calling to mind Christ's life of self-gift.

At the end of his review of post-conciliar literature on the theology of the laity, Jacques Dupuis offers a rich summary that points toward the future work that we still face:

> The real ecclesiological problem, then, consists less in defining the laity's place and role in the Church than in determining the function in it of the hierarchical priesthood, based on the sacrament of order received in the apostolic succession, and in showing how it is related to the basic priestly reality of the People of God. Does not in the last analysis the priest's function in the church community raise a more difficult question than does simply being a member of God's People? And has not our own time been marked by an identity crisis of priests rather than of lay people? Paradoxically, the solution of the problem will not lie in holding fast to distinctions which have resulted in dichotomies and fictitious opposition (clergy-laity, spiritual-temporal, church-world), but in rediscovering the "total ecclesiology" of the communion of all the baptized and of their common participation in the mission of the Church — an ecclesiology in which what unites all disciples of Christ in the Church will prevail, without denying it, over the distinction of charisms, functions and ministries.[54]

Chapter 10

Reflection

JOSEPH NUZZI

THE CONFERENCE PAPERS delivered by John Strynkowski and Edward Hahnenberg both approach a central theme in this post–Vatican II era: the relationship between a priest and other bodies within the Church. Strynkowski addresses the question of the relationship between bishops and priests. Because of the scope of the paper, he limits himself to a mainly theological, and perhaps even idealized, description of this relationship. Yet he does stress the reality that this relationship is lived out differently in different dioceses, and that it is not always lived out according to the Church's vision, as expressed in church documents. Hahnenberg reflects on the relationship between ordained ministry in general (inclusive of bishop, priest, and deacon) and lay ministry. His paper discusses in depth the contemporary problem of the definition of priestly ministry as exercised by the hierarchy versus the priesthood of all the baptized. The explosion of lay ecclesial ministry seems to have exacerbated this problem and called forth renewed efforts to make clear distinctions.

What was striking at the conference was the reaction among the participants to the issues raised in both of these papers. There was a lot of energy and emotional reaction among the participants, both in the general question-and-answer period, as well as in the break-out sessions, to the relationship of the priest to both the bishop and the laity. From the papers and from the comments, I came away with the impression that the priest is the person who is "caught in the middle," which is not a comfortable place to be.

126

What strains the relationship between priest and bishop is that it is simultaneously a ministerial and an administrative relationship. No one expressed any problem with the validity of the vision that the bishop and his priests share in Christ's priestly ministry and shepherding role. As Strynkowski points out, John Paul II, in many documents, calls for a spirit of collaboration, trust, and mutual respect to define the cohesion within the one presbyterate. In fact, many concerns raised at the conference seemed to come from a view that the relationship of most priests to their bishop in reality falls far short of this vision. The problem clearly does not stem from a disagreement over the theology of the episcopacy or the theology of the priesthood.

Instead, questions arose from the other facet of the relationship between bishop and priest: administration. The complaints echoed a concern that most priests do not have adequate access to their bishop and that communication seems to flow in general in one direction: top down. Problems seem to stem from the fact that in the hierarchical administration of the Church, the priest reports to and is responsible to his bishop. While part of this does have its roots in the theology that the bishop is the head of the local church and that the priest assists the bishop to extend his ministry, the reality is that the purely administrative, corporate nature of these roles seems to trump the spirit of collaboration and shared ministry that should exist among fellow ministers in the Church. I heard many at the conference speak of their bishop the way anyone working in a large corporation might speak about their president or CEO. In other words, many times the bishop relates to his priests more as a boss to an employee, instead of as a fellow shepherd charged with overseeing the flock. This seems to be the cause of a lot of anxiety and resentment.

If a priest's distance from his bishop might be a cause for concern and confusion as to what exactly priestly identity is, then the priest's relationship to the laity only makes matters worse. Hahnenberg spends most of his time discussing the way the phenomenon of lay ecclesial ministry has raised fundamental questions as to the very nature of the ministerial priesthood. He traces how Vatican II reversed a long-standing trend to present priestly ministry as over and against the lay state. At the same time, he points out that this

thinking seems to have returned recently to discussions of the role of
the priest in the Church.´ What seems to be at the heart of the matter is that the lived experience of an explosion of lay ministry in the
Church has left many questions. What makes the priest different? Is
his role distinct? Or, are we only left with an arbitrary line which
demarcates who may preside at the sacraments and who may not?
Without going into the details of the situation that Hahnenberg so
clearly delineates, what we fundamentally have today is an identity
crisis in the priesthood.

Vatican II did a wonderful job of clearly defining the role of the
bishop in the Church. His function, status, and role are clear. The
council also did a wonderful job of reclaiming baptism as the primary
sacrament of vocation and of calling all people to live out their baptismal promises. After the council, many lay people felt empowered
to join the priest in ministries which were traditionally reserved for
the clergy. They too developed a clear idea of whom they are and of
their role in the Church. The priest, then, is "left in the middle." He
is clearly not the bishop. And yet he is clearly not the only one who
can "do ministry" in his parish. The notion that only he can preside, specifically at the Eucharist, only begs the question: why? Why
him and not the director of religious education? Why him and not
the youth minister? If the problem of the priest's relationship to the
bishop is one of distance and disenfranchisement, then the problem
of the priest's relationship to the laity, and in particular to his own
people in his own parish, is one of a lack of clear identity. He is stuck
between a bishop to whom he must answer and his parishioners to
whom he is also responsible.

This situation, especially when played out to its extreme ends, can
be very difficult and, at times, sad. One pastor present at the conference made this clear in a very poignant story. Along with the rest of
his diocese, this pastor received a letter from his bishop mandating
a very strong and firm stance against homosexuality in the Church
and against gay unions. This was in a state where this question was
before the legislature for consideration. The pastor, knowing that he
was shepherding a very diverse community that included many gay
as well as gay-friendly parishioners, knew that this policy would be

hurtful to many people. He followed his bishop's mandate and followed through with the policy; subsequently, many in his community were angry and upset. He lamented his decision and shared that in retrospect he would do things very differently. The reason he chose to do what he did was because he was afraid at the time to stand up to his bishop against this policy, even though he knew that it would have been the right thing to do. He was afraid of the repercussions from his "boss," the bishop. What the story made very concrete and real is the fact that our priests occupy an ambivalent position. They stand between the people to whom and with whom they serve and the bishop to whom they have vowed obedience and to whom they are administratively responsible.

Upon reflecting on these papers and on the reactions of the participants to them, it has become clear to me that the problem many of our priests face today stems essentially from a lack of Christian charity and vision within the community as a whole. Vis-à-vis the bishop, many priests and lay people live in a culture of fear. If they believe that the bishop differs, they fear to express what they may believe to be the pastorally right thing to do. Priests also seem to fear, as lay ministry grows more and more with ever more qualified people doing things that the priest used to do that their ministry and role may be undervalued. There is a lot of fear in our Church, and it is adversely affecting all of us. All of this among a people whom the Lord constantly tells, "Do not be afraid."

While I believe that structural changes are needed to address some of the problems and issues raised by these two papers, I also believe that the first step, although not structural, is even more important. We need more courage and more love, all around, to alleviate the pressure the priest feels by being "caught in the middle." We need more charity and collaboration on the part of our bishops toward their priests, especially since it is the priests who effectively make the bishop's ministry a reality on the local level. We also need our bishops to be more courageous in being able to listen and bend, so that their priests can feel confident that they can share very real and difficult situations of pastoral need. We need our priests to be more charitable to the people with whom they share their ministry, so that in loving the gifts of all people, they can feel less threatened by a lack of identity. We need our priests to be more courageous, to be the shepherds of their local community by being its voice in front of the bishop and among the rest of the presbyterate. Otherwise, the local community has no way of having a voice in the hierarchy. Finally, we need the laity to be more charitable toward its priests, who have the difficult role of being placed "in the middle." We need the laity to cherish priestly ministry and to be compassionate toward priests. At the same time, the laity must also be courageous enough to continue to work and to minister in a Church which remains closed off to any real, meaningful recognition of that ministry. Because the culture of fear that exists in our Church speaks volumes about how we do not love each other enough, love and courage are needed all around.

In closing, maybe the role of the priest is precisely to be the person "in the middle." This position, which is fraught with difficulties, may be just the thing that defines the priesthood. The priest does stand "in the middle"; but he also gives a face to Christ's priesthood and a face to the Church, at least within the local community, in doing so. Because of this he is also charged, as a shepherd to his local community, to be the face of that community within the larger Church. He is a shepherd who must at the same time internally attend to and externally advocate for his flock. Maybe the reality of being "in the middle" is not so lamentable; perhaps, it is a powerful source of ministry within the Church.

Part Four

CHALLENGES
FOR THE FUTURE

Chapter 11

Addressing the Priest "Shortage"

Dean R. Hoge

❧❧❧

A S PREPARATIONS got under way for the election of a new pope in April 2005, much attention was paid in the media and academe to problems facing the Catholic Church today. Near the top of most observers' lists of problems was a shortage of priests. In many nations, the priesthood is in decline, and, in a few, a precipitous decline. Sociology can contribute to solving problems in the priesthood by providing reliable information. In this paper, I will review sociological findings on three topics: the distribution of priests in the world, recent changes in priestly identity, and conditions of priestly life today.

Distribution of Priests in the World

We need to look at worldwide statistics on Catholic membership and on numbers of priests. The number of Roman Catholics in the world is increasing. The total now is about 1.07 billion. Table 1 on the following page portrays trends by comparing 1985 figures with the latest data available. The second and third columns in the table show the trends. Catholic membership growth in the world since 1985 has been 26 percent, with the greatest growth in Africa and Asia nearly matching the world's population growth of 29 percent in the same period of time. But growth in the number of priests has been zero.

The trends vary widely from continent to continent. In the United States, membership growth since 1985 has been 23 percent, while the number of priests has fallen off by 16 percent. Europe has seen

Table 1
World Data on Catholic Membership/Number of Priests

	Total Membership in millions (2002)	Change in Membership in percent (1985–2002)	Change in Priests in percent (1985–2002)	Catholics per Priest (2002)	GNP per Capita in dollars (2002)
North America	78.8	+22	−17	1,382	35,390
United States (only)	65.5	+23	−16	1,375	36,110
Europe	279.9	+1	−12	1,374	17,730
Oceania/Australia	8.4	+31	−12	1,732	19,960
Central America	123.5	+26	+44	6,763	7,580
Caribbean	25.4	+33	+27	7,983	7,980
South America	306.6	+27	+24	7,138	6,970
Africa	137.4	+89	+62	4,694	2,100
Middle East	2.8	+21	+2	1,189	6,100
Far East/Philippines/ South Asia	107.5	+54	+65	2,473	4,540
World Total	1070.3	+26	0	2,642	7,590

GNP per capita data are from the *World Population Data Sheet 2004,* published by the Population Reference Bureau, Washington, D.C. All other data are from the *Statistical Yearbook of the Church,* published annually by the Vatican.

---

virtually no growth in membership, while the number of priests has fallen off by 12 percent. Africa and Asia have seen large increases in priests, followed by Central America. By contrast, North America, Europe, and Oceania, which are by far the wealthiest portions of the world, have seen decreases. Sixty percent of Catholics in Oceania are in Australia. Put plainly, the wealthy nations in North America, Europe, and Australia have been losing priests, while the rest of the nations have been gaining priests. And yet it is in the wealthy regions of the world where Catholics have the greatest access to priests.

The fourth column in Table 1 reports the number of Catholics per priest in 2002. Latin America is unique in the large numbers of Catholics per priest, that is, in its dearth of priests. The fifth column shows the relative wealth of the nine regions, measured in gross national product per capita. Note that the wealthy regions, North America, Europe, and Oceania have by far the fewest Catholics per priest (i.e., the most priests in service per 1,000 laity). They are far wealthier than the rest of the world. The poor regions have many fewer priests available. The Middle East is an unusual region with very few Catholics, but it has unusually numerous priests for its rather low economic

Figure 1
Number of Catholics per Priest (2002)

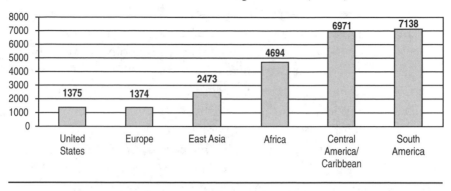

level, and in this respect it is anomalous; it is also unique in other ways. The number of Catholics per priest is summarized in Figure 1.

The falloff in number of priests has occurred in most of the developed nations. Table 2 shows the changes in thirteen of them. With the exception of Poland, all have faced sizable decreases in seventeen years. In sum, the wealthy nations have the money; the poor nations have the people and the seminarians.

Table 2
Changes in Number of Priests: 1985–2002

Europe		Percent Change
	Austria	−22
	Belgium	−34
	France	−35
	(Unified) Germany	−19
	Great Britain	−22
	Ireland	−12
	Italy	−13
	Netherlands	−42
	Poland	+36
	Spain	−15
Western-Oriented		Percent Change
	United States	−16
	Canada	−24
	Australia	−16

The Priest Shortage in the United States

In 2004, there were 1,453 laity per priest in the nation, and that number compares with 652 back in 1950 and with 778 in 1965.[1] In 1900, it was 899. The year 1950 was a highpoint in availability of priests; before that it was lower.[2] Since the 1980s, the number of priests has dropped by 9 to 11 percent per decade, and it shows signs of a continuing decline in the years ahead. Compared with diocesan priests, who fell by about 8 to 10 percent per decade, the drop-off in religious priests has been relatively sharper — about 20 percent per decade. The average age of priests (active and retired) in 2001 was sixty, and the average age of nonretired priests was fifty-six. Diocesan priests average five years younger than religious. Ordinations have varied between 440 and 540 in recent years, but have maintained overall a long-term gradual decline. Today, the American seminaries are producing each year priests at between 35 and 45 percent of the number needed to keep the priesthood at a constant size.

Meanwhile the American Catholic membership has been growing about 12 to 14 percent per decade, largely as a result of immigration and the larger number of children that immigrants have. The number of priests is falling while the number of laity is growing, thus predicting fewer and fewer priests per 1,000 Catholics in America in the future. Many Catholics today are pondering institutional adjustments to ease the problem, since a long-term continuation of present-day trends, they feel, will weaken the Church.

Most Catholics in America, but not all, agree that we have a priest shortage today.[3] There has been some confusion as to what constitutes a "shortage." Let me explain that "shortage" can be defined in three ways. The first is statistical, based on the number of Catholics per priest in different regions, as shown in Table 1. This measure, objective and simple, leads us to conclude that the United States relative to other parts of the world faces no priest shortage. In Latin America, for instance, the number of Catholics per priest is five times as high.

The second definition depends on the *feeling* of lay Catholics in one nation or another that a priest shortage exists. For anyone to feel that there is a shortage, he or she would have had to experience a situation in which more priests were available; either in one's own nation at an earlier time or in another nation. It is instructive to remember that in the United States there was no discussion of a "priest shortage" until the 1980s. At that time, the *recent change* in availability of priests began to produce a perception of shortage. The same kind of feeling would arise if an individual had lived previously in another country where more priests were in service per thousand Catholics. A Catholic moving from the United States to Brazil would feel that there is a shortage of priests; but a Catholic who has always lived in Brazil, where the number of priests has always been chronically lower, since he or she has never known anything else, would say, "What shortage?"

In Latin America, which has never enjoyed a large number of priests, a style of Catholicism which does not require as many priests has grown up over the centuries. Latin Americans have evolved a family-based or home-based Catholicism more than a parish-based Catholicism, with religion being taught by grandmothers and mothers and practiced in the home. There exists no felt need for weekly Mass attendance or frequent sacraments. Put simply, this definition of shortage indicates that there is no shortage in Latin America, because the present situation is *felt* to be normal and customary.

The third definition of "shortage" derives from opportunities lost. It defines "shortage" as not having enough priests to do what is needed. In such countries as Nigeria, Ghana, or India, with millions of people showing signs of readiness for evangelization, additional priests would be a big help. Using this definition, one could conclude that the whole world has a priest shortage. What Catholic community would not benefit from having more active, capable, and devoted priests working in it? In much of the world, in which the harvest is ready, the laborers are lacking. Why should we not strive to *double* the number of priests in the world? In my view, we should, for it would truly advance the cause of Christianity. The only limitation would be financial, that is, how many jobs for priests could we sustain in each country, given the money available?

I should add here that the laity-per-priest ratio in American Protestant denominations is much different from that in American

Catholicism. For Catholics in 2002, the figure was 1,375 laity per priest. For American Protestants, the figure was much lower, between 270 and 300. What causes this difference? One factor is that the more numerous clergy in Protestant denominations is made possible by the higher level of giving by Protestant members; Protestants want more clergy and are willing to pay to get them.[4] I see no reason that American Catholics would not prefer to have more clergy than they have at present or why they would not be willing to pay to get them.

Of the three measures of priest shortage, the second is the operative one. It is the one in the minds of most laity and the one that influences their attitudes. Older American Catholics can remember a time when more priests were available, thus they feel that they are faced with a priest shortage which is a major problem.[5] Many parishes today have no resident priest. In 2003, it was 16 percent; in most parishes, fewer Masses are available each weekend, while more priests are being asked to pastor two or more parishes. Nobody likes the trends. The laity want more sacraments, more presence of priests, and more priestly services, such as weddings and baptisms; the priests desire to pastor one parish and not more than one; the bishops want enough capable priests to staff the parishes for which they are responsible.[6] It is a lose-lose situation.

Are there alternatives? Here are nine possible alternatives. Some represent large departures from present-day discipline and others small. Let me clarify that I will mention only the alternatives which have a minimal relationship to central doctrine and dogma. The age-old apostolic core of the faith must be defended intact; only peripheral adjustments to today's institutions should be countenanced. Also, incremental changes are all that are possible, since any other changes would endanger unity in the Church.

Recruit more seminarians by trying harder

This is the most obvious course of action. It assumes that more men could be attracted to the priesthood if we encouraged them, if we gave them positive previews of seminary life and ministry, and if we portrayed priesthood correctly. I have had twenty years experience working with vocation directors and vocation programs in the

United States, and I do not believe a major increase in seminarians under present circumstances is possible. We are already trying harder, and we are investing immense energy and money into recruiting seminarians. No other Christian denomination is working at recruitment nearly as hard as we are. I would grant that a modest increase might be possible here or there, but not the doubling of ordinations we need. Recruitment should continue, but taken alone it is not a solution.

Make celibacy optional for diocesan priests

The most discussed alternative is to make celibacy optional for diocesan priests. This is favored today by 71 percent of the Catholic laity and by 56 percent of the priests. Yet nobody in the hierarchy talks about it. In 1985, I was given a foundation grant to estimate if the celibacy requirement is a large or a small deterrent in keeping men from entering the priesthood, and on the basis of a survey of Catholic college students, I found that it was the single biggest deterrent. If celibacy were optional for diocesan priests, there would be an estimated fourfold increase in seminarians, and the priest shortage would be over.[7] The priesthood would grow until it hit financial limits.

Priesthood with optional celibacy would cost more to Catholic parishes than a celibate priesthood. In 1987, a team of researchers compared the total costs of celibate Catholic priests — including housing, food, pensions, insurance, and salary — with the costs to Lutherans and Methodists of having married ministers. It was found that Lutheran and Methodist ministers cost about 38 to 40 percent more to have on the job than Catholic priests.[8] A reasonable assumption would be that the cost of a married priesthood to Catholics would be similar. Would Catholic laity contribute the additional funds needed to support married priests? Judging from the American Protestant experience, I believe that if Catholics were well served by a more available cadre of priests, they would. An adjustment in the celibacy requirement is widely discussed in Western nations today, but we need a more careful analysis of its ramifications in the theology of the priesthood and Catholic institutional life.

Institute an honorable discharge for priests

It has been widely noted that young adults today are hesitant about making lifelong commitments. Indeed, there is no occupation in America except Catholic priest or sister that demands a lifelong promise. Since Protestants have a lower theology of ordination, not involving ontology or sacrament, Protestant denominations do not require a lifelong commitment of their ministers. The military, the professions, and the government all use limited appointments or tours of duty. Would the option of having an honorable discharge, modeled on the military, after maybe ten or fifteen years, with optional renewal, aid recruitment to the priesthood? In the 1985 survey of Catholic college students, we tested the idea and found that it would produce many more seminarians. The idea is worth considering, even though it entails an adjustment in the theology of the priesthood, since the adjustment is less drastic than some other options.

Ordain women

The Church could ordain women. A first step would be to ordain celibate women. This was favored by 62 percent of the Catholic laity in a 1999 survey. I have not seen any figures on priests' attitudes on this, but judging from other research, the figure would probably be in the range of 35 to 55 percent in favor. A logical first step would be to ordain vowed women in religious communities. To ordain married women, which would be a more drastic step, was favored by 53 percent of Catholic laity in a 1999 survey.[9]

Bring in priests from other nations

International priests have been brought into the United States for many years. At present, about 16 or 17 percent of all active priests in the United States were born overseas, and the number is growing gradually. In recent ordination classes, 28 to 30 percent were born overseas, and most will stay here. Are there more priests overseas who are available to bring to the United States? Yes, from several countries, especially India, Nigeria, Philippines, and Colombia. But do not those nations have a worse priest shortage than we have (as shown in Table 1, page 134)? This question requires some explanation. Those countries do indeed have many fewer priests per thousand laity than Americans have. But, they have never had as many as we have, so there is no tradition of priests being readily available; and furthermore, as I said earlier, in many of those countries, there is not enough money to sustain a large cadre of priests. Poor nations cannot support a large priesthood.

At present, about 380 to 400 foreign-born priests are brought into the United States each year, of whom about 30 percent were trained in American seminaries. A portion of these men are brought here explicitly to minister to immigrant parishes, e.g., Korean priests invited to minister to Korean Catholics. The majority, however, minister to multicultural parishes or predominantly European American parishes.

A survey in 2004 estimated that about 5,500 international priests who began their ministry in 1985 or later are now serving in the United States, of whom 87 percent are diocesan and 13 percent are religious; the majority do not expect to serve in this country their entire lives. The largest numbers are in the Western and Southwestern states, Florida, and the greater New York City area. They have come mainly from Mexico, Colombia, Philippines, India, Vietnam, Nigeria, and Poland. Their average age is forty-six, which makes them much younger than American-born priests.

With international priests come unique problems. From the point of view of American priests and laity, the most serious of these are inadequate English skills, cultural misunderstandings, and a too-conservative ecclesiology. From the point of view of the foreign-born priests themselves, the main problems are inadequate orientation to American culture and the ways of the American Church, lack of appreciation and respect by American priests, and unfair treatment by diocesan leaders in placements and appointments.[10] These problems could be alleviated by a more careful screening of candidates and better orientation programs for new arrivals.

Increase the number of lay ministers

Today there are more lay ministers working in parishes than priests, and their number is growing rapidly. In ten or twenty years, they will far outnumber the priests. About 80 percent are female, and in a recent survey the average age was fifty-two. Fifty-three percent have received professional training beyond their BA.[11] They are in charge of schools, religious education programs, RCIA, youth ministry, liturgy, music, and administration. Priests sometimes feel threatened by them. This is understandable since many of the lay ministers have received the same education as priests, and since having worked in their parish for a number of years, they know more about it than any new priest just coming in. While lay ministers can do most of the work in running parishes, they cannot celebrate the sacraments. Although their usefulness is limited, lay ministers will be needed. They are an important resource for expanded parish leadership, and steps could be taken to enhance their official status, their ritual participation, and generally their spiritual leadership. Probably, they will do more officiating at communion services and more preaching in the future.

Expand the permanent diaconate

We could investigate ways to recruit more permanent deacons, and we could at the same time revise the theology of the permanent diaconate, so that deacons could administer all sacraments, not just baptism, matrimony, and the last rites. Such a theological revision would be a useful step, but it has ramifications. Nobody, so far as I have seen, has been seriously talking about it.

Accept more married Episcopalian priests

There exists in the Catholic Church a special pastoral provision for allowing married Episcopalian priests and a few ministers of other Protestant denominations to come in as married Catholic priests. The protocol is cumbersome and lengthy, and fewer than two hundred have signed on over a twenty-year period.[12] Why not amend the rules so that the invitation is more enticing? The process now is very slow, and it entails loss of income in the meantime. Why not aim at quadrupling the annual number coming in?

In a 2001 survey, 72 percent of Catholic priests said that the Catholic Church should continue to welcome married Episcopalian priests. The Episcopal Church in America has more clergy than it can place, and some of them would be interested in switching. An increased flow to the Catholic Church may damage ecumenical relations; however, according to my Episcopalian advisors, the damage would not be severe.

Expand the special pastoral provision to include married Catholic priests

We could expand the special pastoral provision to include Catholic priests who have left the priesthood to get married. Estimates of the number of married Catholic priests in the United States, to whom this might apply, range from 12,000 to 20,000. How many would return as married priests? To my knowledge, only one research study has asked, and it found that about 40 percent would return, either full-time or part-time.[13] Let us suppose that there are 16,000 married Catholic priests in the United States and that only 30 percent return. That would mean 4,800 more priests — the equivalent of ten years of ordinations at the present rate. This is a large number, making the option an important one. In a 2001 survey, 52 percent of American priests, when asked whether they supported such a move, responded, "Yes."

Shifts in Priestly Identity

Today any discussion of the priest shortage in the United States is complicated by a marked division among priests themselves over the nature of priestly ministry. Divergent views of priestly identity and role have been discussed repeatedly in the last decade in the Catholic community. Surveys of American priests have found two shifts in priestly self-understanding from the 1960s until today. During and after Vatican Council II, American priests shifted from a "cultic model" of the priesthood to a new "servant leader model," and later many of the new priests again preferred the cultic model.

The cultic model, which had prevailed for a long time, saw the priest as mainly an administrator of the sacraments and teacher of the faith. In this view, the priest needs to be celibate and set apart from other Catholics; his life is a witness to faith in God and an example of holiness. This model emphasizes that priests are different from laity. They are presumably higher in holiness, and they alone can serve as mediators between God and humanity. By contrast, the servant leader model emphasizes that the priest is the spiritual and social leader of the Catholic community. As such, he must interact closely with the laity and collaborate with them in leading parish life. The distinctness of the priest over and against the laity is de-emphasized, as symbolized by the preference of many priests after the 1960s not to wear the clerical cassock and collar. Also, the priests living the servant leader model invest themselves more in community leadership beyond the parish, attempting to have a beneficial effect on the larger society.[14]

The predominant self-understanding of younger American priests shifted from the cultic model to the servant leader model during the 1960s, and then later, beginning in the middle 1980s, the even still younger group shifted back. According to research in 2001, the second transition was already well advanced, and the young priests had moved quite a distance from their elder brothers in their understanding of what a priest is. Specifically, they differed from their elders on whether ordination confers on a priest a new ontological status which makes him essentially different from laity, whether a priest should be a "man set apart," whether celibacy should become a matter of personal choice for priests (the young men were more opposed), and whether the Church should welcome more lay ministers (the young men were more opposed). The younger priests have been more conservative in their theology of the priesthood, as well as in their ecclesiology and in their liturgy. As numerous observers have noted, they tend to be much more rigid on matters of liturgy, morals, and priestly life. They also believe it is important to be seen in priestly attire.

The priests holding to the servant leader model in 2001 were mostly in the fifty-six-to-sixty-five-year-old age cohort — not the very oldest priests. Priests over seventy years old were between the extremes, not clearly upholding either the cultic or the servant leader model. The age differences in the priesthood were large, and they formed a U-shaped curve, with the bottom of the U in the fifty-six-to-sixty-five-year cohort.[15] Many American priests adhere today to one model or the other, which creates an uneasy state of tension. Some priests see the good of both models.

Research findings depict the advantages of the two models. In favor of the cultic model, for instance, is the finding that priests adhering to it have stronger priestly identity. One study had an opportunity to study this question with both 1970 and 2001 data. In both time periods, the priests adhering to the cultic model reported stronger priestly identity and higher morale.[16] Also in favor of the cultic model is that seminaries and dioceses adhering to it have been more successful in attracting vocations.[17] The cultic model affirming a distinctive identity of the priest as a man set apart and seeing the focus of priesthood as administering the sacraments is attractive to more men today. It is closer to the teachings of Pope John Paul II and always received his support.

The argument against the cultic model comes partly from laity and lay ministers, who assert that tomorrow's parishes must be led by collaborations of priests and lay ministers. Since priests holding the cultic model are less open to lay ministers, this will lead to tensions and conflicts. According to a survey of professional lay ministers in 2002, older lay ministers, in fact, felt that cultic model priests were more difficult to work with and undervalued lay ministry.[18] The lay minister who is older typically prefers to work with priests of the servant leader model. In addition, a more complex picture was discovered in the 2002 research, in that younger lay ministers, contrasted with older ones, are more in accord with cultic model priests. An age difference exists. If tensions emerge between lay ministers and priests, they will be between older lay ministers and younger cultic model priests.

Another criticism of the cultic model states that it fosters stronger clericalism in a Church that has already given priests and bishops too much power, privilege, and secrecy. This argument contains both theological and organizational assumptions, some of which are not researchable by social science. It is unclear how many lay people feel this way, but there are hints. A 2003 survey, for instance, found that 77 percent of lay Catholics agreed that "the Catholic Church needs better financial reporting at all levels." In the same survey, 73 percent agreed that "lay people should have some say in who their parish priest will be."[19] American Catholics are ready for the laity to have more input on church governance. Judging from the research on trends, the cultic model of the priesthood will be gaining in power and influence.

New Ordinands

Who are the men being ordained today? Each year since 1998, the United States Conference of Catholic Bishops has made a survey of the newly ordained priests. In 2005, the average age at ordination was 37.3 years; in 1998, only 35.[20] Eighty-eight percent were diocesan, and 12 percent were religious. In 2005, 27 percent were born outside the United States, with the most frequent countries of birth being Vietnam, Mexico, and the Philippines. When the survey asked about race, 10 percent said they were Hispanic, and 12 percent said they were Asian or Pacific. The level of education of priests prior to their seminary education has been climbing. In the 2005 ordination class, 32 percent had completed a graduate or professional degree beyond the baccalaureate prior to entering the seminary. The figure gained markedly from 13 percent in 1998. The trend in recent years has been in the direction of older and more highly educated men entering the priesthood.

Priestly Life Today

Catholic literature has contained repeated laments about low priestly morale.[21] And yet research has not supported the claim that morale is low. Researchers have compared priests with other American men of comparable age and education (borrowing from other studies) and have concluded that the level of happiness and morale was roughly the same for priests and the other men.[22]

Morale has gradually improved. Trend studies in the United States have found that it improved, on average, among priests from 1970 to 2001.[23] For example, on surveys asking the priests if they are thinking of staying or leaving, the percentage saying "I will definitely not leave" rose from 59 to 79 over the thirty-one years. The percentage saying that, if they had the choice again, they would still enter the priesthood rose from 78 to 88. It is possible that a partial explanation for these increases is that 1970 was a time of unusually low morale, which is evidenced by the surge of priestly resignations between 1967 and 1973. Also, a large number of priests, who were probably the unhappy ones, resigned after 1970, thereby raising subsequent average scores for the remaining priests. In any event, the explanation is unclear.

The level of happiness in surveys done in 2001 and 2002 was fairly high. In 2001, 88 percent said that they would choose the priesthood again, and only 5 percent reported that they were thinking of leaving the priesthood. In a *Los Angeles Times* survey in 2002, 90 percent said that they would choose the priesthood again.[24] There was not a morale crisis in the priesthood at that time. It is probable that the sexual abuse crisis from 2002 to 2005 depressed priestly morale; to judge from reports that I have read, nobody knows how much.

Satisfactions and Problems Felt by Priests

The 2001 survey of priests asked them what their main sources of satisfaction were. The top three sources were "joy of administering the sacraments and presiding over the liturgy," "the satisfaction of preaching the word," and "opportunity to work with many people and be a part of their lives." Their satisfaction comes apparently from those public roles, especially the sacramental roles, in which the priest functions in a way specific to priests. A second important satisfaction is personal service to the laity. Religious priests were slightly different, in that their satisfaction was derived less from administering the sacraments and presiding at the liturgy and more from working for charity or engaging in social reform.[25]

What are the main problems priests feel today? In 2001 the top three were "the way authority is exercised in the Church," "too much work," and "unrealistic demands and expectations of lay people." Older priests were bothered more than younger priests by "the way authority is exercised in the Church," while younger priests were more bothered by "too much work" and "unrealistic demands and expectations of lay people." Are many priests thinking of resigning? No. It was estimated in 2002 that between 10 and 12 percent resign within the first five years; how many resign in subsequent years is unknown.[26] The number who would like to be married is also not high. In 2001, it was 12 percent, down from 18 percent in 1970.

Heterosexuality and Homosexuality

The percentage of American priests who have a homosexual orientation is unknown, but the most reliable observers estimate that it is between 25 and 50 percent. The number of active homosexuals is certainly much lower. A widely read book by Donald Cozzens said that homosexual orientation is not a major issue for the priesthood, yet it has one dangerous aspect: the growth of *homosexual subcultures* in seminaries and dioceses. Subcultures may be harmless groupings of priests who prefer to meet together or go on outings together, but they may turn into divisive factions that engage in verbal scuffles with other priests.[27] This situation, which occurs in some seminaries, is spiritually and psychologically dangerous.

The 2001 survey of priests asked them if there is a homosexual subculture in their diocese or religious community. Nineteen percent said, "yes, clearly"; and 36 percent said, "probably." The survey also asked about the seminary the priest had attended. Fifteen percent said that "yes, clearly," there was a homosexual subculture in the seminary, while another 26 percent said, "probably." Young priests reported a much higher number of homosexual cultures in their seminaries than did older priests, and the researchers were unsure if this was because fewer homosexual subcultures existed in the past or because they were more hidden then. Given all of the available information, I would guess that the homosexual subcultures have grown in number. Today, seminary faculties agree that they should be controlled.[28] By contrast, in their view, whether individual seminarians have a homosexual orientation or not is less crucial, so long as they are chaste and responsible.

Summary

In this paper I have described changes in the priesthood since the 1960s and 1970s. The ancient institution of the priesthood is under pressure today, and some adjustments would possibly serve the Church well. Older institutions and rules in the varied religious traditions need to be reevaluated from time to time to see if they are still performing well. We can anticipate a period of debate over what should be done. Parties of opinion will slowly form, divided on whether the priesthood should be defined mainly in terms of ontological status or in terms of how it contributes functionally to the Church's overall mission. Parties will also form over how to restructure or not to restructure parish life in a time of fewer available priests. We can anticipate tensions. Theological and sociological research will be needed, plus abundant goodwill, to help us through the years ahead.

Chapter 12

Is the "Burnout" Real?

JAMES BURNS

Introduction

WHEN I WAS INITIALLY APPROACHED by the coordinators of the Priesthood in the 21st Century conference at Boston College, I was intrigued by the question: "Can you say something about parish priests and burnout?" My instinctive reply was: "Is this to be autobiographical or something more general?" Having for three years been the pastor of two city parishes, in which the people from each parish had a formal if not cool relationship with each other, as well as having counseled and consoled many pastors as a psychologist, I have been left with any number of anecdotes relative to causes and contexts for priestly burnout. However, I decided that perhaps a more instructive and a more useful approach, i.e., if the response of those attending the conference is indicative of a more general interest in this topic, would be to address the theories and underlying constructs related to burnout in general and then specifically how these apply to clergy. By doing so it will be demonstrated that certain themes emerge relative to the challenges clerics face in ministry which can then be formulated in terms of intervention strategies. Anecdotal information will only serve to underscore the reality of priestly challenges.

As a concept "burnout" is of relatively recent origin, beginning roughly in the mid-1970s. Freudenberger in his book *Burnout: The High Cost of High Achievement* first coined the term as "the extinction of motivation or incentive, especially where one's devotion to a cause or relationship fails to produce the desired results."[1] He described more or less the conditions under which burnout occurs.

These conditions included a work environment in which the individual is highly or intensely involved in his work, receives poor remuneration and little recognition, undergoes chronic distress accompanied by a sense of reduced effectiveness, and experiences decreased motivation. The result of this environment is to lead the individual to a series of dysfunctional attitudes and behaviors at work. In many ways, this creates a vicious cycle depleting the person of internal resources.

The construct of burnout received a quantifiable rationale and empirical verification through the work of Maslach, which categorized burnout in terms of job-related stress, in particular, for individuals who work with people in the human services professions.[2] Both Maslach and Freudenberger highlight the relationship of burnout to levels of stress and distress. In fact, one of the more popular psychological models for understanding stress was identified and validated in the mid-1980s. Lazarus proposed that psychological stress was related to a combination of situation-appraisal-outcome variables, i.e., the situation was difficult or perceived as such, the interpretation of the situation led to greater difficulty or a sense of discomfort, and the end result created greater problems or led to greater distress.[3] The properties of these events involving the situation-appraisal-outcome dynamic were identified as having Ambiguity, Novelty, Uncertainty, and Temporality, or time constraints; as an acronym it reads fittingly A-N-U-T. When reflecting on parish ministry one can quickly identify how many of these elements occur on a daily basis.

For example, one priest related that in his new assignment only a few years after ordination he was asked to take responsibility for four parishes, one of which he was to close and two of which were to be merged. However, the people from the parishes were informed that no merger or closings were planned. In this example he experienced role ambiguity as ministerial demands changed from being an assistant to being a pastor, while simultaneously dealing with multiple assignments and responsibilities. This was further complicated when he was informed that the closing parish needed to be closed within ten months, that he was losing through a forced retirement the senior priest who was assisting him, that the vicar general was unable to give him an official authorization from the chancery to carry out the task, and that he was expected to have this process completed within two years. The dynamics related to increased stress were clearly present in that time constraints were unrealistic and in that changes were occurring more rapidly than anticipated. In addition to layers of bureaucratic demands, resources were insufficient, and the preparation necessary to carry out the roles was lacking. All of these factors created uncertainty about the priest's responsibilities and further complicated reporting issues.

In their 2000 study of burnout among clerics, Grosch and Olsen developed a two-pronged model to explain the relationship among the variables related to clergy who face burnout.[4] One prong of the model identifies a set of systemic or external factors related to clerics experiencing burnout, i.e., bureaucratic issues, poor administrative support, difficult work conditions, etc. The other prong implicates intrapersonal factors as important to understanding clerical burnout, i.e., rigidity, perfectionism, feeling constrained, along with certain personality features involving a weak or deficient sense of self, which could be related to a chronic need for attention, admiration, or esteem.

This two-pronged model provides the basis for self-schema themes related to the person of the cleric, i.e., both intra- and interpersonal features. For example, how does the cleric perceive demands placed upon him? These would include physical, psychological, emotional, and spiritual demands that he is likely to experience as he thinks about and relates to himself as well as to others. The systemic themes previously identified also relate to the way the cleric's self-schemas are influenced by and what influences him as a result of interactions with his environment, i.e., all the systems the cleric finds himself involved in both personally and professionally. For example, how does he relate to his own family of origin, as well as his parish families, the parish as a whole, the diocese, society, culture, and politics, etc.?

In order to provide a visual representation of these themes, I have expanded Bronfenbrenner's Ecological Model of Human Development and superimposed the understanding of the cleric, as described above, onto the revised model.[5] In this modified version, Bronfenbrenner's original Ecological Model, which consisted of four levels, is extended to include a temporal and supernatural dimension.[6] The systems that were originally identified consist of the microsystem, the mesosystem, the exosystem, and the macrosystem. Later research identified a fifth system, the chronosystem. The microsystem contains the most intimate levels of existence, including the immediate settings that shape a person's development. It includes an individual's daily activities within these intimate environments as well as the individual's biological, cognitive, and psychological makeup. The mesosystem consists of a complex network of interactive relationships between the individual and those people who are responsible to or for them, such as their parents, teachers, peers, and role models. The exosystem comprises all the external networks that influence the microsystem, such as school, community, mass media, and health agencies. Cultural values, philosophies, political systems, economic patterns, and social conditions encompass the original outermost layer of influence known as the macrosystem. Finally, the chronosystem highlights the changes that take place in the ecological environment over time, and the manner in which these changes continue to influence the person's development.

While the existing model has been shown to be an effective approach to understanding human development, since it surveys the majority of human experiences across multiple spectrums, it was found lacking in the theological grounding necessary for the life and purpose of the Catholic priesthood. Thus, an additional level was needed to incorporate a specifically Christian, more specifically Catholic, perspective. Without it, the model would fail to account for the way in which the Catholic faith is deeply imbued in all the levels of the Catholic individual's functioning. Further, it lacked an appreciation of a specifically Catholic philosophical approach to life. The term "kyros-system" was designated for this purpose. It is understood as the Christological system which encompasses the individual as a member of the Body of Christ. This attempts to appreciate the phenomenological, ontological, and real dimensions of the priest as he experiences his life as incorporation into Christ. In so doing, the system, now encompassed by the trans-historical kyros-system, provides a more comprehensive understanding of the Catholic person and in particular the experience of the Catholic priest.

Clearly, these interacting levels create not only demands but may also provide renewed resources for ministry. Therefore the goal is not so much to completely eliminate the demands or pressure, whether intra-psychic or external, but rather to help the priest to better manage or reduce the stress while simultaneously identifying and developing resources that can provide refreshment to one's ministry. For example, Welch, Medeiros, and Tate identify five key areas that clergy who are burning out are likely to experience as problematic, i.e., physical, intellectual, emotional, spiritual, and social.[7] They then offer potential avenues for remedying the symptoms in these areas. While this medicalized model offers important insight into clerical burnout, it focuses mostly on the micro- and mesosystems and thus offers a rather limited understanding of the causes and contexts as well as the remedies.

As an aid to understanding the issue more holistically especially given the current challenges clergy face in ministry, a few authors have focused on identifying and dealing with "Antagonists to Ministry."[8] Understanding what or who may be antagonizing the ministerial role of the priest, i.e., considering those individuals, groups, or things that contend with, oppose, or act against him, can also be a step toward identifying resources or "agonists" to ministry, i.e., those things that alleviate strain or assist in his ministerial functions. In order to gain a different perspective on this, the current author has divided the potential "antagonists" and "agonists" into domains.

Self

The experience of personal doubts and fears related not only to ministry, but also how these concerns relate to the priest as he understands himself and his humanity with attendant needs, wants, and desires is the focus of this category. This will necessarily involve his perspective on such things as sin and evil, what it means to be a "good priest," the physical, emotional, and psychological demands

Figure 1

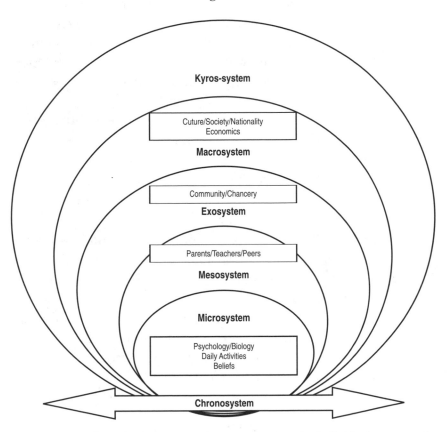

Kyros-system: Christological system that encompasses the individual as a member of the Body of Christ;

Macrosystem: influences of all other systems, including cultural values, philosophy, political systems, economic patterns, social conditions;

Exosystem: external networks that influence the individual, such as school, community, parish, chancery;

Mesosystem: interrelationship between a person and those people with responsible roles in his/her world, such as parents, teachers, peers, role models;

Microsystem: biological, psychological, and cognitive makeup, plus daily activities within immediate settings, such as family or household;

Chronosystem: changes to the ecological environment that continue over time and influence a person's development.

of the self and ministry, an understanding of his realistic limitations, and the need for intimacy and relationships. For example, Fr. Jones entered the seminary with a deep desire to be of service to the people of God and win souls for Christ. He had high ideals and enthusiasm. During seminary he learned of the many different aspects to theological studies, i.e., moral, spiritual, liturgical, etc. However, as he progressed through seminary he had to come to terms with his own understanding of himself as a servant and a leader with his own faults and failings as well as gifts and talents. He became preoccupied with what it meant to be a good priest, which only intensified as he began his early years of ministry. Questions of worthiness and humility frequently entered his mind as he met more and more of the people of God who seemed to have a more mature grasp of their faith and morals. He countered by becoming more intensely rigid in his approach to ministry and by working long hours, extending himself to everyone, but not taking care of himself. Finally in exhaustion he asked his spiritual director if this was what the spiritual writers meant by "burning oneself out in the Lord." To which his director sagely responded that he thought it sounded more like burning up before the Lord and suggested that this young priest develop a more prudent and balanced approach to his ministry.

Laity

The experience of the people of God, of which the priest is a member who has been called to a distinctive role with specific authority and charisms, may result in a dynamic of its own. As a result of interactions with members of the community, there often emerge those who, though small in number, are insidious in their ability to gather others around central themes that surface in parish life, e.g., quibbles about finances; disagreement over school board issues; complaints about staff members; sacred music, or liturgy; and the often long-standing intergroup conflicts between various parish organizations. The common effect, however, is to place the cleric in the center and turn up the heat. For example, the Young family and the Smith family were not at all happy with their new pastor, Fr. Green. They complained he did not do enough for the youth, that he was not involved in the school, and that he was ruining the parish finances. When Father tried to become more involved in the school and youth group, they countered that he had better watch it as there were concerns about the amount of time he was spending with young people. When he attempted to develop a committee to look into the finances and fundraising, a committee to which they were not invited to be members, they claimed he was stacking the committee with "yes" people and reported him to the chancery, while demanding another audit. They harassed the priest to the point that he asked the bishop for a transfer after only two years.

Staff

The concept of the parish staff as an entity to be reckoned with may seem of rather recent origin. However, housekeepers, cooks, maintenance workers, and even members of the pastor's family, who were once the mainstay of Catholic rectory living, have in today's parish been replaced by persons with the titles of music minister, liturgical director, business administrator, and the like. While these people are not necessarily spending a great deal of time in the parish house itself as in past eras, they nevertheless consume a great deal of the priest's time and energy, since they have almost daily contact with him. The dynamic created by these professional staff members can be a great asset when things are running smoothly. When problems arise, however, these members can also create greater demands and strain. Thus, conflicts may frequently revolve around those who would attempt to usurp certain pastoral prerogatives, those who have concern over who has power and decision making responsibility, those difficult staff members who thrive on conflict and dissension, those difficult personality types or disorders, those pastors and other staff who attempt to play favorites or draw attention to a favored status, and those well-intentioned and sincere, but overly intrusive, employees who leave the priest with little personal space for himself or others. The priest has to confront the struggles of dealing with incompetent staff members, along with the stress and strain brought about from hiring or firing personnel, whether this brings relief or not. For example, Fr. Murphy was well known in the diocese for his gifts and talents in sacred music, art, and liturgy. He had his S.T.L. in Sacred Liturgy from a prestigious Roman university. He had also been recently assigned to a new parish known for strong staff personalities. However, no staff member was as powerful a figure as Pat, the director of music. Though Pat lacked formal training in music and liturgy, he styled himself as an expert in liturgy. Fr. Murphy, at a social event held in the parish, commented to a benefactor of the parish that it would truly be a gift if they could establish a center for excellence in liturgy and music at St. Agatha's. The benefactor agreed and provided a generous initial gift to begin the enterprise. Later that week after consulting with Pat, Fr. Murphy realized that should this go forward Pat would attempt to fight him every step of the way. His concerns were warranted as Pat's dissatisfaction materialized. With every initiative related to liturgy that Fr. Murphy engaged in he found Pat was there to undermine his efforts. Nine months later Fr. Murphy was forced to dismiss Pat. However, Pat did not let the issue rest there. Whenever the chance arose Pat would attempt to divide the staff with rumors, innuendo, and outright lies. Fr. Murphy stayed on but only after being treated for chronic stress headaches, depression, and ulcers.

Fellow Priests

Priests and bishops are fond of speaking of the fraternity of the priesthood, *Fratres in Christo,* "Brothers in Christ." In fact the *Catechism of the Catholic Church* states, "All priests, who are constituted in the order of priesthood by the sacrament of order, are bound together by an intimate sacramental brotherhood."[9] While this is a wonderful image and ideal to foster, often the relationships of priests with one another in a given diocese or order are less than Christlike. This can lead to uncertainty and confusion among the younger clergy and cynicism with suspicion among the senior clerics. Where charity and love were intended to prevail, they are replaced by envy and jealousy. Younger clerics become alarmed at the apparent preferential treatment of some young priests over others. Older priests who have become less confident with regard to the ability of diocesan leadership and who worry about the ability of their fellow priests to be understanding and compassionate learn to fear intimacy as a trap that will lead them to penalty whether personal or ecclesial in nature. Those who do not conform to the current paradigm that is dominant in the diocese or religious order face being ostracized and gossiped about. The once clear identity of the priest becomes confused and weakened for lack of fraternal support. The ideals of youth give way to acting more carefully and becoming more isolated. This is especially true with regard to concerns that a given priest might find himself as being seen on the "fringe." Support groups which can often provide a means of healthy coping and stress reduction by building trust and intimacy can also become a means of isolating into factions. They have been reported by some as being places of brutal criticism of the "others" who are not like "us." They can impose unyielding demands on the members. Finally, not a diocese or religious order today is removed from the effects experienced by groups of clerics who seem to oppose one another on theological, liturgical, or spiritual grounds. While this remains an area fraught with tension and delicate intricacies, priests' relationships to one another and to the bishops are also areas for potential resources. In fact, recent research points to the benefit of supportive social networks that act as buffers against the demands of work stress and are related to fewer mental health issues such as anxiety and depression. Further, having the perceived support of those in supervisory roles was an aid in decreasing the need for mental health resources, while the lack of such support often has the opposite effect.[10] For example, in the case of Fr. Black, the jealousy of fellow priests created such tension that the bishop was forced to remove him from the parish. He was regarded for years as unassignable. It all began when word circulated among the presbyterate that Fr. Black was being considered for a new post that would require further studies. Priests who had before been friendly or neutral became suspicious and angry. Those who did not care for Fr. Black became vicious. They sent private memos and e-mails to the bishop claiming all kinds of inappropriate behavior in an attempt to defame him and stop his "progress," as they viewed it. Fr. Black became embittered and disaffected.

Hierarchy

In the Decree Concerning the Pastoral Office of Bishops in the Church (*Christus Dominus*)[11] and in the *Catechism of the Catholic Church* emphasis is placed upon the manner in which priests are to share in the office of the bishop as coworkers and cooperators in the mission of the Church. For example Vatican II states: "The relationships between the bishop and the diocesan priests should rest most especially upon the bonds of supernatural charity so that the harmony of the will of the priests with that of their bishop will render their pastoral activity more fruitful. Wherefore, for the sake of greater service to souls, let the bishop call the priests into dialogue, especially about pastoral matters. This he should do not only on a given occasion but at regularly fixed intervals insofar as this is possible."[12] Moreover, the *Catechism of the Catholic Church* states, "The promise of obedience they make to the bishop at the moment of ordination and the kiss of peace from him at the end of the ordination liturgy mean that the bishop considers them his co-workers, his sons, his brothers and his friends."[13] This is also properly highlighted in the ordination ritual of priests in the Catholic Church. This emphasis is in distinction to a kind of feudalistic relationship that had been the hallmark of episcopal authority in the past. Often the difficulty in this area is the manner in which the bishop relates to his priests. For instance, in some dioceses the bishop could not be more remote from his priests. A priest finds it troublesome even to get an appointment with his bishop, which would make it difficult for the priest to realize the value of his ministry or receive authentic advice and counsel or offer the same in return. In some dioceses the bishop is perceived as too close and overinvolved, as if nothing is permitted without his acknowledgment or nod of the head. This often leads to a feeling of inadequacy among the clergy, who begin to believe that nothing they do is without notice. They perceive more and more the strain of having someone looking over their shoulders. Either style fails in creating that dynamic which allows for cooperation, collegiality, and mutual counsel. Often priests, when discussing their relationship to their bishop, relate the bishop's failures in empathic awareness and mutuality and in the inability of the bishop to relate in what psychology terms intersubjective understanding, i.e., that the one person, in this case the bishop, can for a moment truly place himself in the shoes of the other, in this case his brother and friend, the cleric. If the priest is to allow himself to be known and understood, then the bishop should foster an environment in which to know and understand that priest. This stance highlights one of the great obstacles in priest-bishop relationships, and that is dialogue. This is the very dialogue commended and recommended by the Vatican Council and in other subsequent documents. Breakdowns and failures in communication remain one of the key features of priestly strain and burnout in relation to the episcopacy. For example, Bishop Fritz was known as a reasonable man in general except when it came to the assignments of priests. He was of the mind that when the bishop has spoken the case is closed. He was unable to take the perspective that dialogue was as much a part of episcopal ministry as was any other exercise of his authority. Any number of the priests in the diocese had become disenfranchised with his lack of dialogue and began exercising a kind of Lone Ranger ministry. Other priests sought out greener pastures in a neighboring diocese where that bishop relied on dialogue and understanding by attempting to help his priests to focus on the best way to utilize their unique gifts and talents. In fact this bishop was known to seek out those priests who were hurting or injured in some way. Unfortunately, this made matters more difficult for the priests who remained in Bishop Fritz's diocese, adding greater stress and strain to an already taxed presbyterate.

Conclusion

The categories and examples above identify key elements related to stress and burnout. The reader may find it helpful at this point to review the appendix to this essay, which incorporates a series of questions related to understanding potential areas of burden, while remembering that these can also have the potential to be sources of relief and ease. In fact, an exercise that may be of some benefit could be to return to Figure 1 (page 155) while focusing on the appendix and keeping in mind the domains above. This may help a cleric identify what influences his ministry. This exercise may also aid him in discovering themes that are a part of his world at any particular level in the ecological model. Next, divide the items you identify into resources/refreshment and burdens/pressures. Then rank the importance of the item from 1 (very little) to 10 (very much). This will help you determine how much you believe you are currently experiencing a given burden or resource. Once you have identified these resources and demands you can determine ways that you can actively redefine your emotional, spiritual, physical, and psychological health. For example, you may determine that you need to bolster your emotional and spiritual well-being. Thus, finding a good spiritual director and therapist may be an essential part of a healthier, more holistic manner of functioning for you.

It is important to note that there is hope in all of this. In fact, this exercise should provide opportunities and avenues by which to receive the important aids and blessings to your ministry. Identifying themes and addressing areas where greater emphasis needs to be placed while reducing the pressure from other zones can be the start of a healthy, more fruitful path to an integrated and resilient ministry. Ultimately, only you can make the decision to move forward in creating a healthy, holistic, and sacred experience of priesthood. However, you need not face this alone. There are many individuals and support systems that are available to help and that seek to promote ministerial health and resourcefulness. You may need to reach out to a trusted friend or confidant in a prayerful request, but be assured by Christ's own words: "Come to me, all who labor and are heavy laden, and I will give you rest. Take my yoke upon you, and learn from me, for I am gentle and lowly in heart, and you will find rest for your souls. For, my yoke is easy, and my burden is light" (Matt. 11:28–30).[14]

Appendix

- Do you find that you spend a good deal of time responding to the complaints of a small but vocal minority of parishioners or staff?

- Are those with little understanding of the situation or project continually undermining your efforts?

- Do you find yourself being blamed for nearly all (or most) of the difficulty in the parish or the ministry in which you are engaged?

- Do you usually, or often, receive positive evaluations from others but never from a certain person or group?

- Do you experience an inability to respond to critics because their claims are baseless or false or because by responding to them you would be admitting responsibility for something you did not do?

- Is the usual substance of complaints of a personal nature (i.e., in some way against your person) and not based upon substantive issues? For example, the complaint cannot be categorized according to something that is measurable, accomplished, or concrete.

- Is a person or group difficult to deal with because they are often confrontational and attacking you, using "You" statements and finger pointing? Are they, or were they, often charming and appealing with others or with you in the past?

- Do others misappropriate Sacred Scripture to prove their point, especially when you attempt to take a stand for your good name or rights? For example, do they call you to love everyone, turn the other cheek, and accept their abuse as a sign of the cross?

- Do you experience intraoffice conflict with persons or groups demanding your support and alternately calling into question the attention you pay to other groups or ministries?

- Is the office plagued by gossip or constant whispers of dissatisfaction often aimed at those who have the greatest access to you or who have legitimate demands on your time?

- For those with more than one parish, does interparish conflict magnify the preceding question?

- Do other priests tell you directly, or indirectly through clerical gossip or through inciting antagonistic parishioners, that your ministry is in some way deficient, i.e., liturgically, spiritually, financially, structurally (time, effort, money allocated to the physical plant), or morally?

- Are you concerned about the lack of clerical fellowship due to time or travel, interests, or fear of intimacy (legitimate or not)?

- Do you find diocesan staff or the bishop or superior unable to relate meaningfully to you?

- Do you experience a lack of direction from those who are in a position to give it?

- Do you also experience a lack of validation related to your ministry or person?

- Do you feel pulled between the demands of being part of the presbyterate (brotherhood of priests), while competing demands are placed upon you that keep you from meaningful engagement with others?

- Do you experience "blocked" access to the bishop or superior or feel you have been "blackballed" by chancery staff or other potent priests?

- Are there demands related to obedience that you struggle with? For example, what is your expectation of your leaders and theirs of you, especially in terms of appointments and duties?

- Do you struggle with any aspect of celibacy or sexuality? Is there a fear to admit this in the current climate?

- Do you struggle with the parish or school financial situation?

- Do you struggle with your personal financial situation? Do you feel undervalued and underpaid?

- Do you struggle with the number of registered families or school attendance?

- Are there certain Church teachings and their application that you struggle with?

- Do you experience strain related to your own reactions, parishioner reactions, or reactions of others related to the sexual abuse crisis?

- Do you struggle with issues related to the closing of parishes and the dissolution of their communities?

- Have you experienced strain related to positive developments, e.g., receiving a large donation or endowment, new staff, or growth?

- Are their other stresses or strains that you face?

Chapter 13

The Future of Catholic Ministry

Our Best Hopes

Thomas Groome

Rolling Sea Change in Progress

S INCE THE CLOSE of the Second Vatican Council, a rolling sea change has been in progress for Catholic ministry. This is all the more amazing, given that Vatican II favored an ontological divide between clergy and laity,[1] designating the former for the "sacred" ministries of the Church and assigning the laity to the "secular" work of building up God's reign in the world with occasional opportunities to participate in volunteer "apostolates."[2] Upon checking the index of Abbott's *Documents of Vatican II*, the term "ministry" is not listed, and under "ministers," previously considered a Protestant term, it says, "*see* Clergy; Priests; *etc.*"

Though the council fathers may not have intended as much, Vatican II was, in fact, the catalyst for an "explosion of ministry."[3] The repatterning in function, form, and style of ministry that now unfolds could well be called a *new* paradigm, if it were not so much in continuity with the practices of the first Christian communities. While statistics regarding the "priest shortage" are alarming,[4] there are many positive indices that a sea change in Catholic ministry rather than decline is already under way and rolling along.

There are now some thirty-five thousand lay people engaged in full-time ministries in the U.S. Catholic community, many fulfilling services heretofore reserved to the ordained. The Church refers to them as "lay ecclesial ministers," surely an anomalous term. Likewise there are some fifteen thousand "permanent" male deacons (most of them married); before the council the diaconate was simply the last stepping stone to priesthood.

The 1950s image of the urban U.S. Catholic parish with a rectory of half a dozen priests and a convent with at least a dozen nuns has been replaced by a parish staff of one priest and a host of full-time lay ministers. Formerly, parishioners were seen and saw themselves as passive recipients at a spiritual "service station" with little function beyond "pray, pay, and obey." Now besides living their faith as a vocation in the midst of the world, all are encouraged to contribute their time, talent, and treasure to the life and mission of their parish. In its "call to stewardship" handout, my home parish lists seventy-four different opportunities for parishioners to actively engage in its ministries.

Vatican II catalyzed such change not by its attention to holy orders, but by its reclaiming of baptism. In many ways this summarizes the agenda and outcome of Vatican II: to reclaim a radical theology of baptism, radical in that it is the root of who Christians are and how we should live as disciples of Jesus. So baptism calls all to holiness of life,[5] to exercise our rights and fulfill our responsibilities within "the common priesthood of the faithful," who participate with the ordained "in the one priesthood of Christ."[6]

The council elaborates: "The baptized, by regeneration and anointing of the Holy Spirit are consecrated into a spiritual house and a holy priesthood."[7] It goes on, "These faithful are by baptism made one body with Christ . . . sharers in the priestly, prophetic, and kingly functions of Christ . . . in the mission of the whole Christian people."[8] *Lumen Gentium* sounds an egalitarian note that all the baptized "share a common dignity from their rebirth in Christ, a true equality."[9] In this Body of Christ, no one is any more baptized than anyone else.

The council's Decree on the Laity echoed such sentiments: "The laity, too, share in the priestly, prophetic, and royal office of Christ and therefore have their own role to play in the mission of the whole People of God in the Church and in the world."[10] Such sentiments have been reiterated many times in official church documents since the council; for example, the *Catechism of the Catholic Church* (no. 1268) states, "By baptism, [the baptized] share in the priesthood of Christ, in his prophetic and royal mission. . . . Baptism gives a share in the common priesthood of all believers."

Taking seriously our baptismal bonding with Christ as "priest, prophet, and ruler," Vatican II amplified that baptism calls us to "full, conscious, and active participation" in the Church's worship,[11] to be a priestly community, to side with those "who are poor or in any way afflicted,"[12] to be a prophetic community, "to express [our] opinion on things which concern the good of the Church,"[13] and to be a co-responsible community. In sum, the entire baptized are held responsible for the very mission of the Church, namely, to carry on God's saving work in Jesus Christ. Begun in baptism, affirmed in confirmation, and constantly nurtured through the Eucharist, initiation into the Body of Christ designates all Christians for ministry within and through the Christian community as the sacrament of God's reign in the world.

Reclaiming baptism with such expansive rhetoric made inevitable a "breaking open" of formal ministry, beyond ordained priesthood, out into the whole Catholic people of God. We now recognize that baptism commissions us to participate intentionally in every aspect of Jesus' mission either explicitly within the Christian community or through it into the world. Regardless of what our particular vocation in life might be, the Holy Spirit calls and gifts in varied ways all baptized people to employ their God-given talents with the conscious commitment of Christian faith for the realization of God's reign in Jesus.

Conjoined with the reclaiming of baptism Vatican II championed a communal model of Church. The oft told story of how the chapters in the council's Constitution on the Church were juggled from the original draft that began by focusing first on the hierarchy to the final draft that begins with the Church as mystery and moves on to the Church as "The People of God" reflects the fundamental shift that took place. No longer is the Church "them" and "us." Rather, "we," all who make up the Body of Christ, are the Church; our community is called to approximate the "communion" of the Blessed Trinity.

Now real members of a community participate in its life, are responsible for its common good, have access to its resources, and contribute to its purpose. Based on a radical theology of baptism, this emphasis on the Church as communion, rather than on its institutional, hierarchical, and juridical aspects, called for a massive empowerment of its people. Every member should be an active participant in its mission and ministries, according to charism, calling, and context.

And indeed this is happening. Ordinary Christians are reclaiming their baptismal vocation to "put faith to work" in their daily life and social context, seeing all work when done with the consciousness of Christian faith as contributing to God's reign. More lay people are engaging part-time in varied ministries through their parishes and other Christian agencies, and many are embracing full-time vocations to ecclesial ministries, without ordination or taking on the vowed life. Beyond the clerical pyramid, we now find "concentric circles of ministry, moving from the leaders to all full-time and professionally trained ministers out through levels of part-time ministers to all of the baptized."[14] The future of Catholic ministry has already begun, though this varies from one culture to another. What are our best hopes, the horizon that calls for our commitment now, taking one step at a time?

Christians must always be ready to "give a reason for our hope" (1 Pet. 3:15). Besides the good signs of our times, my greatest hope comes from remembering the ministry of Jesus and of the first Christian communities. This is not to fall into a biblicism, as if how "they" did it then is how we must do ministry now; we cannot go back nor would we find any blueprint to follow. Jesus himself cautioned that "scribes learned in the reign of God" should be like the head of a household who can bring from the treasury "both the new and the old" (Matt. 13:52). So we go back, not to repeat the past, but to be sure to bring with us the "old" that will always be wise and to imagine from this memory the "new" possibilities for our time. Whatever we do as ministry in any age must be congruent for a community of disciples apprenticed to Jesus, albeit inculturated to each time and place.

Kenan Osborne writes, "Jesus' own ministry remains the abiding source, model and dynamism of all Christian ministry."[15] Thereafter and down through history, Christian ministry continues Jesus' mission through the power of God's Holy Spirit, enacted within and through Christian community "for the life of the world" (John 6:51). Jesus' *sense of mission and then what he did as ministry and how he did it* must always be the archetype for our own efforts. I turn, then, to the ministry of Jesus, and with a hermeneutic of what we may hope for and so, by God's grace, work for as our best aspirations for Catholic ministry.

The Mission of Jesus

There seems to be consensus among scholars of the Christian Scriptures that Jesus expressed his sense of mission through the symbol of God's reign. Insofar as we can detect his conscious intent, i.e., something that likely "grew" as his public ministry unfolded, he saw himself as a catalyst for the reign of God. The first time Jesus appeared in public, and Mark's account is likely the most historical, he declared, "This is the time of fulfillment. The kingdom of God is at hand. Repent, and believe in the gospel" (Mark 1:15). Thereafter, Jesus carried on his public ministry, died, and rose again as the Christ of faith in order to bring about God's reign.

Jesus understood this symbol in continuity with his Hebrew tradition and in the context of his time. So it represented for him God's saving activity in the midst of human history, saving *from sin* and its consequences and *for shalom,* for "life abundantly" (John 10:10). This symbol summarized God's desire and will on behalf of which God is ever active, namely, that all people come to live in peace and justice, with love and freedom, wholeness and fullness of life, and the well-being of all creation. It would also symbolize the responsibilities that the divine/human covenant places upon all people to do God's will now, to live in right and loving relationship with God, self, others, and creation, after the model of how God relates with humankind.

Though Jesus lived for the reign of God in continuity with these core convictions of his Jewish faith, he also gave the symbol his own distinctive emphases. He radicalized its law of love to include even enemies; correspondingly, he highlighted the availability of God's mercy for sinners. Likewise, he made clear that all are welcome into God's kingdom, regardless of race or status, with special outreach to the poor, oppressed, and marginalized. His only criterion for membership was commitment to do what God wills, fullness of life for all.

For Jesus, too, the reign of God was a "tensive symbol,"[16] with multiple "both/and" meanings. So in Jesus' preaching and praxis, the reign of God is already and not yet, for here and for hereafter, both personal and communal, both spiritual and social, to shape people's politics as well as their prayers. It is a symbol of hope and command, of promise and responsibility. God's reign is realized only by the power of God's grace, and yet it makes its covenant partners, potentially all humankind, responsible for living according to the *shalom* that God wills for all people. Even as we pray "thy kingdom come," the abiding mission of Jesus' disciples is to do God's will on earth as it is done in heaven.

The Church can never again lose sight of Jesus' purpose as its own;[17] empowered by the Holy Spirit, its mission is "the kingdom of Christ and of God" (Eph. 5:5). As Vatican II summarized, "the Church has a single intention: that God's kingdom may come, and that the salvation of the whole human race may come to pass."[18] That same paragraph of *Gaudium et Spes,* echoing *Lumen Gentium,* went on to describe the Church as "the universal sacrament of salvation." Thus, the Church's mission is to be an effective sign, causing to happen what it signifies (Aquinas's notion of sacrament[19]) as God's reign, demanding appropriate ministries on its behalf in every time and place.

The Ministries of Jesus on Behalf of His Mission

In Jesus' public life, what are the specific ministries that he did on behalf of God's reign? Contemporary work on the historical Jesus highlights various aspects: his role as wisdom teacher, his compassion toward the poor and for all human suffering, his healing ministry, both physical and spiritual, his commitment to peace and justice for all, his gathering of an inclusive community of disciples, epitomized in his table fellowship, his mercy and outreach toward sinners, his life of prayer and worship, the integrity of his commitment to God's reign, and more. Instead of attempting an exhaustive list, I will turn to one text that I find particularly suggestive, the incident in the synagogue at Nazareth on a Sabbath (Luke 4:18–21). I do so because it was his own summary, at least according to Luke, of the ministries that he took upon himself. It also anticipates the schema of ministries that the first Christians embraced as his community of disciples.

Seeing this text in its context within Luke highlights something that we must always emphasize, namely, that Jesus carried on his ministries "by the power of the Holy Spirit." Thomas O'Meara rightly insists that all Christian ministry must be done by the call and power of the Holy Spirit, as was true of the historical praxis of Jesus.[20] Luke recounts that John the Baptist baptized Jesus at the Jordan, at which time "the heavens were opened, and the *Holy Spirit* descended upon Jesus in bodily form, as a dove. And a voice from heaven said, 'This is my beloved Son in whom I am well pleased' " (Luke 3:22). Then, "*Filled with the Holy Spirit,* Jesus returned from the Jordan, and was *led by the Spirit* into the desert for forty days" (Luke 4:1–2). There follows the account of Jesus fasting in the desert and the devil tempting him to pride, power, and presumption. But Jesus resisted, in each case reiterating his allegiance to God alone. Then, "Jesus returned to Galilee *in the power of the Spirit*" (Luke 4:14).

The dramatic scene in Nazareth on a Sabbath day now follows. Jesus went "as was his custom" to the synagogue for worship. His local faith community invited Jesus to read. He took the scroll of Isaiah the prophet, searched out one of its great Messianic texts (Isa. 61:1–2), and read: "The Spirit of the Lord is upon me, and has anointed me to bring good news to the poor, to proclaim liberty to captives, recovery of sight to the blind, to set free the oppressed, and to proclaim God's year of favor." Then, after a pause, Jesus made the dramatic announcement, "Today this scripture has been fulfilled in your hearing" (Isa. 4:18–21).

"Good news to the poor." "Liberty to captives." "Sight to the blind." "To set free the oppressed." This program of ministries issued in "God's year of favor." Scholars agree that this verse refers to the jubilee year as described in Leviticus 25 and 27. The Jubilee was a radical social proposal to recognize that everything belongs to God and to give it back.

From this summary in Luke, we can detect four basic functions to Jesus' ministry: to *preach/teach* the liberating and prophetic word of God; to *care for human suffering* with love and justice; to *call people into a community* of free and right relationship with God, self, others, and creation; and, to encourage people to recognize that everything belongs to God and to so *worship*. To continue the work of Jesus, the Church must always carry on such ministries; it can do so by the power of the Holy Spirit.

Jesus' Style of Ministry

It belabors the point a bit to distinguish between *what* Jesus did as ministry and *how* he did it; his content and process reflected each other. Yet it can stimulate our best hopes for ministry to remember *how* he went about it. Not pretending to be either unbiased or exhaustive, I note four distinctive features that mark Jesus' approach to ministry: first, he built up an inclusive *community* while encouraging it to outreach to all in need; second, beyond service, his style *empowered* people to be agents of their own faith; third, he favored *partnership* with disciples and of them with each other; and fourth, his style promoted *integrity* between life and faith, inviting people to integrate the two into "lived faith."

To Build Up an Inclusive and Outreaching Community

Throughout his public ministry, Jesus' approach was to build up an inclusive community of disciples, with special welcome for the marginalized and sinners, for the poor and oppressed; his approach was truly "catholic." So inclusive was his table fellowship that it scandalized traditional piety and was the first criticism made against him; "Some scribes asked, 'Why does he eat with tax collectors and sinners?' " (Mark 2:16). But his community was neither to be an end in itself nor to serve only its own. Jesus' ministry was an outreach to every human hurt and hurting human. His approach was to care for all: Jew and Samaritan, Roman and Greek, men and women, rich and poor, children and adults, officials and common peasants. This, too, should be the modus operandi of his community today.

To Serve and Empower People

So much of Jesus' public ministry was service to people in need, whatever it might be. Yet he often reached beyond service to empower people, especially those to whom life was being denied. His praxis repudiated the cultural mores that discriminated against people on any basis, treating all with dignity and respect. Even in his miracles of healing, he expected the sick to participate by their faith — to be agents in their own healing rather than dependents on his power. On the one hand we read, "Courage, my daughter, your faith has restored you to health" (Matt. 9:22). On the other, "He did not work many miracles there because of their lack of faith" (Matt. 13:58). Imagine a crowd of poor peasants hearing, "You are the salt of the earth... you are the light of the world" (Matt. 5:13–14); being told to address God as "father" (Matt. 6:9); being assured "not to worry" (Matt. 6:31). The Sermon on the Mount was directed not to the elite but to "the crowds" (Matt. 7:28); how empowered its first hearers must have felt.

To Work in Partnership

From the beginning of his public ministry, Jesus called disciples to be partners with him; "come after me and I will make you fishers of [people]" (Mark 1:17). Once he commissioned as many as seventy disciples and sent them out "in pairs," i.e., in partnership, to prepare the way for his own preaching (Luke 10:1). And they were to pray for more laborers to work with them because "the harvest is abundant." The more partners in this mission, the better. Likewise, Jesus encouraged disciples to avoid both dependency and paternalism; they were to "call no one father" (Matt. 23:9), nor were they to "lord it over" anyone (Mark 10:42). The middle ground between those two is partnership. At the great commission on a hillside in Galilee, the risen Christ addressed "the eleven" as one and gave all the same mandate. They were to work together to evangelize all nations, to baptize and welcome others into his community in the name of the Triune God, the ultimate model of partnership.

To Integrate Life and Faith

I detect a distinctive pedagogy throughout Jesus' public ministry; he encouraged people to bring their lives to faith and their faith to life. So often, and especially by parables, Jesus turned people to look at "the ordinary" of their own lives, things as commonplace as fishermen sorting fish, farmers sowing seed, a woman looking for a lost coin. But he invited people to look at the ordinary of their lives in a whole new way, often turning their perspective upside down. Who would have expected the Samaritan to be neighbor, the father to forgive the prodigal, or the prostitutes and tax collectors to enter God's reign before scribes and elders?

Then Jesus wanted people to reflect on life in the light of their faith, which he taught "with authority" (Mark 1:22). In his preaching and praxis, Jesus affirmed and cherished the tradition of his people, obeyed its precepts, quoted its Scriptures, and said that he had come not to abolish the Law and the Prophets but "to make their teachings come true" (Matt. 5:17). And yet he also felt free to reinterpret the tradition, to point to inadequacies in people's understanding and living of the spirit of the Law. His intent was always to invite greater faithfulness to living in covenant with God and each other. To be a disciple was to follow "the way" that he modeled, to live the life. Indeed it is only by living his teaching that we become disciples and come to know the truth that sets free (John 8:32). It is not the one who proclaims, "Lord, Lord," who enters the reign of God, but the one who does God's will (Matt. 7:21).

While this "life to faith to life" pedagogy is evident throughout Jesus' public ministry, it is epitomized by the Risen Christ on the Road to Emmaus (Luke 24:13–35). The "stranger" meets two despondent disciples, "walks along with them," and asks about what is going on in their lives. Having heard their story, Christ invites them to bring what "happened in Jerusalem these past few days" into dialogue with their faith tradition. "Beginning then with Moses and all the prophets, he interpreted for them every passage of scripture which referred to himself." Instead of telling them what to see, Christ waits for them to come to see for themselves. Now they are ready to take their rekindled faith back to life again, to return to Jerusalem with renewed commitment.

Ministry among the First Christian Communities

Pentecost launched the young Christian community and its mission upon the world. There were "about one hundred and twenty persons" present in that upper room, including "some women and Mary the mother of Jesus" (Acts 1:14–15). Then, with the sound of a "strong driving wind . . . tongues as of fire . . . came to rest on each one of them. And they were all filled by the Holy Spirit" (Acts 2:2–4).

They came forth with a rock-solid conviction that God had raised Jesus from the dead, that he was the Christ, and that they were empowered by the Spirit to continue his saving mission to the world. That very first day, Peter gave a mighty sermon declaring that "God raised this Jesus" (Acts 2:32), making him "both Lord and Messiah" (Acts 2:36). Peter called people to baptism and "about three thousand persons were added that day" (Acts 2:41). Then Acts immediately describes what these first Christians did as ministry: "they devoted themselves to the teaching of the apostles and to the communal life, to the breaking of the bread and to the prayers. . . . They would sell their property and possessions and divide them among all according to each one's need" (Acts 2:42, 44).

Note the original emphasis on "the teaching," on "the communal life," on "breaking the bread," and on caring for human needs; this is how Jesus highlighted his ministries from the messianic promise of Isaiah 61:1–2. From these seeds, the first Christians discerned their central and shared ministries to be carried on by the whole community. The Greek terms are *koinonia* (building up community), *marturia* (witnessing to faith), *kerygma* (preaching the scriptures), *didache* (teaching the faith), *leitourgia* (worshiping God), and *diakonia* (serving human needs). Rather than separate functions, however, they saw these ministries as intertwined and overlapping, all with the common purpose of continuing the mission of Jesus.[21]

By combining some, I summarize them into a fourfold schema: to be a community of witness, word, worship, and welfare. So to serve their mission for God's reign in Jesus Christ, the first Christian communities came to recognize their corporate work as follows:

♦ to be a bonded Christian community (*koinonia*) that bears credible witness (*marturia*) to its faith in Christ, lives by "the way" of Jesus, and works to bring about God's reign in the world;

♦ to preach, teach, and evangelize the word of God (*kerygma/ didache*) as mediated through Jesus, God's word made flesh (John 1:14), through the writings of the New Testament, through the Hebrew Scriptures, and through Christian tradition thereafter;

♦ to assemble as a community of faith for the public work (*leitourgeo*) to worship God and celebrate the sacraments together; and

♦ to render the service (*diakonia*) of caring for people in need of any kind, spiritual, physical, and psychological, promoting human welfare as integral to God's work of salvation.

Of course, the first Christian communities are precisely where Vatican II found its radical theology of baptism, outlined earlier. They were convinced that all baptized Christians are responsible to carry on the mission of Jesus and must work together to fulfill the central ministries of the community. By Paul's rich imagery, they must function now like the Body of Christ in the world, enlivened by the Holy Spirit, with every part playing its role and serving the whole mission. Though the Spirit gives "different kinds of spiritual gifts," none should trump or stifle the others; all are given "for some benefit" to the life and mission of the community (1 Cor. 12:4–7).

In fact, Paul proposed a deep equality within this Body of Christ: "For in one Spirit we were all baptized into one body, whether Jew or Greek, slave or free person, and we were all given to drink of one

Spirit" (1 Cor. 12:13). The varied gifts of the Spirit are all "for building up the body of Christ" and call their recipients to responsibility
that they "may no longer be infants" in their faith (Eph. 4:12, 14).

Thus, the first Christians were convinced that all the baptized are
responsible, according to charism and context, for the general ministries of the Church, both within the community and into the world.
And long after those first communities, into the third century, the
Church made no distinction between laity and clergy; in fact, *laikos*
is never used and all Christians were referred to as *kleros*, regarded
as "holy and chosen."[22]

Beyond the ministry of all the baptized, it is also clear that the early
communities designated particular people for more specific functions
of ministry. The ministries of witness, word, worship, and welfare
required more precise tasks and talents. So someone was needed to
care for the common purse within the community, or to go evangelize
in the neighboring villages, or to lead the community at worship, or
to care for those in particular need. Then the community also noticed
that certain members had the requisite charism to fulfill these more
specific ministerial functions. So the community commissioned them
by the power of the Holy Spirit to do so in its name.

These designated functions of formal ministry varied from one
community to another. Scholars often contrast the functions that
grew up in the Palestinian Church with those that emerged in Pauline
communities, or compare Jewish with Hellenistic Christian communities. Reviewing the variety of designated ministerial functions among
different communities, Scripture scholars count up to twelve; many,
however, may have overlapped or the same functions may have had
different names from place to place. Anyhow, they include: apostle,
prophet, evangelist, teacher, pastor, miracle worker, healer, helper,
administrator, deacon, elder, and overseer (Eph. 4:11–13; 1 Cor.
12:4–11, 12:28–31; Rom. 12:4–8, 16:3–5; 1 Tim. 3:8–13; Acts
20:28).

Some communities bring teacher, prophet, and apostle to the fore
whereas others seem to favor bishop, presbyter, and deacon. But there
is no hierarchical ordering of the ministries according to power.[23]
The configuration seems more like a pie than a pyramid, with all

working together in "holy order." It would appear[24] that the ministry of *word* was served primarily by the apostles (a wider category than the original Twelve), prophets, evangelists, and teachers. The ministry of building up a community of Christian *witness* was served by the pastor, administrator, elder, and overseer. The ministry of service to human was *welfare* served by deacon, healer, helper, and miracle worker. What then of *worship?*

From the very beginning, Christian communities celebrated two central liturgical acts, baptism and Eucharist (Acts 2:41–42). Regarding baptism, there has always been some openness about who presides; to this day, in situations of emergency, a lay person may baptize. What then of presiding at Eucharist?

That the first Christian communities celebrated Eucharist is beyond doubt, but who presided and how they were chosen is far from clear. A common thesis is that the function of presiding fell to the local community leader, not because of a sacral power but because of his or her function as community leader.[25] This was not invariable. For example, the *Didache,* a normative text in many communities, suggests that teachers and itinerant prophets presided at *leitourgeo,* as well as perhaps deacons and bishops.[26] Raymond Brown, the distinguished scholar, carefully summarizes:

> There is simply no compelling evidence for the classic thesis that the members of the Twelve always presided when they were present, and that there was a chain of ordination passing the power of presiding at the Eucharist from the Twelve to missionary apostles to presbyter-bishops. How one got the right to preside and whether it endured beyond a single instance we do not know; but a more plausible substitute for the chain theory is the thesis that sacramental "powers" were part of the mission of the Church and that there were diverse ways in which the Church (or the communities) designated individuals to exercise those powers.[27]

From the first Christian communities, five summary points are worth noting to stimulate our own hopes for the future of ministry.

First, baptism made every Christian responsible for the general ministries of the Church to carry on the mission of Jesus. Second, there was great diversity in functions and a concentric relationship among the designated ministries. Third, there was openness in form by way of whom the Church designated for formal ministries. As far as we can tell there were three conditions: that the person be a baptized and faithful disciple of Jesus Christ; that he or she have the requisite charisms to fulfill the particular function; and, that she or he be designated by a Christian community to act on its behalf. Fourth, there was no clear-cut practice with respect to how the communities designated for formal functions of ministry. Imitating Jewish custom, the Pauline communities had a laying on of hands by the local leaders (1 Tim. 4:14, 5:22) or by Paul himself (1 Tim. 1:6). Such a ritual is mentioned also in Acts 6:6 and 13:3. By the third century, this laying on of hands became the rite for designating bishops, presbyters, and deacons, at least in the Church of Rome, as reflected in the Apostolic Tradition of Hippolytus.[28] In the first and second centuries, however, laying on of hands was not practiced in all the communities, and where it was used, it designated people for a variety of ministries or was simply a symbol of blessing. Those first Christians assumed that every community had people with the necessary charisms to carry on its formal ministries. The Holy Spirit grants the requisite "gifts" to each community; it must recognize them, call them forward, and designate them for such service.[29] Fifth, "the Twelve" had a central leadership role in the first communities, and Peter had a primacy among them. But beyond the apostolic and petrine offices, the first communities lend us no blueprint for how to organize the ministries of the Church in later times and places. The variety, diversity, and openness at the beginning, however, can prompt hope and imagination of new horizons.

Between Then and Now

In a brief paper, I can only make a few summary points of what transpired regarding Christian ministry between those first Christian communities and the Second Vatican Council. For those of any vintage, who grew up in the pre–Vatican II Church, a few indicators will suffice to recall the contrast "between then and now."

Entrusted to carry on the mission of Jesus Christ, guided and empowered by the Holy Spirit, the Church has faithfully evangelized and taught the Scriptures and Christian tradition, has effectively celebrated the sacraments, has built up Christian communities, and has rendered extraordinary service to human need of all kinds. With this faith affirmation in place, however, we must recognize that much of what emerged in the forms, functions, and style of the Church's ministries was the product of history rather than a blueprint from heaven.[30] What history has produced, subsequent history may choose to change, forging more effective structures for new times and contexts. And even while we give thanks for the good ministry that the Church has done over the ages, O'Meara's summary seems warranted: "After the third century we have stasis and reduction, and after the sixth century, diminution. Ministry has fewer forms or is institutionalized; ministry becomes priesthood and is grafted on to canonical positions."[31]

Salient Points

First, baptism was a fundamental turn toward discipleship in Jesus, and this first sacrament of Christian ministry was lost, in large part, as Christianity received preferred status in the Roman Empire beginning with Constantine. The rigor of the catechumenate receded, and baptism became a cultural expectation more than a call to lifelong *metanoia* and to active participation in the Church's mission.

Second, the multiple ministries of the first Christian communities became subsumed into the sacerdotal category with the designation by ordination to the "degrees" of priesthood. For these priests, presiding at Eucharist defined their central function.[32] Brown summarizes: "The priesthood represents the combination or distillation of several distinct roles and special ministries in the New Testament church."[33]

Third, priests became clergy in the sense that they were given significant social privileges and civic responsibilities in the Empire, both

East and West, for a variety of cultural reasons. Primarily, it seems that Christian priests were expected to fill the civic roles of the old pagan priesthood.

Fourth, priesthood became sacral in the sense that it was considered as a divine power possessed by the individual priest and independent of any Christian community. This was epitomized in the Catholic practice of referring to the ordained alone with the revered title *alter Christus,* assigned to act *in persona Christi,* ignoring that the call to "put on Christ" (Gal. 3:27) and to be "ambassadors" of Christ (2 Cor. 5:20) was addressed to all the baptized.

The sacralizing of priesthood was augmented by the polemics of the Reformation. As the Reformers rejected the ontic power of priesthood in order to emphasize the "priesthood of all believers," Catholicism placed increased emphasis on the sacral nature of priests and their qualitative difference from the laity. In the *Catechism of the Council of Trent,* the most influential text in promulgating that council's decrees, we read this extraordinary statement: "Priests and bishops ... act in this world as the very person of God. It is evident that no office greater than theirs can be imagined. Rightly have they been called angels (Mic. 2:7), even gods (Exod. 22:28), holding as they do among us the very name and power of the living God."[34]

Fifth, priesthood became hierarchical, not in the sense of concern for "holy order" (the etymology of the word *hier arche,* the opposite of *an arche*) but describing descending levels of canonical authority and sacramental power. Thus, the bishop possesses the fullness of priesthood, priests to a lesser degree, and the diaconate is a stepping-stone to priesthood. Below diaconate, the *Catechism of the Council of Trent* counted five lower orders, and, within priesthood, five ascending levels: priest, bishop, archbishop, patriarch, and "superior to all of these ... the bishop of Rome."[35]

And sixth, designated ministries became exclusive as they were reserved to those in holy orders, and the Church attached the requirements of maleness and celibacy for priesthood, though the New Testament lists neither as preconditions for ministry. Regarding women in priesthood, the Pontifical Biblical Commission appointed to evaluate this question concluded that there is no biblical warrant for their continued exclusion. Further, and modeled on the example of Jesus, this commission's report noted that women participated actively in the ministries of the early Church and shared in functions later subsumed into priesthood.[36]

The Western Church practice to require celibacy of its bishops and priests has a long and complex history; the influence of monasticism, a negative theology of marriage, Jewish purity laws regarding the priest before offering sacrifice, and concern for church property are typically on the list of causes.[37] The first decisive step toward obligatory celibacy was taken at the Second Lateran Council (1139), which declared that marriages of priests were not only unlawful but invalid. Thereafter, celibacy for priests has been a law in the Western Church, but has never been accepted by Eastern Orthodoxy or by Eastern Catholic rites in union with Rome. Whatever the origins of mandatory celibacy, like the exclusion of women, it was more the product of cultural influences than a mandate of the Christian scriptures. In light of present exigencies surrounding the priesthood, it would seem wise for the Roman Catholic Church to make celibacy optional for its priests.[38]

Our Best Hopes

Our first and best hope must be that the good work begun by Vatican II to reclaim baptism will continue. Baptism initiates the common vocation of all Christians as fully fledged members of this "holy priesthood" (1 Pet. 2:5); every member is responsible to consciously participate in carrying on the mission and ministries of Jesus Christ. Regardless of what people's particular vocation in life might be, we must reclaim "vocation" as an inclusive term.[39] The Holy Spirit calls and gifts every baptized person to employ his or her God-given talents with the conscious commitment of Christian faith for the realization of God's reign in the Church and world.

The baptized must employ their varied charisms both within the Church and through the Church into society and must carry on the fourfold functions of Christian ministry in both places. They must build up the Church community as a credible sacrament of God's reign and contribute to the common good of society; they must evangelize through the witness of lived Christian faith, and, as appropriate, explicitly share God's word; they are called to assemble weekly with their faith community for liturgy, to live the values of worship and Sabbath, and in society to state that all belongs to God. They must fulfill the social responsibilities of their faith, working for justice, compassion, peace, and reconciliation, within the Church and in society.

What then of the formal ministries of the Church? I have been referring to them as "designated" ministries. The Catholic Church now seems to favor "ecclesial" ministries. A creative suggestion at the Boston College conference was to call them "ordered" ministries. By whatever name, I am referring to formal functions of ministry that are carried out explicitly in the name of a Christian community.

The most hopeful configuration for all ecclesial ministries would seem to be a concentric circle instead of the top-down pyramid that separates more than distinguishes the ordained from all other ministries and that creates a chasm for "the laity." Better by far to forge concentric circles with ordained ministry renewed at its center, circling out into the many functions of designated ministries that people embrace as their vocation, then rippling out to include people who render any service in the name of a Christian community — all the volunteer ministries of a parish — and who then bring God's word of "liberating salvation" into "every level and strata of society."[40] Such ecclesial ministries would be marked by diversity in function and openness in form.

Diversity in Function

I hope the Church will continue to retrieve the diversity in functions that marked the formal ministries of the first Christian communities. Of course, these ministries have continued over the centuries but were subsumed into priesthood, as if any one person could have all the requisite charisms. Or they were done, but not recognized as ministries. One thinks immediately of the extraordinary heroism and generosity, volume, and diversity of ministries carried on by vowed religious women. Other than the sacramental, they have borne the brunt of the Church's ministries in education, health care, and human services.

I propose that ecclesial ministry include any specific function of service and empowerment that is rendered by a baptized Christian who, gifted with the requisite charism from the Holy Spirit, is commissioned for that particular work by, with, and on behalf of a Christian community, in order to continue Jesus' mission of God's reign to the world. Although many have subfunctions within them, a partial list of such formal ministerial functions would be:

- evangelizing and preaching the kerygma of Christian faith;
- formation and education of the community in Christian identity;
- presiding and assisting at worship and the celebration of the sacraments;
- caring for the psychological and spiritual well-being of people;
- caring for immediate human needs with compassion;
- engaging in works of peace making and social justice;
- administering and promoting good stewardship of the community's material assets;
- studying scripture and tradition to lend ready access to their spiritual wisdom; and
- encouraging and coordinating the charisms of all members of a faith community to work with "holy order" within the Church and "for the life of the world" (John 6:51).

Within the concentric circle of those ministries, I hope the ministry of priests will be constituted by three constitutive functions: to preside with the community at worship and in celebrating the sacraments; to preach the scriptures and traditions of Christian faith, especially at the liturgical assembly; and, to coordinate and empower the other ministries of a Christian community, enabling all to "work well together" (*hier arche* at its best).[41]

I hope bishops will fulfill a similar function as the priest, with the added responsibility of oversight (*episkope*) for a diocese. As such, a

bishop cares for the faith life of an integral Christian Church and promotes its communion with other dioceses of the region and within
the universal Church. By way of who gets designated, it does not
seem likely that Catholicism will return soon to the criteria for bishops outlined in 1 Timothy 3:2–10. However, the emphasis there on
being "a good manager of one's own household" surely implies that
a pastoral charism be a non-negotiable requirement. Beyond this, we
should hope that the Church will soon return to the common practice
of the first millennium that gave real voice to the baptized and the
presbyterate in selecting their bishop.[42]

The revival of the "permanent" diaconate has had mixed reception throughout the Church, with some dioceses recruiting for it
and others discouraging it. However, the fact remains that there are
now some fifteen thousand permanent deacons in the United States
Catholic community alone. According to the gospel criterion ("by
the fruits"), I believe the permanent diaconate should be embraced
as the work of the Holy Spirit. It may also be the beachhead that first
welcomes women into ordained ministry; the one extended reflection
on the diaconate in the New Testament presumes that women are
included (1 Tim. 3:8–13).

Regarding the ministerial functions of deacons, I hope they will
share in all the ministries of priesthood, except presiding at sacraments that are reserved to priests and bishops. More specifically, the
defining ministry of deacons should be service to human needs. The
word "deacon" has this etymological meaning. The New Testament
text typically identified with diaconal ministry (Acts 6:1–7) has them
appointed to distribute food to those in need. The argument that the
deacon's function is primarily liturgical reflects the reduction of ordained ministry to the sacramental. Reclaiming the original diversity
of ministries is an opportunity to return the diaconate to its primary
function of caring for human needs.

Openness in Form

Regarding the forms for ecclesial ministry, the requirements to be so
designated by the Church, I hope for return to the original openness
of the first communities, enforcing only the three criteria that we find

there. In contemporary language: first, that the person has the charism needed for the particular function and then the requisite theological education and spiritual formation to perform it well; second, that the person has enthusiasm for the particular ministry and a sense of calling to perform it; this reaches beyond ability to an aptitude for it; and third, that the person be designated to her or his function of ministry by and on behalf of a Christian community. Whether by ordination or installation no one can appoint himself or herself as an ecclesial minister; each person needs the commission of the Church to act in its name.

Beyond these three (preparation, inclination, and designation), I hope the Church will impose no further conditions for fulfilling any function of ecclesial ministry. Theologically, there seems to be no adequate warrant to retain maleness or celibacy as prerequisites for ordained ministry; spiritually and pastorally there seems to be compelling reasons to discontinue both. Thus, I have four hopes for the approach taken by Christian ministries; they parallel those I noted in the style of the historical Jesus.

First, all Christian ministry must be deeply communal, being both *for* and *through* the Christian community. The Holy Spirit gives charisms "for building up the body of Christ" (Eph. 4:12), for building up community. A Christian community must be radically inclusive, or let us say, truly "catholic," welcoming saints and sinners and the whole rainbow of God's people. Then such an inclusive community must be for mission. When the Risen Christ assembled the small community on that hillside in Galilee (Matt. 28), it was to send them out. In sum, the Church's mission is to be a sacrament of God's reign in the world, a credible community of faith, hope, and love that by God's grace through the Holy Spirit causes what it symbolizes.

Christian community must always be outward bound. The Church reaches out into the world by "bringing the Good News into all the strata of humanity ... transforming humanity from within and making it new," participating in God's work of "liberating salvation." This is what John Paul II intended by a "new" evangelization. If the "old" evangelization put emphasis on "bringing them in" (anyone not already Christian), the "new" emphasizes "bringing Christians out" of the Church and into the world with lived and joyful witness to our faith. We are to share the truth we know and the faith we believe by living *for life and for all.*

Following on from community, I hope for partnership, that all functions of ministry may work together in "holy order." Much of the current literature on the practice of ministry calls for collaboration among the ministries and with the people whom they serve.[43] Indeed, the business world is shifting to encourage partnership, to engage and maximize the gifts of everyone involved in an enterprise. Apparently such collaboration is more productive than top-down management.[44]

Christian ministry has better reasons for partnership than increased productivity, though the latter should not be dismissed. We believe in a God who within Godself and toward us is a Triune partnership of loving relationship; surely a people of God should attempt to reflect as much. The communal nature of the Church — its *koinonia* — and Paul's riveting image of it as the Body of Christ calls for partnership in ministry. Jesus' dire warning to the disciples that they not "lord it over" anyone (Mark 10:42), repeated in one way or another six times throughout the Gospels, surely demands a partnership approach to ministry.

Third, I hope Christian ministry will reach beyond "service" toward empowerment. Now direct service will always be needed and expected of Christian faith, e.g., to feed people who are hungry. Yet Christian ministry must also reach beyond immediate need, making it possible for people to feed themselves and, indeed, to challenge the social structures that cause their lack of food in the first place. To empower people to help themselves and each other requires eliciting the gifts of each person, affirming and mentoring as needed, and encouraging them to "work well together."

My last hope for now is that ecclesial ministries, regardless of their specific functions, will take on a style that mediates effectively between faith and life, between gospel and culture, encouraging people to integrate their lives and their faith into a faith alive and lived in the world. We need a style that challenges what Vatican II described as one of "the more serious errors of our age," namely, "the split between the faith which many profess and their daily lives."[45]

My hope here is for more than a "correlation" between life and faith; we need a style of ministry that encourages people to *integrate* their lives into their Christian faith and their Christian faith into their lives. I have written about this approach as "bringing life to faith, and faith to life."[46] Every function of ministry should attend to what is "going on" in people's lives and their social context, lend ready access to the wisdom, sacraments, and ethic of Christian faith, and then encourage people to live their faith in the everyday of life. This was the approach of Jesus. I hope his respectful and empowering style may come to mark the Church's ministries as well.

Chapter 14

Reflection

THOMAS MAHONEY

T HE SIMPLE FACT that I am a priest of the Archdiocese of Boston in 2005 explains my interest in the topic of "the Roman Catholic priesthood in the 21st Century." Participation in a conference where scholars demonstrate their love for the Church, offer the fruits of their scholarship as food for thought, promote open, frank discussion, and creatively analyze the evolution of priestly ministry from its beginnings to the present, revives my hope, despite alarming evidence of recent decline, for continued growth and renewal in the Roman Catholic Priesthood, and indeed in the Roman Catholic Church. This conference provides a refreshing encounter with a relatively small but energized and inspired group focused on the future of the Catholic Church. How unusual it feels to reflect on the future of priesthood in the presence of life-giving hopes and dreams, instead of in the presence of the all too familiar defensiveness and ineffectiveness of those most empowered to create a blueprint for its future.

The formal presentations at the conference are clearly the result of careful reflection, serious study, and professional scholarship. In addition to theological concepts and statistical data, we find much anecdotal evidence of what in Boston and elsewhere is regularly referred to as a "morale problem" among priests. A chorus of both clergy and laity who work in the Church in various ministries harmoniously voices a common refrain: "something has to change." Yet for those with the greatest concentration of power, and hence the most potential for becoming agents of that needed change, the word

190

itself evokes fear. Current hierarchical leadership neglects the opportunity to renew its vision of priestly ministry by delving ever more deeply into the historical study of the development of what is currently accepted as orthopraxis — as if, to honor tradition, it must regress to the customs of an era that produced a period of homeostasis. However, the comfortable and unquestioning acceptance of such a status quo permitted devastating harm to be done to individuals, which led in turn to a chasm between hierarchy and laity.

This regression, a defensive response, belies the fact that throughout church history leaders, prompted by the Holy Spirit, have successfully collaborated with serious scholarship to address the foibles and failings of previous generations, although admittedly not without difficulty and uncertainty in the process. A contributing cause for this negligence is the lack of credibility given by those far more willing to assign labels such as relativist, dissident, or even heretic, than to engage in honest dialogue or to do the real work of integrating the gospel message into the lived experience of a changing world to the scholars of our day. This engagement with a thoughtful approach to the questions of the future begs the question of whether the Church works primarily for the maintenance of its ecclesiastical leadership or for the engagement of all people in a life-changing, heartfelt encounter with the living God.

The sociological analysis of the purported priest shortage offered by Dean R. Hoge yields for me new insights and conclusions. Hoge suggests that differing expectations of priesthood and varying experiences with regard to the role of the priest are important determining factors in drawing conclusions about the severity of the priest shortage and its long-term effects. Hoge makes the case that there may be no real priest shortage in the United States. Other parts of the world with large and even growing populations of Catholics function with far fewer priests. In these faith communities, more is expected of the laity. In places where a shortage is perceived, even without consideration of women who discern a call to priesthood, there is a ready pool of qualified lay ministers, who are functioning already in important ways within the limits imposed by the Church's authoritarian hierarchy. Thomas Groome's presentation suggests a return to the original

meaning of "holy order," which would empower qualified lay ministers and which would enable the whole Christian community, freed
from an inappropriate, hierarchical authoritarianism, to "work well
together."

Adding to the impact of the sociological study, James Burns adds
a fundamental mental health perspective. An examination of the psychological phenomenon of deteriorating ability to function known
as "burnout" furthers the implication that the expectations and demands placed on the priest in today's American Catholic Church
often supersede the capability of the diminishing number of clergy,
which suggests a needed adjustment in our expectations of what is
strictly a priestly or clerical role. As a priest honestly engages practical
questions of how to function in relationship to self, to the laity, to professional staff, to other priests, and to the hierarchy, he must struggle
with differing and sometimes contradictory expectations within the
limits of his own human potential.

Admitting that the call to priesthood will always require reliance
on sacramental grace to transcend the inadequacies of the individual
priest does not negate the need to integrate the spiritual role within
the human context. This does not mean that we should pare down
the role of the priest by simply stripping out duties that can adequately be performed by the nonordained. Rather, we must reform
our vision of the kingdom of God, in its beginning here and now, and
more fully recognize and empower the gifts imposed by baptism. The
"best hopes" that Groome advocates capture much of the spirit of
reform that is needed in our understanding and practice of Church
and outline the clear and desirable implications for priesthood. These
"best hopes" are deeply founded in both ancient practice and the
modern collaborative genius of the Second Vatican Council.

The emphasis Groome places on the retrieval of baptism and on
the situation of holy orders in good order within the faith community touches a nerve that has been rubbed raw in the anxious and
contentious atmosphere of American Roman Catholicism. Groome's
approach for me offers a charismatic balm to soothe the wounds of
our failures. We priests too often fail to call forth from within those
we have baptized the fire we ourselves ignite. Therefore, we often

find ourselves alone or lonely in the vineyards in which we toil. We baptized fail to do the hard work that is necessary to keep the flame of faith alive and burning brightly in our parish communities, and we allow our potential to languish. In the face of the needs of our human family, these failures loom large.

The framework of Groome's "best hopes" takes its shape around these human needs and the capacity of the Christian community to provide for these needs. His view of designated ministry accounts for the broad spectrum across which human need and the Holy Spirit's inspired response are sprinkled and the splendid, varied ways in which Christ chooses to make himself present in the meeting of gift and need.

As a cleric trained in the seminary system, I nevertheless feel constrained by the limits of my understanding, imagination, and skills, as I attempt pastoral outreach to the people of my faith community and beyond, both of whom I am called by baptism and ordination to serve. Faced with the partial list of ministerial functions in Groome's presentation, and even prior to reflecting on the morale problem among priests, I am practically paralyzed. How life-giving it would be for me as a priest to hear my bishop, recognizing the needs of the human community and the Christian response required, encourage me to carefully discern, encourage, and coordinate the charisms of all the members of my parish to work together to meet those needs. How that message differs from the concerns of an entrenched, dysfunctional, and clerical corporate culture.

Although Groome reminds us of the Second Vatican Council's amplification of the baptismal role of sharing in the priesthood of Christ, two significant obstacles seem to thwart progress toward making that a lived reality in our faith communities. This reform is resisted by the clerical culture that has not been trained to navigate the challenges of collaboration on a broad scale and by a leadership that has not implemented such a model, which has resulted in the second obstacle. The continued emphasis on canonical authority, sacramental power, and the ontological distinction of the ordained continues to form a laity that has not widely understood or received the invitation to a more responsible and participatory role.

The precipitous decline in the number of men expressing interest in or seeking admission to our seminaries will certainly have an impact for generations to come. The only reasonable prediction is for continued decline until, as the presentations and spirit of this conference suggest, our Church promotes a clerical leadership that will embrace collaboration with highly qualified lay leaders, and that will engage in open dialogue, so that together we can rebuild the Church, in order to become what our God always intends, a community of love, which seeks only to make the love of Christ present and clearly visible in our midst.

Chapter 15

The Charism of the Priesthood Today

Eugene Lauer

(✤)

M Y TASK IN THIS VOLUME is to attempt to identify the special
charism of the Catholic priesthood that would be most valuable and fitting for the Church of the twenty-first century in the
United States. I have analyzed carefully the preceding articles in this
book. I listened attentively to the stimulating discussions that accompanied the presentations that all the authors made at the Boston
College conference that occasioned the writing of this book. In the
following pages, I have summarized some of their most significant
observations and some insights from many of the enthusiastic conference participants, and I have dared to suggest, at the very end of
this chapter, a charism that I think is one of the most valuable for
understanding and re-visioning the ministry of the Catholic priest in
the twenty-first century. In order to begin this task with clarity, it will
be helpful to give a concise explanation of some of the terms that are
crucial for this analysis and summary.

An Understanding of "Charism"

A charism, in our understanding of Scripture and its unfolding meaning in Christian tradition, is a gift given to a person or persons by
the Spirit for the sake of the community — the Christian community
and the whole of the human community that it touches. Hence, it is
not necessary to think of a charism as a gift given only to an individual. It could be a gift given to the whole of the Christian community

through which the meaning of priesthood is significantly developed and new dimensions of priesthood revealed.

In attempting to name the charism of the priesthood for the twenty-first century, we must be attentive to three basic questions of our scriptural/theological tradition:

* What, if anything, comes from the "Christ event" itself, i.e., from the teachings of Jesus, especially those recorded in Scripture?

* What comes simply from practical, historical adaptation?

* What comes from the Spirit guiding the Christian community through history as the meaning of Jesus' teaching is unfolded?

One insight from Dean Hoge's sociological analysis is especially important for my task. He observes that the "shortage of priests" that we experience in the United States today does indeed depend on how we define or perceive "shortage." Catholics in the United States may *feel* that there is a dramatic shortage because we have far fewer priests in 2005 than we had in 1950. Yet we still have more priests per number of Catholics than almost any other area of the world. It is his final observation about how to look at "shortage" that is the most important one for my task, viz., do we have enough priests to do *what is needed*. What do we need the ordained for? Our investigation into the special charism of the priesthood will help us to answer this very practical question.

Use of the Term "Priest"

When we use the word "priest" we are obviously speaking about those men who have been ordained to this special ministry. However, it will be helpful to give a more exact description of what we mean by the term in this analysis, since the priesthood has taken on many different forms throughout history, and priests have been assigned to, or pursued, scores of different tasks. Note that in the preceding chapters in this book, there is for the most part the assumption that "priest" means the ordained person who is ministering to a local community in some leadership role, always with the special function of presiding at the Catholic sacraments. As James Bacik pointed out in quoting Karl Rahner, "The Church, as event, is necessarily a local and localized community."[1] Hence, the parish is the highest degree of actuality of the Church. This does not mean that priests who are doing other functions are not carrying out genuine ministry. It only assumes that the core role, the fundamental role, of priest has been and will be ministering to the local Christian community and that the other roles for priests that have evolved throughout the centuries must in some way support and enhance this fundamental role.[2]

Earliest Description of Christian Ministers/Priests

As John Baldovin pointed out, the term 'priest' is never used by Jesus for those whom he called to spread the gospel and care for the community. The term is used in the New Testament only for Jesus himself, and in only one source, the Letter to the Hebrews. The apostles and disciples were not a distinctly privileged class as were priests in the Jewish hierarchy. The apostles and disciples of Christ were instructed on many occasions not to "lord it over" others but to be the servants of all, like true shepherds. "If anyone wishes to be first, he shall be the last of all and the servant of all" (Mark 9:35).

The primary commission to the New Testament leaders was that they were to spread the gospel, to evangelize just as Jesus himself did. This ministry is probably summarized best in the famous passage when Jesus first appears in the synagogue in his hometown: "The Spirit of the Lord is upon me, and has anointed me to bring good news to the poor, to proclaim liberty to captives, recovery of sight to the blind, to set free the oppressed, and to proclaim God's year of favor" (Luke 4:18–21). Thus, the primary element in the description of a minister in the New Testament is *one who evangelizes.*

It is natural that those who carry out the evangelical mission of gathering and forming a community of believers are the ones who are deeply involved in *overseeing the shaping* of the early communities, the second descriptive characteristic. In so doing, it is clear in Scripture that they look to others to take certain roles in the shaping of the community, roles that Paul tells us are gifts of the Spirit (1 Cor. 12:7–11).

The third characteristic of the New Testament leaders follows from this. They do not do everything themselves. They are ministers among ministers. They *empower others* because the community needs the gifts of all its members. The leaders ensure that ministry is provided but they do not attempt to do it all themselves.

As Thomas Groome pointed out, this kind of leadership led to the fourth major function, *presiding at the table of the Lord.* As Raymond Brown's research has concluded, there is no compelling evidence that these designated leaders were the only ones who ever presided at the "breaking of the bread."[3] Naturally, those who brought a community of believers together by their evangelizing efforts and who had a major role in shaping that community and in empowering the members of that community to use their own gifts for the sake of the community would also be the ones to lead the community at Eucharist. Presiding at Eucharist is indeed the "summary role" of ministry. The priest leads the community into the quintessential experience of intimate union with Christ.

Finally, the Scriptures tell us what kind of person should be selected for such leadership. The Letter to Titus gives the best New Testament summary of this point: "You should appoint elders in each town, in accordance with the principles I have laid down. Are they men of unimpeachable character? Is each the husband of one wife? Are their children believers, not open to any charge of dissipation or indiscipline? He must not be overbearing or short-tempered or given to drink; no brawler, no money-grubber, but hospitable, right-minded, temperate, just, devout, and self-controlled. He must keep firm hold of the true doctrine, so that he may be well able both to appeal to his hearers with sound teaching and to refute those who raise objections" (Titus 1:5–9). In a sentence, the leaders must *model the teachings of Christ* which they bring to the community.

In summary, there are five elements in the description of the ministry of the bishop/priest/minister/leader in the first two centuries of Christianity: first, to evangelize, to teach the Word of God; second, to take a leadership role in forming the Christian community; third, to empower others to participate in ministering to the community; fourth, to preside at the eucharistic table; and fifth, to model the teachings of Jesus in striving to live out the Christian message.

I think that James Bacik is accurate when he asserts that the "Good Shepherd" is the key summary metaphor for the early Church leaders. The leadership qualities of a shepherd fitting for the New Testament minister are immediately obvious, even to the person who has been raised in the industrialized cities of the twentieth century: one who leads with loving care, nurtures, is intimately related to the flock, the one who "knows" the deep needs of those entrusted to him or her. We call this today "servant leadership."

Four Significant Historical Developments

In the complex evolution of the nature and function of priesthood, there are four very significant stages of development that need some analysis in order to determine a charism of priesthood for the twenty-first century. Even though these theological and pastoral revisions may seem to have moved our tradition away from the biblical and ancient Church descriptions of priesthood presented above, they may still have some genuine value in leading us to our goal.

As we review these developments, it is important to keep in mind the following understanding of the nature of Christian theology. All theologizing is an attempt to unfold Christian meaning, to express more and more clearly in human terms transcendent realities. The expressions themselves, the language used and the philosophical explanations, are not our Christian teaching. Our teachings, our defined dogmas, reside in the *meaning* of those expressions and explanations. Even expressions and philosophical explanations that were very narrowly crafted or moved in unfortunate directions were attempts for the most part to "get at" the ultimate meaning of faith. Hence, we need to analyze the four revisions that will be presented here in this light. Were they attempting to "get at" something in the meaning of priesthood that could be valuable to us today in discovering the charism of the priesthood for the twenty-first century, even though the language or philosophical explanations that they used may no longer be the most appropriate for the contemporary world?

First, the gradual separation of the priest from a necessary connection with a local community beginning in the fourth century significantly changed the reality of what a priest was to be. In order to counter this growing trend, the Council of Chalcedon mandated in 451 that "no one can be ordained priest or deacon in an absolute manner . . . unless a local community is clearly assigned to him."[4] The ordination of monks and the special roles given to priests in some areas of the post-Constantinian Church had contradicted this assumption. Gradually, *ordination in itself became an ultimate value,* i.e., that a person could bring down God's saving grace to earth through his very being. It also gave an ordained person a privileged status in the community. The Old Testament notion that was then applied to the Christian priest as one set apart from the community in a privileged caste to attend to the realm of the sacred enhanced this concept of absolute ordination.

The theologians who developed this approach were trying to articulate the deepest level of the value of ordination. Indeed there is a deep and mysterious value here. It is very valuable to have as leaders persons designated by the community to be symbols of the unity of the community, to model what the Christian life should be, and to preside at the Eucharist. However, this value is never solely for the benefit of the ordained person. It is a value that has meaning only in relation to the Christian community. Ordination is always for the sake of the community. Our theology of priesthood must, therefore, always indicate how the ordained minister engages and enhances the development of the local community and, as we shall see later in this article, how ordination in some way brings the universal priesthood/ministry of all the faithful to its fullness.

Second, this separation of the priest from ministry to a local community led also to a definitive distinction between clergy and laity. Through ordination, the priest became a different kind of person and, in this fallible world, lived in a different realm, the realm of the holy and transcendent, the realm of the sacred. This notion was solidified by the philosophical/theological assertion in the twelfth and thirteenth centuries that an *ontological* change took place at ordination. The very being of the one ordained was changed.

The theologians who developed this theology of ontological change were searching for a way to express something about the special role of the priest. However, in so doing, they used philosophical categories that spoke of a personal change rather than a relational change. Ordination does indeed bring about a relational change between the priest and the rest of the community, a designation for a special role in overseeing and taking a leadership role in the ministry of the community, in presiding at the table of the Lord and in being a symbol of the unity of the community.

Third, since this specially transformed person was the only one to preside at Eucharist, our scholastic philosophy of the twelfth and thirteenth centuries developed a theory to explain this phenomenon, a theory of the passing on of spiritual power. Through an unbroken series of ordinations from the time of the apostles to the present moment, the spiritual power to consecrate at Eucharist and to forgive sins was preserved on earth in the person of the priest.

The theologians who gave us the language of spiritual power and the theory of an unbroken series of ordinations to pass on that power were intent on giving an explanation of how/why only certain persons in the community could and, in fact, did lead the community in worship and administer the sacraments. However, the metaphor of "power" (and, remember, all theological language is analogy or metaphor) seems to focus on controlling the act of worship rather than on being designated to preside at worship. Such language seems to focus too strongly on the role of the priest rather than on recognizing that it is Christ who is effecting the transcendent reality. In the best of our biblical/ancient tradition, leadership both in overseeing the community and in leading worship is better expressed as a servant role, not as a controlling role. Hence, it is probably more helpful — and more accurate — to use language that indicates that the priest is the one who is designated to act in union with Christ in leading the community into the mysterious reality of communion with the Divine at the eucharistic meal.

Fourth, gradually in the post-Constantinian period, the priest subsumed virtually all of the diverse ministries that had been shared in
the apostolic community and in the early centuries. Eventually the
priest also absorbed the duties of the deacons. The result was that
ministry itself was for the most part identified with the priest (and
bishop). Other members of the community might indeed "help" the
ordained in their work, but they were not doing ministry itself in the
proper sense of the word.

Perhaps the most obvious critique of this theory is that it sets the
ordained priest in an impossible situation. No one person could possibly do all of the ministries necessary for forming an ideal Christian
community. The Pauline phrase of "being all things to all people" was
not referring to ministries; it was referring to being open to all peoples
and cultures, being open to their differences and personal needs.

Finally, the biblical/ancient model of ministry seems to be also the
most practical one. Every member of the Christian community has
his or her special gifts. The rite of initiation has given to every one
of the faithful a role in ministry. It does make great practical sense
that there be a leader to oversee and organize these ministries into
an organic whole, but it is quite a stretch to suggest that all of these
ministries belong of their very nature to the ordained person.

The Charism of the Priesthood in the Twenty-First Century

What is the charism of the priesthood for the twenty-first century
in the light of the earliest Christian description of those who ministered, and in the light of the intent of theologians in these four major
transitions in the theology of priesthood?

I need first to point out one major contemporary development
that is of enormous importance for answering this question. According to data from a recent survey by the National Pastoral Life
Center in New York, this contemporary development may be the
beginning of one of the most significant transitions in ministry in
the history of the Church in the United States, and perhaps in the
universal Church. Today in the United States, there are about thirty-
one thousand paid professional lay ministers working either full-time

or at least twenty hours a week in our Catholic parishes. They are
the contemporary expression of the passage: "To each individual
the manifestation of the Spirit is given for some benefit. To one is
given through the Spirit the expression of wisdom; to another the
expression of knowledge...to another faith...to another gifts of
healing...to another mighty deeds; to another prophecy; to another
discernment of spirits; to another varieties of tongues; to another interpretation of tongues. But one and the same Spirit produces all of
these, distributing them individually to each person" (1 Cor. 12:7–
11). However, their gifts are named differently today from those in
the Scripture passage: directors of religious education, pastoral associates, youth ministers, social service ministers, directors of parish
life, liturgical ministers, music ministers, and many others.

Within this context, I am suggesting that the charism of the priesthood for the twenty-first century is not a special gift of the Spirit to
individual priests or to the whole of the presbyterate. Rather, it is a
special gift of the Spirit within the whole Church, the whole of the
laity, presbyterate, and episcopacy together. It is the gift of a vision
of priesthood in the light of the evolving dramatic development of
lay ministry. To put it in theological terms, it is the gift of seeing the
ordained priesthood within the context of the entire priesthood of
the faithful: pope, bishops, priests, deacons, religious, and laity. It is
the Spirit touching the whole of the Church to discern the authentic
reality of lay ministry and the authentic reality of priesthood as inter-
woven ministries, functions, and realities, whereby the Church can
reach its fullest expression. It is a gift that raises our consciousness
to be aware that we can know the full meaning of ordained priesthood and the full meaning of the priesthood of the baptized only by
viewing them together.

The priest of the twenty-first century should certainly continue to
do those functions that were at the very core of ministry from the
Church's beginning: to teach the Word of God and evangelize, to
lead and nurture an evangelized community of believers, to empower
the members to use their gifts for the faith community and the larger
human community, to attempt to model the teachings of Jesus, and

consequently to lead the community in worship and sacrament. However, in the context of the developing tradition of lay ministry in the
United States, and in the light of our observations about the "four
significant historical revisions" noted above, we may find that a revised model of how the priest does those ministries may be evolving.
Perhaps evolving also may be a revised model of how candidates
are selected and designated for the priestly ministry of presiding. In
order to articulate this evolution more specifically, we need to ask
the following questions about the relationship between lay ecclesial
ministry and priestly ministry. How do they fit together? Do they
overlap? Does the ministry of one group intrude on the ministry of
the other? Are there some ministries that belong solely to one group
that the other can never do?

Here follows some observations about the actual experience of lay
ministry today that can help us to answer these questions and describe
the charism. The Church, at least in the United States, seems to have
decided by customary practice and language that what lay ecclesial
ministers do is indeed ministry, and not simply an apostolate. It is a
ministry that comes from baptism. As Edward Hahnenberg pointed
out, a recent Roman decree attempted to distinguish the ministry
of the priest from the work of the laity, stating that what the laity
does is "apostolate" but not ministry in the strict theological sense.[5]
However, the consciousness of the Christian community seems to
have decided that such a separation simply does not fit reality.

The two concentric circles suggested by Groome and Bacik seem to
be the best metaphor for expressing the reality of the relationship between the ministry of priests and the ministry of the faithful. We are
all initially in the larger outer circle of "the faithful," laity, religious,
deacons, priests, bishops, and pope. We all have an authentic commission to minister by virtue of our baptisms. Then, some within that
circle, by virtue of ordination, are given a more focused commission
to bring that ministry to its fullness, especially through leadership at
worship.

Michael Himes had a very practical way of expressing this phenomenon when he lectured regularly on this topic at the Hesburgh
Center at Notre Dame. He said that the priest does professionally,

full-time, and in a leadership way what all the faithful are commissioned to do. The priest thereby is a sign of the unity of the faithful and has the burden/responsibility to model the Christian life in his own person. And, because of this, the priest leads the faithful in worship.

What is apparent in this description is that, in a very real experiential sense, full-time lay ecclesial ministers today often are doing four of the five functions of ministry described above very successfully and faithfully as pastoral associates, hospital chaplains, parish life administrators, etc. Is it really that simple? Do lay ecclesial ministers evangelize and teach the Word of God, help to shape and oversee local Christian communities, empower many other members of those communities to share in their ministry, and attempt to model the teachings of Jesus in their own lives and work? Do lay ecclesial ministers do virtually everything that priests and bishops do except preside at Eucharist and administer the sacraments of confirmation, reconciliation, orders, and anointing?

Putting these questions in a very experiential mode, if a priest preaches a homily on a Scripture passage and a lay ecclesial minister gives a reflection on the same passage, and the hearers in both cases are moved to a deeper union with Christ, is there any real, actual difference in what they have done within the ministry of Christ? If a priest does a hospital visitation, comforts and prays with a sick person, and a lay ecclesial minister does the same, and both sick persons experience a prayerful touch of the healing Spirit, has anything different actually happened in this ministry?

We can conclude, in this view of ministry, that there is no essential (or, ontological) difference in the ministries themselves, but that the real difference comes from the designation (ordination) to a specific role. The priest is ordained/designated to oversee and summarize the ministry of the community and consequently to preside at the Eucharist; and thus, he stands in a new and unique relationship to the rest of the community.

Where does this view of a charism lead us? It could be that those who are already ministering very effectively out of their baptismal call and who have been accepted by the Christian community for their ministry might be the ones who in the future will be called into the special circle of presiders at Eucharist and ministers of the sacraments. Practically speaking, they could be an ideal pool of candidates. According to the lay ministry survey just completed by the National Pastoral Life Center, 48 percent of them have master's degrees, and 70 percent presently state that they wish to be involved in ministry for the rest of their lives. Unlike seminarians, many and perhaps most have already passed the test of experience in their local communities and have been accepted as healthy, competent ministers of the gospel. Given the present numbers of lay ecclesial ministers, actually a superabundant pool of candidates, the Church could be very selective in determining how many and which ones should be designated to preside at the Eucharist and minister the sacraments.

There is another way of viewing the conclusion that has just been suggested. If lay ministers are really doing four of the five major functions of pastoral ministry very effectively, and there are over thirty-one thousand of them in the United States today, then perhaps we can conclude that there is no shortage of "ministers" in the Church. Rather, there is a shortage of those who can preside. And, if there is no shortage of ministers, could we possibly conclude that Catholics in the United States are actually being ministered to more carefully, frequently, and effectively than they were fifty years ago when ordinations to the priesthood were at their highest level?

An example that a priest told me in a conversation about the NPLC survey on lay ministry illustrates this observation very convincingly. He said that when he was ordained to the priesthood some forty-five years ago, there were three full-time priests at his first assignment, a large suburban parish of over two thousand families. Today there is one full-time priest there with some part-time assistance from another priest. Plus, the parish has grown considerably.

However, when he was stationed at the parish, he directed all the religious education programs, was in charge of the youth program (called CYO in those days), was charged with oversight of liturgical planning and parish social services, along with a score of other duties like taking communion to a long list of homebound parishioners, hospital visitation, teaching part-time in the grade school, etc. In that era, these were considered to be standard duties for an assistant pastor. There were no professional lay ministers at the parish.

Today there are three full-time and three part-time paid lay ministers, a deacon, and a much larger number of volunteer parish ministers who visit and take communion to the homebound, visit hospitals, and attend to numerous other ministries of care in the parish. Such a situation raises the interesting and challenging question suggested here: overall, are the parishioners of that parish being ministered to more carefully, frequently, and effectively than they were forty-five years ago? And is the real need of that parish and hundreds, perhaps thousands, of other parishes essentially a need for more presiders, those who are ordained or designated to preside at the Eucharist and minister the other sacraments? Perhaps this gift of the Spirit to the whole Church, this charism of being able to view priesthood in the light of the dramatic evolution of lay ministry, will carry us into a new era, an era remarkably similar to the Church of the apostles.

Notes

Chapter 1 / Priesthood, Susan Wood, S.C.L.

1. Daniel Donovan, *What Are They Saying about the Ministerial Priesthood?* (New York: Paulist Press, 1999), 3.

2. Hervé Legrand, "The Presidency of the Eucharist according to the Ancient Tradition," *Worship* 53 (1979): 432.

3. Susan Wood, "Presbyteral Identity within Parish Identity," in *Ordering the Baptismal Priesthood: Theologies of Lay and Ordained Ministries,* ed. Susan Wood (Collegeville, Minn.: Liturgical Press, 2003), 175–94.

4. Donovan, *What Are They Saying?*

5. Synod of Bishops, *Ultimis Temporibus,* in *Vatican II: More Postconciliar Documents,* ed. Austin Flannery (Grand Rapids, Mich.: Eerdmans, 1982).

6. Bishops, *Ultimis,* "Description of the Situation," sections 1–4.

7. Congregation for the Clergy, *The Priest and the Third Christian Millennium: Teacher of the Word, Minister of the Sacraments, and Leader of the Community* (Boston: Daughters of St. Paul, 1999).

8. Congregation for the Clergy, *The Priest and the Third Christian Millennium,* 18.

9. Congregation for the Clergy, *The Priest and the Third Christian Millennium,* 55.

10. Congregation for the Clergy, *The Priest and the Third Christian Millennium,* 19.

11. John Paul II, post-synodal apostolic exhortation, *Pastores Dabo Vobis* (March 25, 1992).

12. John Paul II, *Pastores Dabo,* no. 6.

13. John Paul II, *Pastores Dabo,* no. 7.

14. John Paul II, *Pastores Dabo,* no. 11.

15. John Paul II, *Pastores Dabo.*

16. John Paul II, *Pastores Dabo,* no. 12.

17. Susan Wood, *Sacramental Orders* (Collegeville, Minn: Liturgical Press, 2000), 20.

18. Wood, *Sacramental Orders,* 16.

19. Donovan, *What Are They Saying?* 8.

20. This is true of the draft document on Lay Ecclesial Ministry, which has been widely circulated for review. It is also the use of the text issued by a number of Vatican dicasteries, "Instruction on Some Aspects of the Collaboration of the Lay Faithful with the Ministry of Priests," *Ecclesiae de Mysterio* (August 15, 1997): AAS 89 (1997), 852ff.

21. Congregation for Divine Worship and the Discipline of the Sacraments, *Redemptionis Sacramentum* (March 25, 2004).

22. David Power, "Priesthood Revisited: Mission and Ministries in the Royal Priesthood," in *Ordering the Baptismal Priesthood,* 110.

23. Power, "Priesthood Revisited," 111.

24. Dean R. Hoge and Jacqueline Wenger, *Evolving Visions of the Priesthood: Changes from Vatican II to the Turn of the New Century* (Collegeville, Minn.: Liturgical Press, 2003), 47–59; Susan Wood, "The Search for Identity," in *Evolving Visions of the Priesthood: Changes from Vatican II to the Turn of the New Century,* ed. Dean R. Hoge and Jacqueline Wenger (Collegeville, Minn.: Liturgical Press, 2003), 167–73; Philip Rosato, "Priesthood of the Baptized and Priesthood of the Ordained: Complementary Approaches to Their Interrelation," *Gregorianum* 68 (1987): 215–66; and David Coffey, "The Common and the Ordained Priesthood," *Theological Studies* 58 (1997): 209–36.

25. Richard Gaillardetz, "The Ecclesial Foundations of Ministry within an Ordered Communion," in *Ordering the Baptismal Priesthood,* 40.

26. Daniel Buechlein, "The Sacramental Identity of the Ministerial Priesthood: 'In Persona Christi,' " in *Priests for a New Millennium* (Washington, D.C.: United States Catholic Conference, 2000), 37–52; Sarah Butler, "The Priest as Sacrament of Christ the Bridegroom," *Worship* 66 (1992): 498–517; "Priestly Identity: 'Sacrament' of Christ the Head," *Worship* 70 (1996): 290–306; "Quaestio Disputata. 'In Persona Christi.' A Response to Dennis M. Ferrara," *Theological Studies* 56 (1995): 61–80; Dennis Ferrara, "In Persona Christi: Towards a Second Naivete," *Theological Studies* 57 (1996): 65–88; Dennis Ferrara, "Representation or Self-Effacement? The Axiom In Persona Christi in St. Thomas and the Magisterium," *Theological Studies* 55 (1994): 195–224; Mark O'Keefe, *In Persona Christi: Reflections on Priestly Identity and Holiness* (St. Meinrad, Ind.: Abbey Press, 1998); Susan Wood, "Priestly Identity: Sacrament of the Ecclesial Community," *Worship* 69 (1995): 109–27; Thomas Rausch, "Priest, Community, and Eucharist" in *Finding God in All Things,* ed. Michael Himes and Stephen Pope (New York: Crossroad, 1996), 262–75; and Thomas Rausch, "Priestly Identity: Priority of Representation and the Iconic Argument," *Worship* 73 (1999): 169–79.

27. David Power, "Church Order: The Need for Redress," *Worship* 71 (1997): 296–309.

28. Yves Congar, *I Believe in the Holy Spirit,* vol. 3 (New York: Crossroad, 1983, 1999), 235–36.

29. Congar, *I Believe in the Holy Spirit,* 236.

30. Congar, *I Believe in the Holy Spirit,* 234.

31. "Instruction on Some Aspects of the Collaboration," 852ff.

32. Zeni Fox, "Laity, Ministry and Secular Character," in *Ordering the Baptismal Priesthood,* 121–51; Aurelie Hagstrom, "The Secular Character of the Vocation and Mission of the Laity: Toward a Theology of Ecclesial Lay Ministry," in *Ordering the Baptismal Priesthood,* 152–74; and Susan Wood, "Conclusion: Convergence Points toward a Theology of Ordered Ministries," in *Ordering the Baptismal Priesthood,* 256–67.

33. *Apostolicam Actuositatem,* no. 5.

34. Ten theologians, Michael Downey, Zeni Fox, Richard Gaillardetz, Aurelie Hagstrom, Kenan Osborne, David Power, Thomas Rausch, Elissa Rinere, R. Kevin Seasoltz, and Susan Wood, met to articulate a contemporary theology of lay and ordained ministries. The results are in *Ordering the Baptismal Priesthood.*

35. U.S. Lutheran–Roman Catholic Dialogue, "The Church as Koinonia of Salvation: Its Structure and Ministries" (Washington, D.C.: United States Conference of Catholic Bishops, 2004).

36. Susan Wood, "Presbyteral Identity within Parish Identity," in *Ordering the Baptismal Priesthood,* 175–94.

37. John O'Malley, "Priesthood, Ministry and Religious Life: Some Historical and Historiographical Considerations," *Theological Studies* 50 (1989): 527–47; and "Diocesan and Religious Models of Priestly Formation: Historical Perspectives," in *Priests: Identity and Ministry,* ed. Robert Wister (Wilmington, Del.: Glazier, 1990), 54–70.

Chapter 2 / The Priest as Sacramental Minister, John Baldovin, S.J.

1. All references to Council documents come from Walter Abbott, S.J., ed., *The Documents of Vatican II: in a New and Definitive Translation, with Commentaries and Notes by Catholic, Protestant, and Orthodox Authorities* (New York: Crossroad, 1989). For elaboration, see *Lumen Gentium,* no. 28; and *Presbyterorum Ordinis,* nos. 4–6.

2. Ray Noll, *Christian Ministerial Priesthood: A Search for Its Beginnings in the Primary Documents of the Apostolic Fathers* (San Francisco: Catholic Scholars Press, 1993).

3. Paul Bradshaw, *Liturgical Presidency in the Early Church* (Bramcote, Nottinghamshire: Grove Liturgical Studies, 1983).

4. John Baldovin, "The Fermentum at Rome in the Fifth Century: A Reconsideration," *Worship* 79 (2005): 38–53.

5. St. John Chrysostom, trans. Graham Neville, *Six Books on the Priesthood* (Crestwood, N.Y.: St. Vladimir's Seminary Press, 1984); and Theodore of Mopsuestia, *Mystagogical Catecheses,* in *The Awe-Inspiring Rites of Initiation,* ed. Edward Yarnold, 2nd ed. (Collegeville, Minn.: Liturgical Press, 1994), 165–250.

6. Alexander Schmemann, *Introduction to Liturgical Theology* (Crestwood, N.Y.: St. Vladimir's Seminary Press, 1966), 72–86.

7. Bernard Cooke, *Ministry to Word and Sacrament: History and Theology* (Minneapolis: Fortress Press, 1976), 557.

8. Paul Beaudette, " 'In the World but Not of It': Clerical Celibacy as a Symbol of the Medieval Church," in *Medieval Purity and Piety: Essays on Medieval Clerical Celibacy and Religious Reform,* ed. Michael Frassetto (New York: Garland, 1998), 23–46; Michael Frassetto, "Ritual Purity in Roman Catholic Priesthood: Using the Work of Mary Douglas to Understand Clerical Celibacy" (Ph.D. dissertation, Graduate Theological Union, Berkeley, 1994); Cooke, *Ministry,* 558; and Daniel Callam, "Clerical Continence in the Fourth Century: Three Papal Decretals," *Theological Studies* 41 (1980): 3–50.

9. Cyrille Vogel, *Medieval Liturgy: An Introduction to the Sources*, trans. and rev. William Storey and Niels Rasmussen (Washington, D.C.: Pastoral Press, 1986), 156–59.

10. Wendelin Knoch, *Die Einsetzung der Sakramente durch Christus: eine Untersuchung zur Sakramententheologie der Frühscholastik von Anselm von Laon bis zu Wilhelm von Auxerre* (Münster: Aschendorff, 1983).

11. Louis-Marie Chauvet, *Symbol and Sacrament* (Collegeville, Minn.: Liturgical Press, 1995), 453–68; and Liam Walsh, "Sacraments," in *The Theology of St. Thomas Aquinas*, ed. Rik van Nieuenhove and Joseph Wawrykow (Notre Dame, Ind.: University of Notre Dame Press, 2005), 326–64.

12. John Paul II, *Dominicae Cenae* (Holy Thursday Letter to Priests, 1980), no. 8; and Encyclical *Ecclesia de Eucharistia* (2003), no. 29. The phrase is used as well in documents from the council, e.g., *Lumen Gentium*, nos. 10, 28; *Sacrosanctum Concilium*, no. 33; *Christus Dominus*, no. 11; and *Presbyterorum Ordinis*, nos. 2, 6. Also see *Catechism of the Catholic Church*, 2nd ed. (Washington, D.C.: United States Catholic Conference, 2000), no. 1548.

13. Most famously, St. Jerome, Letter 146 (to Evangelus), *Patrologia Latina* 22:1192–1195, *www.newadvent.org/fathers/3001146.htm;* also see Cooke, *Ministry*, 80.

14. *Lumen Gentium*, nos. 26–27.

15. Karl Rahner and Angelus Häussling, *The Celebration of the Eucharist* (New York: Herder & Herder, 1968), 54–60.

16. St. Augustine, *Confessions*, trans. Henry Chadwick (Oxford: Oxford University Press, 1991), 9:11:27.

17. Cooke, *Ministry*, 582.

18. Cooke, *Ministry*, 594–604.

19. For the papal rejection of Anglican Orders (*Apostolicae Curae*, 1896) and the formal response of the archbishops of Canterbury and York (*Saepius Officio*, 1897), see Christopher Hill and Edward Yarnold, eds., *Anglicans and Roman Catholics: The Search for Unity* (London: SPCK, 1994).

20. Cooke, *Ministry*, 610–13.

21. *Lumen Gentium*, nos. 26–27.

22. *Lumen Gentium*, nos. 23, 28; *Presbyterorum Ordinis*, nos. 4–5.

23. *Lumen Gentium*, no. 10; *Presbyterorum Ordinis*, no. 2.

24. Council of Trent, *Canons on Sacraments in General*, DS 1606; also see 1611–1612 (Canons 11–12) on the worthiness of the minister.

25. *Sacrosanctum Concilium*, no. 7; *General Instruction on the Roman Missal*, no. 27.

26. L. William Countryman, *Living on the Border of the Holy: Renewing the Priesthood of All* (Harrisburg, Pa.: Morehouse Publishing, 1999), 138–39.

27. Council of Florence, Decree for the Armenians, DS 1312.

28. Johan Auer and Joseph Ratzinger, *Dogmatic Theology 6: A General Doctrine of the Sacraments and the Mystery of Christ* (Washington, D.C.: Catholic University of America Press, 1995), 108–12.

29. David Kertzer, *The Kidnapping of Edgardo Mortara* (New York: Vintage, 1998).

30. Auer and Ratzinger, *Dogmatic Theology*, 109.

31. Beaudette, " 'In the World but Not of It.' "
32. Sarah Coakley, "The Woman at the Altar: Cosmological Disturbance or Gender Subversion?" *Anglican Theological Review* 86 (2004): 75–93; Elizabeth Johnson, *She Who Is: The Mystery of God in Feminist Theological Discourse* (New York: Crossroad, 1993), 151–56.
33. Cooke, *Ministry*, 609.
34. *Catechism of the Catholic Church,* nos. 1547, 1551.
35. Edward Kilmartin, *Church, Eucharist and Priesthood* (New York: Paulist Press, 1981).
36. René Girard, *I See Satan Fall Like Lightning,* trans. J. G. Williams (Maryknoll, N.Y.: Orbis Books, 2001); James Alison, *Knowing Jesus* (London: SPCK, 1993); Raymund Schwager, *Must There Be Scapegoats?* trans. Maria L. Assad (New York: Crossroad, 2000); and on God's *kenosis* or self-emptying in Christ, David Power, *Love without Calculation: A Reflection on Divine Kenosis* (New York: Herder and Herder, 2005).

Chapter 3 / Reflection, Amy Strickland

1. All references to Council documents come from Walter Abbott, S.J., ed., *The Documents of Vatican II: in a New and Definitive Translation, with Commentaries and Notes by Catholic, Protestant, and Orthodox Authorities* (New York: Crossroad, 1989). *Presbyterorum Ordinis,* no. 13, states: "The daily celebration of Mass is strongly urged, since even if there cannot be present a number of the faithful, it is still an act of Christ and of the Church." Also, *Code of Canon Law,* canon 276, echoes: "In leading their lives, clerics are especially bound to pursue holiness because they are consecrated to God by a new title in the reception of orders as dispensers of God's mysteries in the service of His people. In order for them to pursue this perfection... they are to nourish their spiritual life from the twofold table of Sacred Scripture and the Eucharist; priests are therefore earnestly invited to offer the sacrifice of the Eucharist daily."
2. *Lumen Gentium,* no. 11.
3. General Audience, May 12, 1993.
4. Address to the council of European Episcopal conferences, October 11, 1985.

Chapter 4 / The Priest as Pastor, James Bacik

1. Walter Abbott, S.J., ed., *The Documents of Vatican II: in a New and Definitive Translation, with Commentaries and Notes by Catholic, Protestant, and Orthodox Authorities* (New York: Crossroad, 1989); all references to Council documents come from Abbott, *Documents;* Bernard Cooke, *Ministry to Word and Sacraments* (Philadelphia: Fortress Press, 1980); Roger Haight, *Christian Community in History,* vol. 1, *Historical Ecclesiology* (New York: Continuum, 2004); Nathan Mitchell, *Mission and Ministry: History and Theology in the Sacrament of Order* (Collegeville, Minn.: Liturgical Press, 1990); Kenan Osborne, *Priesthood: A History of Ordained Ministry in the Roman Catholic Church* (New York: Paulist Press, 1988); James Puglisi, *The Process of Admission to Ordained Ministry: Epistemological Principles and Roman Catholic Rites,* vol. 1 (Collegeville, Minn.:

Liturgical Press, 1996); Edward Schillebeeckx, *Ministry: Leadership in the Community of Jesus Christ* (New York: Crossroad, 1981); Edward Schillebeeckx, *The Church with a Human Face* (New York: Crossroad, 1985).

2. Gerhard Lohfink, *Jesus and Community: The Social Dimension of Christian Faith* (New York: Paulist Press, 1984), 10.

3. Lohfink, *Jesus and Community*, 70.

4. Osborne, *Priesthood: A History*, 3–29.

5. Osborne, *Priesthood: A History*, 217–18.

6. Walter Kasper, *Leadership in the Church: How Traditional Roles Can Serve the Christian Community Today* (New York: Herder & Herder, 2003), 58–59.

7. Schillebeeckx, *Ministry: Leadership*, 5–37.

8. Schillebeeckx, *Church with a Human Face*, 203.

9. Schillebeeckx, *Church with a Human Face*, 205.

10. Jay Dolan, *The American Catholic Experience: A History from Colonial Times to the Present* (New York: Doubleday, 1985), 158–94.

11. Susan Wood, "Presbyteral Identity within Parish Identity," in *Ordering the Baptismal Priesthood*, ed. Susan Wood (Collegeville, Minn.: Liturgical Press, 2003), 176.

12. Karl Rahner, "The Theology of the Parish," in *The Parish from Theology to Practice*, ed. Hugo Rahner (Westminster, Md.: Newman Press, 1958), 23–35.

13. Rahner, "Theology of the Parish," 25.

14. Rahner, "Theology of the Parish," 26.

15. Rahner, "Theology of the Parish," 30.

16. Schillebeeckx, *Ministry: Leadership*, 38–74.

17. Schillebeeckx, *Ministry: Leadership*, 38.

18. James Coriden, *The Parish in Catholic Tradition: History, Theology and Canon Law* (New York: Paulist Press, 1997).

19. Haight, *Christian Community*, 169–91.

20. Haight, *Christian Community*, 268–74.

21. Cooke, *Ministry*, 84.

22. Haight, *Christian Community*, 323.

23. Cooke, *Ministry*, 118.

24. Haight, *Christian Community*, 411–12.

25. Haight, *Christian Community*, 412.

26. Coriden, *Parish in Catholic Tradition*, 31.

27. Osborne, *Priesthood: A History*, 248–79.

28. Dolan, *American Catholic*, 349–417.

Chapter 5 / The Priest Preaching in a World of Grace, Thomas O'Meara, O.P.

1. On the sacramentality of the word in Karl Rahner, Otto Semmelroth, and Edward Schillebeeckx, see Paul Janowiak, *The Holy Preaching: The Sacramentality of the Word in the Liturgical Assembly* (Collegeville, Minn.: Liturgical Press, 2000).

2. Jean-Pierre Torrell, "La pratique pastorale d'un théologien du XIIIe siècle: Thomas d'Aquin prédicateur," *Recherches Thomasiennes* (Paris: Vrin, 2000): 282–314.

3. Karl Rahner, "The Great Church Year," in *The Best of Karl Rahner's Homilies, Sermons, and Meditations* (New York: Crossroad, 1993).

4. Thomas O'Meara, "The End!" *Celebration* (October 2003): 468.

5. Chris Chatteris, S.J., "Who Can Preach?" *Grace and Truth* 19 (2002): 39–46.

6. Karl Rahner, "The People of God in History," in *The Content of Faith* (New York: Crossroad, 1992), 420.

7. Thomas O'Meara, "Forum: What a Bishop Might Want to Know." *Worship* 68 (1994): 55–63.

8. Wilfried Engemann, *Einführung in die Homiletik* (Tübingen: Francke, 2002).

9. Andrew Wisdom, *Preaching to a Multi-Generational Assembly* (Collegeville, Minn.: Liturgical Press, 2004).

10. Both are from Paulist Press. Also see Peter Phan, "Cultures, Religions, and Power: Proclaiming Christ in the U.S. Today," *Theological Studies* 65 (2004): 714–40.

11. John Paul II, a master of religious theater, played into the dynamics of individualization and entertainment. Individual Catholics under the age of forty-five like the pope as a public figure, but a theatrical papacy dampened their attention to a magisterium.

12. Vincent Miller, "The Cell-Phone, the iPod, and the Parish," in *The Institute of Pastoral Studies: 40th Anniversary Celebration* (Chicago: Loyola University, 2005), unpublished.

13. Karl Rahner, "The Situation of Faith: Concern for the Church," in *Theological Investigations* 20 (New York: Crossroad, 1981), 13.

14. Thomas Aquinas, *Summa theologiae* I-II, q. 106, a. 1.

15. John Donahue, *The Gospel in Parable* (Minneapolis: Fortress, 1990), 215; and Madeline Boucher, *The Parables* (Wilmington, Del.: Glazier, 1981).

16. Karl Rahner, "Unity of the Love of Neighbor and Love of God," in *Theological Investigations* 6 (Baltimore: Helicon, 1969), 244.

Chapter 6 / The Moral Rights of Priests, James Keenan, S.J.

1. James Keenan, "Framing the Ethical Rights of Priests," *Review for Religious* 64, no. 2 (2005): 135–51; "Ethics and the Crisis in the Church," *Theological Studies* 66, no. 1 (2005): 117–36; "The Ethical Rights of Priests," *Touchstone* (Fall 2004): 6, 19–20; and "Toward an Ecclesial Professional Ethics," in *Church Ethics and Its Organizational Context*, ed. Jean Bartunek, Mary Ann Hinsdale, and James Keenan (Lanham, Md.: Sheed and Ward, 2005).

2. Brian Tierney, *The Idea of Natural Rights: Studies on Natural Rights, Natural Law and Church Law* (Atlanta: Scholars Press, 1997).

3. Caroline Bynum, "Did the Twelfth Century Discover the Individual?" *Journal of Ecclesiastical History* 31 (1980): 1–17.

4. Michael Papesh, "Farewell to the Club," *America* (May 13, 2002): 8–9; *Clerical Culture: Contradiction and Transformation* (Collegeville, Minn.: Liturgical Press, 2004); and David Gibson, "Clericalism: The Original Sin," in *The Coming Catholic Church* (San Francisco: HarperCollins, 2004), 197–219.

5. "Nec te moveat, quod initium sapientiae huic demum loco dederim, et non priori. Ibi quippe in quodam quasi auditorio suo docentem de omnibus magistram

audimus Sapientiam, hic et suscipimus; ibi instruimur quidem, sed hic afficimur. Instructio doctos reddit, affectio sapientes. Sol non omnes, quibus lucet, etiam calefacit;
sic Sapientia multos, quos docet quid sit faciendum, non continuo etiam accendit ad
faciendum. Aliud est multas divitias scire, aliud et possidere; nec notitia divitem
facit, sed possessio. Sic prorsus, sic aliud est nosse Deum, et aliud timere; nec cogni-
tio sapientem, sed timor facit, qui et afficit. Tunc sapientem dixeris, quem sua scientia
inflat? Quis illos sapientes nisi insipientissimus dicat, qui cum cognovissent Deum,
non tanquam Deum glorificaverunt, aut gratias egerunt? Ego magis cum Apostolo
sentio, qui insipiens cor eorum manifeste pronuntiat (Rom. 1: 21). Et bene initium
sapientiae timor Domini; quia tunc primum Deus animae sapit, cum eam afficit ad
timendum, non cum instruit ad sciendum. Times Dei justitiam, times potentiam; et
sapit tibi justus et potens Deus, quia timor sapor est. Porro sapor sapientem facit,
sicut scientia scientem, sicut divitiae divitem." (Bernardus Claraevallensis, *Sermones
in Cantica Canticorum,* Sermo 23, 14. *Migne.* PL 183, cols. 0891d–0892a).

6. See online *www.law.washington.edu/courses/tucker/A534/Documents/Union
%20Pacific%20v.%20Botsford.pdf* (September 16, 2005).

7. See online *www.caselaw.lp.findlaw.com/cgibin/getcase.pl?court=us&vol=277
&invol=438* (September 16, 2005). Also see Alan Westin, *Privacy and Freedom* (New
York: Athenum, 1967); and James Keenan, "The Right to Privacy," in *The New Dictionary of Christian Social Thought,* ed. Judith Dwyer (Collegeville, Minn.: Liturgical
Press, 1994), 783–85.

8. Brian Johnstone, "The Right to Privacy: The Ethical Perspective," *American
Journal of Jurisprudence* 29 (1984): 73–94; and Richard McCormick, "The Moral
Right to Privacy," in *How Brave a New World* (Garden City, N.Y.: Doubleday,
1981), 352–61.

9. On April 14, 2005, Mary Zahn of the *Milwaukee Journal Sentinel* reported,
"Priests in the Catholic Archdiocese of Milwaukee can be required to consent to
unannounced searches of their homes at any time of the day or night if church
officials suspect or know they have been involved in sexual conduct, alcohol or
drug abuse, or other behavior deemed inappropriate by Archbishop Timothy Dolan,
according to a policy change announced to clergy last week.

"As the archdiocese deems necessary, clerics will have to sign a form agreeing to
the searches and other restrictions, according to the policy documents. 'Failure to
comply with the restrictions could cause a reduction in salary and/or benefits provided to the member by the Archdiocese of Milwaukee,' the documents state." Zahn
adds, "Priests would be subject to searches: Archdiocese says target is 'inappropriate'
behavior." *www.jsonline.com/news/metro/apr05/318559.asp* (May 6, 2005).

10. Cardinal Avery Dulles, "The Rights of Accused Priests: Toward a Revision of
the Dallas Charter and the 'Essential Norms,' " *America* (June 21, 2004): 19–23.

Chapter 8 / The Priest's Relationship to the Bishop, John Strynkowski

1. Bernard of Clairvaux, *On the Song of Songs I,* trans. Kilian Walsh (Kalama-
zoo, Mich.: Cistercian Publications, 1971), 85.

2. The Latin word used for "presbyterate" is *presbyterium.*

3. John Paul II, Address to the Bishops of Region IX, November 26, 2004, no. 2, *www.vatican.va/holy_father/john_paul_ii/speeches/2004/November/documents/hf _jp-iisp* (November 29, 2004).

4. John Paul II, *Novo Millennio Ineunte, Origins* (January 18, 2001).

5. John Paul II, *Novo Millennio Ineunte,* no. 43.

6. John Paul II, *Novo Millennio Ineunte,* no. 44.

7. Raniero Cantalamessa, O.F.M. Cap., "God's Humility and World Religions," *Origins* (May 23, 2002): 25.

8. John Paul II, *Reconciliatio et Paenitentia, Origins* (December 20, 1984).

9. John Paul II, *Reconciliatio,* no. 25.

10. John Paul II, *Pastores Gregis, www.vatican.va/holy_father/john_paul_ii/ apost_exhortations/documents/hf_jp-ii_exh*(June 6, 2005), no. 45.

11. This canon acknowledges that if the bishop is "legitimately hindered from doing so personally, he may do so through the coadjutor or auxiliary bishop, through a vicar general or Episcopal vicar, or through another presbyter."

12. John Paul II, *Pastores,* no. 46. For a history of the pastoral visit, see Andrew Slafkosky, *The Canonical Episcopal Visitation of the Diocese* (Washington, D.C.: Catholic University of America Press, 1941).

13. John Paul II, *Rise, Let Us Be On Our Way* (New York: Warner, 2004), 73–77.

14. John Paul II, *Rise,* 76.

15. Congregation for Bishops, *Directory for the Pastoral Ministry of Bishops* (Vatican City: Libreria Editrice Vaticana, 2004), nos. 220–24.

16. *Directory for the Pastoral Ministry of Bishops,* no. 223.

Chapter 9 / One Priestly People, Edward Hahnenberg

1. Of the over two hundred uses of the words "minister" and "ministry" in the council documents, only nineteen apply to lay activity. Elissa Rinere, "Conciliar and Canonical Applications of 'Ministry' to the Laity," *The Jurist* 47 (1987): 204–27. All references to Council documents come from Walter Abbott, S.J., ed., *The Documents of Vatican II: in a New and Definitive Translation, with Commentaries and Notes by Catholic, Protestant, and Orthodox Authorities* (New York: Crossroad, 1989).

2. Hans Küng, *The Church* (New York: Sheed and Ward, 1967), 388–480.

3. Paul VI, *Ministeria Quaedam,* in *The Rites of the Catholic Church,* vol. 2 (New York: Pueblo, 1980), 7–8. For further extensions of the word "ministry" to the laity in the papal magisterium, see also Paul VI, *Evangelii Nuntiandi,* no. 73; John Paul II, *Christifideles Laici,* no. 23; *Ecclesia in America,* no. 44; *Novo Millennio Ineunte,* no. 46; and *Pastores Gregis,* no. 37.

4. John Coleman, "The Future of Ministry," *America* (March 28, 1981): 243. Dolores Leckey, the first director of the U.S. Bishops' Committee on the Laity, who went to work for the bishops in 1977, describes the imprecision surrounding the term lay ministry: "There were few specifics attached to the concept, but there was the conviction that lay ministry was to be encouraged, that it had considerable energy behind it, and that it was of the Spirit." Dolores Leckey, *Laity Stirring the Church: Prophetic Questions* (Philadelphia: Fortress, 1987), 87.

5. Coleman, "Future of Ministry," 245.

6. Coleman, "Future of Ministry," 245.

7. Congregation for the Clergy, et al., "Instruction: On Certain Questions regarding the Collaboration of the Nonordained Faithful in the Sacred Ministry of Priests," *Origins* (November 27, 1997): 399.

8. Congregation for the Clergy, "Instruction," 403. The instruction prohibits the nonordained faithful from assuming the titles "pastor," "chaplain," "coordinator," "moderator," or others that might confuse their role with that of the pastor. The instruction continues the trajectory set in 1983 by the revised *Code of Canon Law*, which, through its careful application of the word "ministry" to lay activity, presented ministry as a fulfillment of the hierarchical *munera*. Laity may be brought into "ministry" by hierarchical invitation only. Rinere, "Conciliar and Canonical Applications of 'Ministry' to the Laity," 219.

9. John Collins, *Diakonia: Re-interpreting the Ancient Sources* (New York: Oxford University Press, 1990); *Are All Christians Ministers?* (Collegeville, Minn.: Liturgical Press, 1992); and *Deacons and the Church: Making Connections between Old and New* (Harrisburg, Pa.: Morehouse Publishing, 2002).

10. Collins, *Diakonia*, 5–45. Summarized in John Collins, "Fitting Lay Ministries into a Theology of Ministry: Responding to an American Consensus," *Worship* 79 (2005): 156–60. H. W. Beyer, *"diakoneo, diakonia, diakonos"* in *Theologisches Wörterbuch zum Neuen Testament*, ed. Gerhard Kittel, vol. 2 (Stuttgart: Kohlhammer, 1935), 81–93.

11. While Collins rejects an undifferentiated "baptismal ministry," he does not limit ministry to the traditional ordained ministries, and he does not believe ministry should be clericalistic or male-dominated. He argues for a revitalization of ministry rooted in its meaning in the Christian Scriptures.

12. "Nevertheless on some points I have written to you rather boldly by way of reminder, because of the grace given me by God to be a minister of Christ Jesus to the Gentiles in the priestly service of the gospel of God, so that the offering of the Gentiles may be acceptable, sanctified by the Holy Spirit" (Rom. 15:15–16).

13. *Presbyterorum Ordinis*, no. 4. The council understands this ministry of the presbyter in relationship to the primacy of preaching in the bishop's ministry: "Among the more important duties of bishops, that of preaching the Gospel has pride of place" (*Lumen Gentium*, no. 25).

14. Karl Rahner, "What Is the Theological Starting Point for a Definition of the Priestly Ministry?" in *The Identity of the Priest*, ed. Karl Rahner (New York: Paulist Press, 1969), 80–86.

15. Donald Cozzens, *The Changing Face of the Priesthood: A Reflection on the Priest's Crisis of Soul* (Collegeville, Minn.: Liturgical Press, 2000), 84.

16. Michael Downey, "Ministerial Identity: A Question of Common Foundations," in *Ordering the Baptismal Priesthood: Theologies of Lay and Ordained Ministry*, ed. Susan Wood (Collegeville, Minn.: Liturgical Press, 2003), 13.

17. Cozzens, *Changing Face of the Priesthood*, 87.

18. *Dei Verbum*, no. 8.

19. *Ad Gentes*, no. 16; *Lumen Gentium*, 35; *Ad Gentes*, no. 23; *Sacrosanctum Concilium*, no. 2; *Lumen Gentium*, no. 11; and *Apostolicam Actuositatem*, no. 11.

20. John Paul II, *The Vocation and the Mission of the Lay Faithful in the Church and in the World: Christifideles Laici* (Washington, D.C.: USCC, 1988), no. 9.

21. John Paul II, *Christifideles Laici,* no. 15. This claim must be read in the context of the preceding statement that *"all the members* of the Church are sharers in this secular dimension but *in different ways."*

22. John Paul II, *Christifideles Laici,* no. 23.

23. Congregation for the Clergy, "Instruction," 399.

24. "The Instruction: An Explanatory Note," *Origins* (November 27, 1997): 409.

25. *Acta Synodalia Sacrosancti Concilii Oecumenici Vaticani II,* III/1 (Rome: Typis Polyglottis Vaticanis, 1974), 282. Also see *Acta Synodalia* III/3, 62; Edward Schillebeeckx, "The Typological Definition of the Christian Layman according to Vatican II," in *The Mission of the Church* (New York: Seabury Press, 1973), 90–116; Joseph Komonchak, "Clergy, Laity, and the Church's Mission in the World," *The Jurist* 41 (1981): 429; and Richard R. Gaillardetz, "Shifting Meanings in the Lay-Clergy Distinction," *Irish Theological Quarterly* 64 (1999): 123.

26. Komonchak, "Clergy, Laity, and the Church," 429.

27. This understanding of the secular characteristic as a typological description also helps to explain the exceptions noted by the council. On the one hand, the documents admit that clergy are often involved in secular affairs and sometimes hold secular occupations (*Lumen Gentium,* no. 31; *Presbyterorum Ordinis,* no. 8; and *Gaudium et Spes,* no. 43). On the other hand, the documents also note the many ways in which laypeople work within and directly serve the church community (*Lumen Gentium,* nos. 33, 35, 41; *Apostolicam Actuositatem,* nos. 22, 24; and *Ad Gentes,* nos. 15–17, 23–24, 26).

28. *Gaudium et Spes,* no. 40.

29. The leaven metaphor appears in six different passages: *Lumen Gentium,* no. 31; *Apostolicam Actuositatem,* no. 3; *Ad Gentes,* no. 5; *Gravissimum Educationis,* no. 8; *Perfectae Caritatis,* no. 11; and *Gaudium et Spes,* no. 40. Gaillardetz, "Shifting Meanings," 124–25.

30. Giovanni Magnani, "Does the So-Called Theology of the Laity Possess a Theological Status?" in *Vatican II: Assessment and Perspectives,* ed. René Latourelle, vol. 1 (New York: Paulist Press, 1988), 600.

31. Magnani, "Does the So-Called Theology?" 611; and, Gaillardetz, "Shifting Meanings," 122–23.

32. *Gaudium et Spes,* no. 40.

33. Gaillardetz, "Shifting Meanings," 126.

34. *Gaudium et Spes,* no. 3.

35. *Gaudium et Spes,* no. 40.

36. Jon Sobrino, "Toward a Determination of the Nature of Priesthood: Service to God's Salvific Approach to Human Beings," in *The Principle of Mercy: Taking the Crucified People from the Cross* (Maryknoll, N.Y.: Orbis, 1994), 137.

37. Sobrino, "Toward a Determination," 116.

38. Sobrino, "Toward a Determination," 129.

39. Sobrino, "Toward a Determination," 118.

40. Miller argues that the pervasive power of consumerism has transformed even religion itself into a kind of commodity. Vincent Miller, *Consuming Religion: Christian Faith and Practice in a Consumer Culture* (New York: Continuum, 2003).

41. Thomas Aquinas, *Summa Theologiae* III 82, 1, ad 2, in *Summa Theologiae,* vol. 56 in "The Sacraments," ed. David Bourke (New York: McGraw-Hill, 1975).

42. Pius XII, "*Mediator Dei:* Encyclical of Pope Pius XII on the Sacred Liturgy," in *The Papal Encyclicals 1939–1958,* ed. Claudia Carlen (New York: McGrath, 1981), 134. Despite an affirmation of the laity's share in Christ's priesthood, *Mediator Dei* envisions the priesthood of believers as generally passive, spiritually internal, and subordinated to the hierarchical priesthood.

43. Such was the critique of Bishop Emile De Smedt of Bruges. See *Acta Synodalia* III/4, 142–44.

44. Pius XII, *Magnificate Dominum,* November 2, 1954, *AAS* 46 (1954): 669.

45. Melvin Michalski, *The Relationship between the Universal Priesthood of the Baptized and the Ministerial Priesthood of the Ordained in Vatican II and in Subsequent Theology: Understanding "essentia et non gradu tantum"* (Lewiston, N.Y.: Edwin Mellen, 1996), 12.

46. Peter Drilling, "Common and Ministerial Priesthood: *Lumen Gentium,* Article Ten," *Irish Theological Quarterly* 53 (1987): 83.

47. David Power, *Gifts That Differ: Lay Ministries Established and Unestablished* (New York: Pueblo, 1985), 135.

48. Drilling suggests that the ease with which the council participants adopted the word "essence" in this context follows from their common background in scholastic philosophy. They understood essence to be, in a general sense, that which makes a thing 'what it is' and 'what it is not.' "In this general sense *Lumen Gentium* is saying that the common priesthood is what it is and the ministerial priesthood is what it is and neither is what the other is." Drilling, "Common and Ministerial Priesthood," 96.

49. *Lumen Gentium,* no. 10. The *Catechism of the Catholic Church,* 2nd ed. (Washington, D.C.: United States Catholic Conference, 2000), no. 1547, elaborates: "While the common priesthood of the faithful is exercised by the unfolding of baptismal grace — a life of faith, hope, and charity, a life according to the Spirit — the ministerial priesthood is at the service of the common priesthood."

50. Edward Kilmartin's reflections on the liturgical anamnesis offer fruitful directions for imagining the priest as a minister of memory. See Edward Hahnenberg, "The Ministerial Priesthood and Liturgical Anamnesis in the Thought of Edward J. Kilmartin, S.J.," *Theological Studies* 66 (2005): 253–78.

51. Dennis Ferrara, "Representation of Self-Effacement? The Axiom *In Persona Christi* in St. Thomas and the Magisterium," *Theological Studies* 55 (1994): 195–224.

52. Downey, "Ministerial Identity," 3.

53. Yves Congar, "My Path-Findings in the Theology of the Laity and Ministries," *The Jurist* 32 (1972): 169–88. This insight was developed in the context of a comprehensive theology of ministry in Thomas O'Meara, *Theology of Ministry,* rev. ed. (New York: Paulist Press, 1999).

54. Jacques Dupuis, "Lay People in Church and World: The Contribution of Recent Literature to a Synodal Theme," *Gregorianum* 68 (1987): 389–90.

Chapter 11 / Addressing the Priest "Shortage," Dean R. Hoge

1. The Center for Applied Research in the Apostolate, CARA, summarizes Catholic trend data, *www.cara.georgetown.edu* (April 15, 2005).

2. United States Conference of Catholic Bishops, "The Study of the Impact of Fewer Priests on the Pastoral Ministry," unpublished report, June 15, 2000.

3. Sullins argues that no priest shortage in the American Catholic Church exists. He maintains that while the number of priests in service is declining, Mass attendance among American Catholics is also declining, and a sharp increase in lay ministers is allowing pastors to delegate major leadership responsibilities. Thus, fewer priests are needed. D. Paul Sullins, "Empty Pews and Empty Altars," *America* (May 13, 2002): 12–16. Also see Robert G. Kennedy, "Will We Ever Have Enough Priests?" *America* (September 13, 1997): 18–22.

4. Research has shown that American Protestants contribute to their churches, as a percentage of family income, two to three times as much as do Catholics. Evangelical Protestants contribute at an even higher rate than mainline Protestants. Dean R. Hoge, Charles Zech, Patrick McNamara, and Michael Donahue, *Money Matters: Personal Giving in American Churches* (Louisville: Westminster John Knox Press, 1996), 13, 32.

5. After the problem of sexual abuse of young people by priests, Catholics rated the priest shortage as the second most urgent problem confronting the Church. James Davidson and Dean R. Hoge, "Catholics after the Scandal: A New Study's Major Findings," *Commonweal* (November 19, 2004): 13–17.

6. A recent study by a sociologist, who visited parishes without resident priests, found that the laity much preferred having resident priests in their parishes, and that the visiting priests serving more than one parish were overextended. Ruth Wallace, *They Call Him Pastor: Married Men in Charge of Catholic Parishes* (New York: Paulist Press, 2003).

7. The Protestant seminaries have been growing in the last two decades, and they produce more ordinations than there are positions available. The only shortages in the Protestant denominations are in small or marginal parishes, in which newly ordained ministers do not want to serve. The United Methodist Church has an appointment system similar to that of the Catholic Church, which alleviates the placement problem. The Lutheran Church–Missouri Synod accepts only male ministers and carefully monitors seminarians. It has only a modest clergy shortage. James Davidson, "Fewer and Fewer: Is the Clergy Shortage Unique to the Catholic Church?" *America* (December 1, 2003): 10–13.

8. Dean R. Hoge, Jackson Carroll, and Francis Scheets, O.S.C., *Patterns of Parish Leadership* (Kansas City, Mo.: Sheed and Ward, 1988), 58.

9. William D'Antonio, James Davidson, Dean R. Hoge, and Katherine Meyer, *American Catholics: Gender, Generation, and Commitment* (Walnut Creek, Calif.: AltaMira Press, 2001), 109.

10. Dean R. Hoge and Aniedi Okure, O.P., "Two Important Issues Concerning International Priests," *Touchstone* (Winter 2005): 6–7; also see Dean R. Hoge and Aniedi Okure, O.P., *International Priests: New Ministers in American Catholicism* (Collegeville, Minn.: Liturgical Press, forthcoming).

11. Philip Murnion and David DeLambo, *Parishes and Parish Ministers: A Study of Parish Lay Ministry* (New York: National Pastoral Life Center, 1999); Dean R. Hoge and Jacqueline Wenger, *Evolving Visions of the Priesthood* (Collegeville, Minn.: Liturgical Press, 2003), 127–31.

12. Joseph Fichter, *The Pastoral Provisions: Married Catholic Priests* (Kansas City, Mo.: Sheed and Ward, 1989).

13. Andrew Greeley, *The Catholic Priest in the United States: Sociological Investigations* (Washington, D.C.: United States Catholic Conference, 1972), 292.

14. Hoge and Wenger, *Evolving Visions*, 58–59, 113–15; also see Katarina Schuth, *Seminaries, Theologates, and the Future of Church Ministry* (Collegeville, Minn.: Liturgical Press, 1999).

15. Hoge and Wenger, *Evolving Visions*, 54–59.

16. Hoge and Wenger, *Evolving Visions*, 124–25.

17. Rodney Stark and Roger Finke, *Acts of Faith: Explaining the Human Side of Religion* (Berkeley: University of California Press, 2000), 182–84.

18. Hoge and Wenger, *Evolving Visions*, 124–32.

19. Davidson and Hoge, "After the Scandal," 16.

20. Dean R. Hoge, "Report on Survey of 2005 Priestly Ordinations" (Washington, D.C.: United States Conference of Catholic Bishops), *www.usccb.org/comm/archives/2005/05-089.shtml* (April 22, 2005).

21. An essay on how to raise priestly morale appeared in 1989: NCCB Priestly Life and Ministry Committee, "Reflections on the Morale of Priests," *Origins* (January 12, 1989): 497–505.

22. Hoge and Wenger, *Evolving Visions*, 28.

23. Hoge and Wenger, *Evolving Visions*, 32–41.

24. Stephen Rossetti, "Post-Crisis Morale among Priests," *America* (September 13, 2004): 8–10.

25. Hoge and Wenger, *Evolving Visions*, 26–27.

26. Dean R. Hoge, *The First Five Years of the Priesthood* (Collegeville, Minn.: Liturgical Press, 2002), 2–3.

27. Donald Cozzens, *The Changing Face of the Priesthood* (Collegeville, Minn.: Liturgical Press, 2000), 99–102.

28. Hoge and Wenger, *Evolving Visions*, 105–10.

Chapter 12 / Is the "Burnout" Real? James Burns

1. Herbert Freudenberger, *Burnout: The High Cost of High Achievement* (New York: Doubleday, 1980).

2. Christina Maslach, *Burnout: The Cost of Caring* (Englewood Cliffs, N.J.: Prentice-Hall, 1982).

3. Richard Lazarus and Susan Folkman, *Stress, Appraisal and Coping* (New York: Springer, 1984).

4. William Grosch and David Olsen, "Clergy Burnout: An Integrative Approach," in *Journal of Clinical Psychology* 56, no. 5 (May 2000): 619–32.

5. Urie Bronfenbrenner, *The Ecology of Human Development: Experiments by Nature and Design* (Cambridge, Mass.: Harvard University Press, 1979).

6. Bronfenbrenner, *Ecology of Human Development*, 22.

7. Ira Welch, Donald Medeiros, and George Tate, *Beyond Burnout: How to Enjoy Your Job Again When You've Just About Had Enough* (Englewood Cliffs, N.J.: Prentice-Hall, 1982).

8. Guy Greenfield, *The Wounded Minister: Healing from and Preventing Personal Attacks* (Grand Rapids, Mich.: Baker Books, 2001); and G. Lloyd Rediger, *Clergy Killers: Guidance for Pastors and Congregations under Attack* (Inver Grove Heights, Minn.: Logos, 1996).

9. *Catechism of the Catholic Church*, 2nd ed. (Washington, D.C.: United States Catholic Conference, 2000), no. 1568.

10. Rena Repetti, "Linkages between Family and Work Roles," in *Applied Social Psychology Annual,* vol. 7, ed. Stuart Oskamp (Beverly Hills, Calif.: Sage, 1987).

11. All references to Council documents come from Walter Abbott, S.J., ed., *The Documents of Vatican II: in a New and Definitive Translation, with Commentaries and Notes by Catholic, Protestant, and Orthodox Authorities* (New York: Crossroad, 1989).

12. *Christus Dominus,* no. 28.

13. *Catechism of the Catholic Church,* no. 1567.

14. *English Standard Version Bible* (Wheaton, Ill.: Good News, 2001).

Chapter 13 / The Future of Catholic Ministry, Thomas Groome

1. All references to Council documents come from Walter Abbott, S.J., ed., *The Documents of Vatican II: in a New and Definitive Translation, with Commentaries and Notes by Catholic, Protestant, and Orthodox Authorities* (New York: Crossroad, 1989). Regarding "the common priesthood of the faithful and the ministerial or hierarchical priesthood," *Lumen Gentium,* no. 10, notes that "they differ from one another in essence and not only in degree." Some participants in the Boston College conference, "The Roman Catholic Priesthood in the 21st Century," suggested that a shift from a "substance" to a "relational" ontology offsets any negative implication of this distinction. By ordination, the priest enters into a new relationship with the community whereby he publicly sacramentalizes the priestly character of all the baptized. As Himes writes, "What is given to all must be sacramentalized by some." See Michael Himes, "Lay Ministry and Ordained Ministers," in *Lay Ministry in the Catholic Church,* ed. Richard Miller II (Liguori, Mo.: Liguori Press, 2005), 85. The *Catechism of the Catholic Church*, 2nd ed. (Washington, D.C.: United States Catholic Conference, 2000), no. 1547, seems to favor a relational ontology between the baptized and the ordained: "The ministerial priesthood is at the service of the common priesthood. It is directed at the unfolding of the baptismal grace of all Christians."

2. Edward Hahnenberg, *Ministries: A Relational Approach* (New York: Crossroad, 2003), chapter 1.

3. Thomas O'Meara, *Theology of Ministry,* rev. ed. (Mahwah, N.J.: Paulist Press, 1999), 6.

4. Dean R. Hoge's essay, pages 133–149 in this collection.

5. The title of Chapter 5 of *Lumen Gentium,* "The Call of the Whole Church to Holiness," makes this point boldly.

6. *Lumen Gentium,* no. 10.

7. *Lumen Gentium,* no. 10.

8. *Lumen Gentium,* nos. 31, 57.

9. *Lumen Gentium,* nos. 32, 58.

10. *Apostolicam Actuositatem,* no. 2.

11. *Sacrosanctum Concilium,* no. 14.

12. *Gaudium et Spes,* no. 1.

13. *Lumen Gentium,* no. 37.

14. O'Meara, *Theology of Ministry,* 6.

15. Kenan Osborne, *Priesthood* (New York: Paulist Press, 1988), 3.

16. Norman Perrin, *Jesus and the Language of the Kingdom* (Philadelphia: Fortress Press, 1975), 31.

17. The Church has interpreted this symbol variously throughout history. The tendency in catechesis was to favor Matthew's phrasing "kingdom of heaven." The phrase was understood to refer to the afterlife in heaven only. This understanding encouraged Christians to disregard the phrase's intra-historical meanings and perhaps even consequently their own Christian responsibilities. See Benedict Viviano, *The Kingdom of God in History* (Wilmington, Del.: Michael Glazier, 1988).

18. *Gaudium et Spes,* no. 45.

19. Thomas Aquinas, *Summa Theologiae,* III, q. 62, a.1, ad 1 (Leonine ed., 12:20a).

20. O'Meara, *Theology of Ministry,* especially chapter 2.

21. Bernard Cooke, *Ministry to Word and Sacrament: History and Theology* (Philadelphia: Fortress Press, 1976), 36ff.

22. Alexandre Faivre, *The Emergence of the Laity in the Early Church,* trans. David Smith (New York: Paulist Press, 1990), 211. Faivre points out that the etymology of *kleros* refers to inheritance and the ones chosen to inherit, the heirs or *kleronomai.* But having been "chosen" (Eph. 1:11), all Christians are "heirs of God and joint heirs with Christ" (Rom. 8:7).

23. *Lumen Gentium,* nos. 32, 58.

24. Power comments that "studies of ministry in the New Testament seem to indicate that it is next to impossible to give a clear factual description of the state of ministries in that era." See David Power, *Gifts That Differ, Lay Ministries Established and Un-established* (New York: Pueblo, 1980), 88–89.

25. Of the first communities, Faivre writes: "There was no independent priestly function that was exercised by a special caste or minister" (Faivre, *Emergence of the Laity,* 7).

26. "The Didache: The Teaching of the Twelve Apostles," in *Ancient Christian Writers,* vol. 6, trans. James A. Kleist (Westminster, Md.: Newman Press, 1948), 178. The term that Kleist translates as "ministry," the Greek *leitourgeo,* comes after instructions about the celebration of the Eucharist. The text implies that bishops and deacons render the same liturgical ministry as teachers and prophets.

27. Raymond Brown, *Priest and Bishop* (Paramus, N.J.: Paulist Press, 1970), 41.

28. *The Apostolic Tradition of Hippolytus,* trans. Geoffrey J. Cuming (Nottingham, U.K.: Grove Books, 1976). For the laying on of hands, see chapter 2 regarding bishops; chapter 7, priests; and chapter 8, deacons.

29. Schillebeeckx comments, "The modern situation in which a community might not be able to celebrate the eucharist because no priest is present is theologically inconceivable in the early church." See Edward Schillebeeckx, *Ministry: Leadership in the Community of Jesus Christ* (New York: Crossroad, 1981), 41.

30. A pseudepigrapha attributed to Denys the Areopagite (often called Pseudo-Dionysius) claimed that the Church's ministries on earth should be ordered hierarchically to reflect the Celestial Hierarchy.

31. O'Meara, *Theology of Ministry,* 47.

32. Since a priest was required to preside, priesthood gained dominance as the Church emphasized the sacrificial nature of the Mass. By the beginning of the third century, previously distinct roles, presiding at Eucharist and the more institutional functions of elder (*presbyteros*) and overseer (*episcopos*), were being united in one sacerdotal role, which was identified as priest, a term not used in the New Testament of a particular person other than of Christ as High Priest (Heb. 4:14–16).

33. Brown, *Priest and Bishop,* 20.

34. *The Roman Catechism,* trans. Robert Bradley and Eugene Kevane (Boston: St. Paul Editions, 1985), 308.

35. Trent lists the lower orders as "Porter, Lector, Exorcist, Acolyte, and Sub-deacon" and remarks that all derive their function from "the consecration and administration of the Holy Eucharist, for which they are principally instituted." The clergy "assumed a physiognomy...very like that used by the state, even down to the vocabulary" (Power, *Gifts that Differ,* 71).

36. Pontifical Biblical Commission, "Can Women Be Priests?" *Origins* (July 1, 1976): 92–96. For insightful commentary and church documents since then on this issue, see Deborah Halter, *The Papal No: A Comprehensive Guide to the Vatican's Rejection of Women's Ordination* (New York: Crossroad, 2004).

37. The attempt to legislate celibacy as a precondition for priesthood may have begun at the Spanish Council of Elvira (circa 309), a gathering marked by severe disciplinary penalties and permeated by Manichaean influence. When the rulings of Elvira were proposed at the general Council of Nicea (325), they were not accepted. Mandatory celibacy for all priests was encouraged by the monastic movement, which became the paradigm for holiness of life and which required of its members vows of poverty, chastity, and obedience. The Church also desired to prevent the alienation of its properties into the possession of the families of priests. While the Church condemned Manichaeism as heretical to Christian faith, the intensely negative attitude toward sexuality and marriage rubbed off. St. Jerome was articulating an emerging sentiment (circa 400), which only deepened over the years, that married people are inferior to virgins and celibates. See Faivre, *Emergency of the Laity,* 200. Bainton observes that "the campaign for clerical celibacy had been waged with a general disparagement of marriage and of woman, who was portrayed as the gateway to hell." See Roland Bainton, *Christianity* (Boston: Houghton Mifflin, 1987), 176. For the historical roots of celibacy, see John O'Malley, "Some Basics about Celibacy," *America* (October 28, 2002).

38. There always has been resistance to the clerical, male paradigm. The Beguines, a movement of lay women begun in the twelfth century, insisted on doing apostolic works and on taking seriously the spiritual life. The Brothers of the Common Life, founded in the fourteenth century by Geert de Groote, endeavored to perform formal ministry outside of the clerical paradigm. Beginning with Angela de Merici and the Ursulines in the sixteenth century, many orders of vowed religious women were founded, contrary to the decree of Trent forbidding women to "work alongside of priests," for public ministry. The consequent "shrinkage" of ministry disadvantaged

both the ordained and the baptized. The clericalization, sacralization, and hierarchalization of ministry led to the idealization of priests. The disempowered laity was allowed to neglect its baptismal rights and responsibilities. Restricting priesthood to celibate men has diminished the Church's mission in the world.

39. Edward Hahnenberg, "Wondering about Wineskins: Rethinking Vocation in Light of Lay Ecclesial Ministry," *Listening: Journal of Religion and Culture* 40 (2005).

40. Pope Paul VI, "On the Evangelization of People" (Washington, D.C.: United States Catholic Conference, 1975), nos. 9, 18.

41. The early Christians likely understood *hier arche*, literally "holy order," as meaning to enable a community "to work well together." My description of the ministry of priests follows the now preferred portrayal of Jesus as "priest, prophet, and ruler." Many commentators now identify corresponding sacramental, prophetic, and "shepherding" functions. See Howard Bleichner, *View from the Altar: Reflections on the Rapidly Changing Catholic Priesthood* (New York: Crossroad, 2004), chapters 10–12. "Shepherd," certainly a rich term, has a more positive effective history than "king" or "ruler." However, it implies that the laity is passive. We must remember that when Jesus offered himself as the Good Shepherd and called disciples, he did not intend "come and be sheep" but "come and be shepherds." All of the baptized share in this calling. I prefer to retrieve the priestly function of "holy order," in order to revive the threefold function of the priest, who presides and preaches, but who also encourages, or enables, the laity "to work well together."

42. "Throughout the second through the tenth centuries, laity and clergy participated in the calling and election of their ordained leaders." See Francine Cardman, "Who Did What in the Church in the First Millennium?" in *Lay Ministry in the Catholic Church: Visioning Church Ministry through the Wisdom of the Past: A Symposium,* ed. Carolyn Osiek and Richard Miller (Liguori, Mo.: Liguori, 2005), 30.

43. Letty Russell, *Growth in Partnership* (Philadelphia: Westminster Press, 1981); Fran Ferder and John Heagle, *Partnership: Women and Men in Ministry* (Notre Dame, Ind.: Ave Maria Press, 1986); and Loughlan Solfield and Carroll Juliano, *Collaboration: Uniting Our Gifts in Ministry* (Notre Dame, Ind.: Ave Maria Press, 2000).

44. Peter Senge, *The Fifth Discipline: The Art and Practice of the Learning Organization* (New York: Doubleday, 1990); Robert Greenleaf, *Servant Leadership: A Journey into the Nature of Legitimate Power and Greatness* (New York: Paulist Press, 1977); and *The Servant Leader Within: A Transformative Path* (New York: Paulist Press, 2003).

45. *Gaudium et Spes,* no. 43.

46. Thomas Groome, *Sharing Faith: A Comprehensive Approach to Religious Education and Pastoral Ministry* (San Francisco: HarperSanFrancisco, 1991), chapter 4.

Chapter 15 / The Charism of the Priesthood Today, Eugene Lauer

1. Karl Rahner, "The Theology of the Parish," in *The Parish from Theology to Practice,* ed. Hugo Rahner (Westminster, Md.: Newman Press, 1958), 26.

2. A great deal of research has been done on the Greek terms used in the Christian Scriptures and in the apostolic Church to designate leaders of the Church. Those terms are ordinarily translated as "overseers," "presbyters," or "elders." Scholars do not agree on the precise manner in which these roles evolved into the roles that we recognize today as the roles of bishop, priest, elder, or minister. Most Catholic scholars do agree that the early leaders of the Church assumed those major ministries which thereby clearly allowed them to be ordained, or to be designated, to preside at Eucharist. In general, these ministries gradually evolved into those performed by a priest in the contemporary Catholic Church.

3. Raymond Brown, *Priest and Bishop* (New York: Paulist Press, 1970), 41.

4. See Edward Schillebeeckx, *Ministry: Leadership in the Community of Jesus Christ* (New York: Crossroad, 1981), 22.

5. Congregation for the Clergy, "Instruction: On Certain Questions regarding the Collaboration of the Nonordained Faithful in the Sacred Ministry of Priests," *Origins* (November 27, 1997): 397–409.

Contributors

James Bacik, ordained in 1962, received his Ph.D. in theology from the University of Oxford, England. The pastor of Corpus Christi University Parish in Toledo, he also serves as campus minister and adjunct professor of humanities at the University of Toledo. His books include *Apologetics and the Eclipse of Mystery, Contemporary Theologians*, and, more recently, *Catholic Spirituality: Its History and Challenges*.

John Baldovin, S.J., received his Ph.D. from Yale University. From 1984 to 1999 he taught at the Jesuit School of Theology in Berkeley and participated actively in the doctoral program of the Graduate Theological Union there. He has served as president both of the North American Academy of Liturgy and of the international ecumenical Societas Liturgica. He is currently a professor of historical and liturgical theology at Weston Jesuit School of Theology in Cambridge. His most recent books include *Worship: City, Church, and Renewal* and *Bread of Life, Cup of Salvation: Understanding the Mass*.

James Burns earned his Ph.D. in counseling and applied psychology from Northeastern University and his M.Div. from St. Paul Seminary School of Divinity. His current research explores how recent crises in the Church have impacted pastoral leadership.

Donald Dietrich, professor of theology at Boston College, has focused his research and publications on German Catholic experiences, ranging from the Tübingen School of Theology to the Third Reich. Most recently, he has edited *Christian Responses to the Holocaust: Moral and Ethical Issues* and has completed a book manuscript, *The German Catholic Experience with Human Rights* (forthcoming). He is a member of the Church Relations Committee at the United States Holocaust National Museum.

Elizabeth Donnelly is writing her doctoral dissertation in the Department of Government at Harvard University on the topic of the Catholic Church's advocacy of debt relief for the world's poorest countries. She received a B.S.F.S. from Georgetown University's School of Foreign Service and an M.T.S. in social ethics from Harvard Divinity School. She has worked as a consultant on the issue of Third World debt for the U.S. Catholic Conference and the Global Public Policy project of the Brookings Institution.

Thomas Groome holds the equivalent of an M.A. in divinity from St. Patrick's Seminary in Carlow, Ireland, and an M.A. and a Ph.D. in religious education from Fordham University and Union Theological Seminary. He currently serves as professor of theology and religious education as well as director of the Institute of Religious Education and Pastoral Ministry at Boston College. He wrote *Educating for Life, A Spiritual Vision for Every Teacher and Parent* and is the primary author of various religion textbooks, most recently the *Coming to Faith* series. His latest book is *What Makes Us Catholic: Eight Gifts for Life.*

Edward Hahnenberg received both his M.A. and Ph.D. in systematic theology from the University of Notre Dame. He is assistant professor in the Department of Theology at Xavier University, Cincinnati, where he teaches theological foundations, ecclesiology, liturgy, and sacraments. Hahnenberg is a theological consultant to the U.S. Bishops' Subcommittee on Lay Ministry. He has authored *Ministries: A Relational Approach* and is currently at work on a book tentatively entitled *A Concise Guide to the Documents of Vatican II.*

Dean R. Hoge received his B.D. from Harvard Divinity School and his M.A. in sociology from Harvard Graduate School of Arts and Sciences. From 1969 to 1974, he served as assistant professor at the

Princeton Theological Seminary. He is currently professor of sociology at Catholic University. His most recent publications include *Evolving Visions of the Priesthood: Changes from Vatican II to the Turn of the New Century, The First Five Years of Priesthood,* and *Young Adult Catholics: Religion in the Culture of Choice.*

James Keenan, S.J., received his M.Div. from Weston Jesuit School of Theology. He studied moral theology at the Gregorian University in Rome, where he received an S.T.L. and a doctorate. He taught at Fordham University, and since 1991 has been teaching at Weston Jesuit School of Theology. He has recently been appointed to Boston College. His newest book is *The Works of Mercy: The Heart of Catholicism.* His earlier work includes *Goodness and Rightness in Thomas Aquinas's Summa Theologiae,* and *Moral Wisdom: Lessons and Texts from the Catholic Tradition.*

Eugene Lauer, a priest of the Diocese of Pittsburgh, directs the National Pastoral Life Center in New York. He began his ministry as a parish priest in his home diocese, serving both inner-city and suburban parishes. After completing his doctorate in historical theology at the Gregorian University in Rome, he served on the theology faculties of Duquesne University, La Roche College, Wheeling Jesuit University, and the University of Notre Dame. At the University of Notre Dame, he served as the director of the Hesburgh Renewal Center.

Thomas Mahoney, ordained for the Archdiocese of Boston in 1988, served the first five years of his priesthood at Sacred Heart Parish in Middleborough, Massachusetts. Currently assigned to St. Patrick Parish in Watertown, Mass., he also serves as the chairman of the board of directors of the Boston Priests' Forum.

Joseph Nuzzi graduated from Villanova University with a B.A. in religious studies and philosophy. He completed his M.A. in biblical studies at the University of Notre Dame. Currently, he works as a pastoral associate at the Church of the Presentation in Upper Saddle

River, New Jersey, where he is responsible for adult faith formation. In addition to teaching courses in Sacred Scripture and Catholic theology, he conducts retreats and missions.

Thomas O'Meara, O.P., a priest of the Dominican order, did his doctoral studies at the University of Munich with Heinrich Fries and Karl Rahner. From 1966 to 1979, he taught at the Aquinas Institute. He has been visiting professor of theology at the Weston Jesuit School of Theology, the Seminary of Sts. Peter and Paul, and the Wartburg Theological Seminary. He has been president both of the Catholic Theological Society of America and of the North American Paul Tillich Society. Among his recent publications are *Theology of Ministry,* rev. ed., and *Thomas Aquinas, Theologian.*

Amy Strickland, a canon lawyer for the Archdiocese of Boston, has an M.A. in theology from the Dominican House of Studies in Washington, D.C., and a S.T.L. in canon law from St. Paul University, Ottawa. For the past several years, her work for the archdiocese has focused on the canonical resolution of allegations of misconduct by priests and deacons.

John Strynkowski, ordained a priest for the Diocese of Brooklyn in 1963, obtained his doctorate in theology from the Gregorian University in Rome. He worked in the Vatican for eight years and then returned to the United States to teach systematic theology at the Seminary of the Immaculate Conception in New York, where he was rector from 1985 to 1995. After serving as a pastor from 1995 to 2000, he was assigned to the United States Conference of Catholic Bishops, where he was executive director of the Secretariat for Doctrine and Pastoral Practices. He is currently rector of the Cathedral-Basilica of St. James in Brooklyn.

Susan Wood, S.C.L., a Sister of Charity of Leavenworth, Kansas, received her Ph.D. in systematic theology from Marquette University. A member of the U.S.A. Lutheran–Roman Catholic Dialogue, she has participated in consultations on baptism and theological anthropology, as well as on the nature and purpose of ecumenical dialogue, sponsored by Faith and Order of the World Council of Churches and the Joint Working Group. She is professor of theology at Marquette University. Her published work includes *Spiritual Exegesis and the Church in the Theology of Henri de Lubac* and *Sacramental Orders.*

Index

Of Related Interest

Edward P. Hahnenberg

MINISTRIES
A Relational Approach

This comprehensive text for every student, minister and teacher offers excellent scholarship and a visually enhanced presentation of the concept and practice of ministry. Dr. Hahnenberg sheds light on the various aspects of modern ministry offering a prophetic vision of the church as ordered communion.

"Takes a giant and welcome step toward narrowing the gap between our experience of ministry in today's church and our ability to understand and express it theologically."

–H. Richard McCord, Ed.D., Executive Director,
U.S. Conference of Catholic Bishops, Committee on the Laity

0-8245-2103-X, paperback

Walter Cardinal Kasper

LEADERSHIP IN THE CHURCH
Theological Reflections

This book offers a timely and profound look at the enduring meaning of church office, and the guidance it is called to provide in light of a changed world and a challenging future. Topics addressed include: the universal vs. local church; the ministry of the bishop, priest and deacon; apostolic succession; and the practical application of canonical norms.

"A must-read for those who indeed exercise church leadership."

–*America*

0-8245-1977-9, hardcover

crossroad

Of Related Interest

Christopher Ruddy
TESTED IN EVERY WAY
The Catholic Priesthood in Today's Church

"*Tested in Every Way* brings together a wide variety of voices on the state of the contemporary priesthood. Christopher Ruddy works a small miracle in gathering disparate viewpoints, weighing the hard facts, and connecting it all with Scripture and church tradition to provide a remarkably engaging study of the Catholic priest today. This new study is essential reading."
— James Martin, S.J., author of *My Life with the Saints*

0-8245-2427-6, paperback

Check your local bookstore for availability.
To order directly from the publisher,
please call 1-800-707-0670 for Customer Service
or visit our Web site at *www.cpcbooks.com.*
For catalog orders, please send your request to the address below.

THE CROSSROAD PUBLISHING COMPANY
16 Penn Plaza, Suite 1550
New York, NY 10001

All prices subject to change.

crossroad